Upgrading your Laptop or Desktop PC

Robert Penfold

Bernard Babani (publishing) Ltd
The Grampians
Shepherds Bush Road
London W6 7NF
England
www.babanibooks.com

Please note

Although every care has been taken with the production of this book to ensure that any projects, designs, modifications, and/or programs, etc., contained herewith, operate in a correct and safe manner and also that any components specified are normally available in Great Britain, the Publisher and Author do not accept responsibility in any way for the failure (including fault in design) of any projects, design, modification, or program to work correctly or to cause damage to any equipment that it may be connected to or used in conjunction with, or in respect of any other damage or injury that may be caused, nor do the Publishers accept responsibility in any way for the failure to obtain specified components.

Notice is also given that if any equipment that is still under warranty is modified in any way or used or connected with home-built equipment then that warranty may be void.

British Library Cataloguing in Publication Data

A catalogue record for this book is available from the British Library

ISBN   978 0 85934 593 4

Cover Design by Gregor Arthur

Printed and bound in Great Britain for Bernard Babani (publishing) Ltd

Preface

Since its introduction in 1981 the IBM PC has undergone continuous changes and developments. IBM themselves led the way initially, but in recent times the various "clone" manufacturers have introduced many innovations of their own, and developments are now largely the work of Intel and the other computer chip manufacturers. In fact the PC has now developed so far that it has little in common with the original PC of 1981. Software for the early PCs might actually run on a modern PC, but things move on, and few of the early PC add-ons will work with a modern PC.

A factor that has certainly aided the popularity of PCs, and aided rapid development, is their open architecture. IBM published the full specification of the PC expansion slots, making it easy for third party suppliers to produce and sell PC expansion cards of various types. This has led to numerous specialist add-ons for the PC being produced, as well as a good range of mainstream products. PCs and their interfaces have moved on over the years, but there still an open approach to things that has encouraged the development of countless add-ons that enable PCs to work well in numerous everyday and specialist applications.

While expanding a PC is, in the main, a reasonably straightforward affair, there are inevitably a few complications to most aspects of PC upgrading. The main purpose this book is to first explain the basics of PC hardware, and to then help untangle the difficulties that can arise when undertaking the more popular of PC upgrades. The topics covered include hard disc drives, memory expansion, processor upgrades, CD-ROM and DVD drives, external drives, ports, modems, and BIOS upgrades. The rate of change in the PC world is such that often the only way of upgrading the processor is to change the motherboard and memory as well. This type of upgrade is also covered.

Do-it-yourself upgrading is a daunting task for those with little experience of dealing with PC hardware. However, most upgrading does not require much in the way of manual skills or tools. If you have a medium size cross point screwdriver you probably have all the tools needed for computer upgrading, but a pair of pliers might also come in useful. You need to be a reasonably practical person, but no real expertise is required. Provided you do not have a history of do-it-yourself disasters there should be no difficulty in undertaking PC upgrades. Many computer components are easily damaged, so you should make sure that you understand the simple handling precautions that are needed before undertaking any upgrading. Computer upgrading should then be reasonably problem free, and should cost much less than having the work done professionally.

Robert Penfold

Trademarks

Microsoft, Windows, Windows XP, and Windows Vista are either registered trademarks or trademarks of Microsoft Corporation.

All other brand and product names used in this book are recognised trademarks, or registered trademarks of their respective companies. There is no intent to use any trademarks generically and readers should investigate ownership of a trademark before using it for any purpose.

Contents

6

Video and audio 103

7

Adding ports 111

Hard and floppy drives 129

CD-ROM and DVD drives 191

External storage 201

11

Power supplies 211

12

The BIOS 223

13

Modems 259

14

Troubleshooting 269

1

PC overview

Modular computer

It is possible to come up with many factors that have led to the unrivalled popularity of the IBM PCs and the numerous compatible machines, which have been the standard business microcomputer for many years now. There are also many millions of PCs in home use. At one time "PC" was a general term, simply meaning "personal computer". The dominance of IBM compatible computers is such that the term is now mainly used to mean this particular type of PC.

One contributory factor to the dominance of the PC is certainly their enormous expansion potential. The basic computer, or "system unit" as it is generally called, is unusable on its own. It requires the addition of disc drives, a monitor, a keyboard, and even such things as an add-on display generator before it will provide any useful function. This modular approach has been the cause of a certain amount of criticism, but in truth it is a very good way of doing things.

If all you require is a very basic computer with an inexpensive processor, a hard disc drive of modest capacity and a small monitor for text use, then you can buy a PC of that type. You do not need to spend money on expensive disc hard drives, up-market processors, or large monitors that you do not need.

If, on the other hand, you are interested in graphics applications and require high-resolution true-colour graphics plus a large and fast hard disc drive, you will have a choice of several PC compatible systems that offer a suitable specification. With requirements for computer systems that fall somewhere between these two extremes you are likely to be spoiled for choice, with a vast number of suitable systems to choose from. Whatever your requirements, it is likely that there will be a PC that closely matches them. Some PC suppliers will actually build a PC to your specifications.

In the unlikely event that you can not find something that exactly meets your requirements, then it is possible to buy a basic computer system and add in suitable peripherals yourself. Due to IBM's so-called "open architecture" policy (publishing full technical details of their microcomputers so that third party manufacturers can produce add-ons for them), the range of add-on boards and other peripherals for the original PCs ran into many hundreds. Although many of the original PC standards are now obsolete, the "open to all" approach has been maintained, and the current range of PC components and add-ons is probably greater than ever before.

Approach

In this book we will mainly be concerned with the hardware side of PC compatible computing. In this first chapter we will take a look at PC hardware in general, going into detail on some subjects, but mainly considering things in a superficial manner. The practical side of PC upgrading is covered in chapter 2. Subsequent chapters provide detailed information on a range of specific upgrades that are not fully discussed in this chapter (disc drives, memory, etc.).

Those who are not familiar with PC hardware should study this chapter and the next one in some detail before progressing to any of the other chapters that cover a topic of particular interest to them. Proceeding without understanding the basics such as anti-static handling precautions could prove costly. Trying to expand a PC without understanding the differences between the various types of PC and their general make-up could also lead to some costly mistakes. You need to know where a PC fits into the overall scheme of things in order to judge whether or not it is feasible or worthwhile trying to upgrade it.

On the face of it, the modular approach makes any PC fully upgradeable to the latest specification. In reality things do move on, and things such as expansion slots and the standard ports have evolved over the years. Upgrading some PCs to a modern specification would involve replacing virtually everything, and would produce what was virtually a new PC rather than an upgraded PC. You may feel that this is a viable approach, and it can certainly be an interesting exercise, but most people would probably prefer to buy a new PC and use the old one as a standby computer.

Compatibility issues

The term "compatibility" in a PC context originally referred to the ability (or lack of it) to run standard IBM PC software designed to operate under either the PC-DOS or MS-DOS operating systems, which were essentially the same. These days it refers to the ability of hardware to run under Windows and peacefully coexist with the other hardware in the system. In theory, PC hardware is supplied with driver software that integrates it with Windows and everything else in the system, or it uses standard Windows drivers that should also guarantee perfect results.

Superficially, it appears as though compatibility issues are a thing of the past, and that any hardware can be used with any PC. It is just a matter of installing the driver software, and then everything will work fine. In practice it is not as simple as this, especially when upgrading older computers. The first point to bear in mind is that some items of hardware will only work if the computer's hardware meets certain minimum requirements. The same is true of any major item of software. While the minimum requirements are mostly fairly modest, they could still be beyond the capabilities of an ageing PC. Also, the minimum requirement is the lowest specification needed in order to run the software or use the hardware at all. Results might not be very good with a PC that barely meets or only just exceeds the bare minimum specification. There is often a recommended minimum specification, and this is a more reliable guide. The new hardware or software should run in a very usable fashion if it meets this specification.

The more usual compatibility problem is that the hardware will simply not work with the old operating system used on the computer that is being upgraded. In most cases the hardware is perfectly capable of working with older PCs, but there is no suitable driver software available. These days even the simplest item of hardware is unlikely to work unless the correct driver software is installed on the computer. The operating system and application software will ignore the hardware unless it is properly integrated into the operating system by a suitable driver program, and without this software installed, the new hardware might as well not be there.

It is crucial to realise that different drivers are needed for each version of Windows. There are some exceptions, but using (say) a Windows XP driver with Windows Vista is unlikely to produce usable results, and the operating system might block the installation of unsuitable driver software. Modern versions of Windows are usually well supported by the hardware manufacturers, but it is relatively rare for modern items of hardware to be supplied complete with drivers for older versions or Windows. Before buying any new piece of computer hardware, always check that it is compatible with the operating system you are using.

BIOS

The BIOS used to be an important factor for good compatibility with PC hardware and software, but a BIOS chip that works properly is something that can be taken for granted these days. The complexity of modern PC hardware is such that there can be occasional problems with the BIOS, but these are usually sorted out quite quickly by the motherboard and computer manufacturers. What exactly is the BIOS, or ROM BIOS as it is sometimes called?

ROM stands for "read only memory", and it is a component (or two in the case of some older computers) which contains a computer program. This program contains the BIOS, or "basic input/output system." The first function of the BIOS is to run a few diagnostic checks at switch-on to ensure that the computer is up and running properly. It then looks on the disc drives in search of the operating system, which it then loads into the computer's memory. The operating system then takes over, but the BIOS contains software routines that can be utilized by the operating system and applications programs.

You will often encounter the term "booting" or "booting-up", which refers to this process of the operating system being automatically loaded from disc and run. This term is derived from the fact that operating system appears to load itself into the computer's memory, which is akin to pulling oneself up by ones bootlaces. Of course, the operating system only appears to be loading and running itself. The truth of the matter is that routines in the BIOS are carrying out this process.

The software in the BIOS, or "firmware" as programs in this form are often termed, must be designed to suit the particular hardware used on the computer's main board. Accordingly, each model of computer tends to have a BIOS program that is different to every other model of computer. The differences will often be quite minor, with each BIOS manufacturer having a core program that is modified to suit each new PC design. Several companies produce BIOS chips, including Phoenix, Award, and AMI.

Modern PCs have some low power CMOS memory that is powered from a battery when the main power source is switched off. This memory circuit is actually part of a built-in clock/calendar circuit, which the operating system uses to set its clock and calendar during the booting process. It is also used by application software, such as a word processor when it automatically adds the date into a letter or other document. This memory stores the BIOS database, which contains numerous pieces of data that the computer needs in order to function properly.

PC versions

The PCs and compatibles have evolved over a period of years, and the more up-market systems in use today have specifications that bear little resemblance to the original IBM PC, which was launched in 1981. The original had just 64k of memory, a monochrome text only display, and included a cassette port. The PC I am using to produce the text and illustrations for this book has 2 gigabytes (well over 2 million kilobytes) of RAM, a colour graphics board and an LCD monitor that can handle up to 1600 by 1200 pixels with 16 million colours, plus a CD/DVD rewriter, and a 250 gigabyte fast hard disc. It also uses a microprocessor that renders it several thousand times faster than the original PC.

Despite this, in some respects it is still highly compatible with the original computer. It can almost certainly run any software that will run on the original version of the computer, including old operating systems such as MS-DOS. It also has the standard parallel and serial ports that can be used with older peripherals, but it has to be admitted that these are conspicuously absent on many modern PCs. In common with most modern PCs, it lacks compatibly with the original expansion cards and it will only take the modern PCI and PCI Xpress varieties.

Compatibility between modern hardware and software and older PCs is less good. There is much software and a lot of expansion cards that will work in my PC, but are unusable with the original PC. In fact it could be hard to find any modern PC hardware or software that will run on an early PC. It is primarily this factor that produces the need to upgrade PCs or move on to newer and better ones. You buy a new PC that works fine with the software and hardware bought at the same time, but it will not necessarily work properly with new hardware and software purchased in a few years time. PCs perhaps change at a somewhat slower rate than in the past, but it is still likely that an upgrade of some kind will be needed before too long in order to use future software and hardware with the computers of today.

The "PC" in IBM PC merely stands for "personal computer". This is a possible cause of confusion since the IBM PCs and modern compatibles are often referred to simply as "PCs", but this is also a general term for any microcomputer which is primarily intended for business rather than home use. In fact these days it is a term that applies to computers for home use as well. Anyway, in this book the term "PC" will only be used to refer to computers that are the modern descendants of the original IBM PCs.

In 1983 the original PC was replaced with a slightly improved version called the PC XT, with the "XT" part of the name being an abbreviation for extended.   Rather than trying to speed up the PC and PC XT computers, IBM produced what was effectively a completely new design, but one which largely maintained software and hardware compatibility with the PC and PC XT. This computer was the PC AT, and the "AT" part of the name stands for "advanced technology."   Modern PCs are effectively AT compatible computers that have evolved into what is really a new design that has little in common with the original.

Multiple Cores

All modern PCs are based on an Intel Pentium processor, or a compatible processor from AMD. These are much faster and more complex devices than the 8088 processor used in the original PCs. The 8088 was used at a clock rate of 4.77MHz, which compares to around 3 gigahertz (3000 megahertz) for modern Pentium processors. A Pentium is not simply faster, but it also has extra hardware that can handle additional instructions. It also contains what is effectively a second processor that handles any complex mathematics.

Things are taken a stage further with some modern PC processors, with dual or even quad cores. This basically just means that there are two or four processing units contained on a single chip. The idea of using dual processors is quite an old one, and PCs based on two separate microprocessors have been around for many years. Having more than one processor can enable a PC to multitask more efficiently, with two programs being handled by their own processor.

Things are essentially the same with a multi-core processor, but the processing units are in a single chip rather than in the form of separate components. Also, with a multi-core processor it is usually the case that significant amounts of the hardware are shared by the cores. In general, the less that is shared the better the chip will perform. You tend to get what you pay for though, with less sharing resulting in a more complex and expensive component.

The 8088 used in the early PCs handled data internally in 16-bit chunks, but it only had an 8-bit data bus. In other words, it could only exchange data with memory and other parts of the computer eight bits at a time. The 8088 was not actually all that efficient by the standards of the time, and processor technology has certainly moved on a great deal since those days. The processors used in modern PCs have a minimum of a 32-bit bus and internal processing. Some are actually 64-bit types, which can be of practical importance. In order to run a 64-bit version of an operating system it is essential to have a processor that can handle 64-bit instructions. There are 64-bit versions of some application programs, which also require a 64-bit compatible processor in order to run properly. However, normal 32-bit versions of Windows and other operating systems should run properly on any PC, regardless of whether its processor is a 32-bit or 64-bit type. The same is true of normal PC application software.

Cache

When dealing with computers you are likely to encounter the term "cache" from time to time, and in a computer context it normally means a certain amount of memory that is not part of the computer's normal contingent of memory. It is a term that is often encountered when looking at the processor section of a computer's specification. This cache memory is high-speed memory that is used to store recently processed data. It is likely that this data will need to be accessed again, and having it available in high-speed memory ensures that it can be processed very efficiently when it is needed. In virtually all practical applications this significantly speeds up the rate at which data can be processed.

Early Pentium processors had only about 32k of built-in cache memory, with several times this amount fitted on the motherboard. These are known as level 1 and level 2 caches respectively. Level 1 cache is faster, but there are practical limits on the amount of cache memory that can be included in the processor. However, with modern processors there can be several megabytes of on-chip cache memory.

You might also encounter cache memory when dealing with disc drives. The idea is much the same as for cache used with a microprocessor. Any data that has recently been written to the disc drive is stored in the cache, and if necessary, it can be read back almost instantly because the cache can be accessed much more quickly than reading the data from the disc itself. At one time it was quite common for a large section of the computer's main memory to be used as a large cache for the main hard disc drive. The operating systems of the day were unable to make proper use of large amounts of memory, and this was a means of putting otherwise unused memory to good use. Modern operating systems can manage large amounts of memory, but the disc cache lives on as an internal part of most hard disc drives, and some other types such as DVD and CD-ROM drives.

Repair upgrade

It will probably be apparent that there have been massive changes to PCs over the years. The days when it was possible to repair practically any PC, no matter how old it happened to be, are now long gone. The early PCs are now collectors' items, as are any remaining spare parts for them. Trying to repair early PCs is likely to prove expensive, and in most cases will be impossible. The situation is not really much different with the early AT class PCs, or with the early Pentium based computers. Things have moved on, and most modern PC components are simply not compatible with PCs of this vintage.

On the other hand, it should be possible to effect most repairs quite easily and at reasonable cost with PCs that are up to about five years old, and in some cases somewhat older PCs can be fixed quite easily and economically. It obviously depends to a certain extent on the precise nature of the problem. However, unless something pretty catastrophic happens, such as dropping the PC from a second floor window, it should be economic and worthwhile repairing this type of PC.

Rather than opting for a straightforward repair you may decide to undertake a major upgrade instead. This will probably cost more than simply replacing the faulty part with a new one, but for the extra money you may well obtain a vast improvement in performance. After the upgrade it might be possible to use hardware and software that were previously beyond the capabilities of the computer. Some spare parts for older PCs have quite high prices, so it is conceivable that an upgrade will sometimes be cheaper than a straightforward repair.

The best choice depends on the particular PC you have, and how badly (or otherwise) you require an increase in performance. It also depends on the nature of the fault. There is probably little point in opting for a major upgrade if a replacement CD-ROM drive is all that is needed. On the other hand, if a motherboard becomes faulty it would probably be worthwhile replacing the processor and memory as well, to bring the PC up to a more modern specification.

With this type of thing you might be lucky, and there could be a motherboard at a good price that will take the original processor and memory. In practice it can often be difficult to find something suitable at all, let alone at a reasonable price. Local computer fairs are often the best source of older components, and the prices are usually very low, but there will probably not be a worthwhile guarantee with these "bargain bin" components.

System make up

A traditional PC is a so-called three-unit style computer. These three separate units are the keyboard, the main computer unit, and the monitor. They are connected together by cables, although wireless connections are sometimes used for the keyboard and peripherals. The three-unit arrangement is a convenient one in that it makes it easy to accommodate everything on practically any computer desk. Bear in mind though, that PCs are mostly quite large and heavy, and likely to prove both too big and too heavy for a low cost computer desk designed for a small home computer or a laptop.

Of course, laptop and notebook computers are not in the traditional three-unit style, but instead have everything combined in one compact unit. Most of these computers can be connected to an external keyboard and monitor, and can therefore be used in a normal three-unit system when back at base. Laptop and notebook computers are clearly radical departures from the traditional desktop PC though, and have relatively limited upgrade potential.

Some of these computers have more upgrade potential than others, and some upgrades must be done professionally at the factory or an official service centre. Upgrades such as hard disc and memory types are often a practical proposition for the user, but are significantly different to the equivalent upgrades for desktop PCs. Consequently, upgrades to laptop PCs will be covered in the same chapters of this book as the desktop PC equivalents, but in separate sections at the end.

Incidentally, the terms "laptop" and "notebook" seem to cause a certain amount of confusion. They are often used as general terms to describe any portable PC, and have largely become different words for the same thing. Strictly speaking though, theses are two different types of computer. A notebook is a lighter and slimmer version of a laptop, although the differences are now relatively slight. Notebook PCs have tended to become generally bigger and better while laptops have shrunk slightly, or at least stayed about the same size. Anyway, in this book the term "laptop" will be used as a generic term to cover any normal laptop or notebook PC, but not really small computers such as palmtop types, which are not covered by this publication.

Returning to the subject of desktop PCs, the main unit is comprised of several sub-units. The main ones are the case, power supply unit, motherboard (or mainboard), and one or more disc drives. Additionally, certain expansion cards must be present on the main board for the system to function, although in modern PCs there is a tendency integrate things like the ports, disc controllers, audio, and video circuits with the main board, so this does not necessarily apply any more. A basic multimedia PC would consist of something like the following list of main parts.

Keyboard and mouse
Case
Motherboard fitted with BIOS and memory modules
17 or 19 inch colour monitor
Integrated graphics
Hard disc drive
CD-ROM/DVD writer
Integrated sound
Speakers

A more up-market PC might have the following set of main components.

Keyboard and mouse
Case
Motherboard fitted with BIOS and memory modules
19 or 21 inch colour monitor
2-D/3-D display card with at least 256 megabytes of RAM
Large hard disc drive
TV/radio card
DVD writer
CD-ROM writer
Upmarket sound card and speakers
Modem or broadband modem for Internet connection

Some of these constituent parts, plus more specialised forms of expansion are discussed in later chapters, but there are a few aspects of these main parts that we will take the opportunity to discuss here.

Keyboards

The original PC keyboard was an 84 key type, but this is now long obsolete and was replaced by the 102 key type, which was in turn usurped by the 105 key type. All current standard keyboards seem to have the 105 key layout. Of course, there are also fancy keyboards having all sorts of additional functions available, but these are used interfaced to the computer in the same ways as standard 105 key units. Keyboards of this type should be supplied complete with any driver software needed to make the additional keys and functions perform properly.

Modern keyboards have a connector of the PS/2 variety (see G.1 in the Colour Gallery), or the keyboard connects to the computer via a USB port. There is no big advantage to either type of connection, but using the PS/2 keyboard port avoids taking up one of the USB ports

Motherboards

Unless you get into DIY PC assembly or undertake large scale upgrades you may not need to know too much about motherboards, although background information of this type often proves to be invaluable from time to time. At one time there were two main motherboard categories: the PC/PC XT type, and the AT type. However, these are now well and truly obsolete, and have been replaced by ATX boards. ATX motherboards have a modified AT layout that puts the processor to one side of the expansion slots. Modern processors, when complete with heatsinks and cooling fans, tend to be quite tall and can obstruct several of the expansion slots. This prevents the slots from being used with the longer expansion cards. By moving the processor to one side this problem is avoided, and it is possible to use long expansion cards in any of the expansion slots. However, unless the board layout is well designed there can be problems with large heatsinks being obstructed by the power supply unit or one of the drives.

There are other differences between the two types of board, such as the different power supply requirements and the on-board ports of ATX boards. ATX boards can be categorised by size (full, mini, and micro), and subdivided according to the processors that they support. A full-size type is shown in G.2 of the Colour Gallery. When buying a replacement motherboard you must therefore make sure that it has a suitable form factor for the case in use, and that it supports the make and type of processor you are using. Obtaining a motherboard to suit an early Pentium processor, or even one of the slightly later Pentium processors, can be very difficult these days. Either a new motherboard, processor and memory has to be fitted, or it has to be accepted that the computer has reached "the end of the road" and that it is time for it to be recycled.

Chipsets

When looking at the specifications for PC motherboards you will inevitably come across references to chipsets. These are the integrated circuits that provide various essential functions that are not included in the processor itself. In the original PCs these functions were provided by dozens of ordinary logic integrated circuits. Even though a modern PC requires much more help from the supporting electronics, there are normally just two support chips, and in some case only one. Intel has manufactured various Pentium support chipsets, but there are also numerous chipsets from other manufacturers.

When looking at the descriptions of motherboards you will inevitably encounter the terms "North bridge" and "South bridge". Most chipsets consist of two chips, which have been given these two generic names. The "bridge" part of the name presumably refers to the fact that the chips provide a bridge between the processor and other parts of the system such as the hard disc and the memory.

The North bridge chip is responsible for handling the memory and the graphics port. The South bridge chip handles things like the IDE ports for the drives, USB ports, and any so-called legacy ports such as the standard serial and parallel types. In fact the South bridge chip handles all input and output functions apart from memory and the graphics card. The North and South bridge chips are linked via a high-speed interface that usually operates at 266 megahertz or more in modern PCs. Although most PCs are based on North and South bridge chips from the same manufacturer, this is not invariably the case.

Maths coprocessor

The maths coprocessor used to be an integrated circuit which looked very much like the main microprocessor in most cases. It was normally fitted into a special socket on the motherboard. Any PC processor from the full 80486DX onwards has the maths coprocessor built-in, and not as an add-on chip. There is no need to worry if you obtain software that needs the services of the maths coprocessor. Unless you are using a very old PC it will already be present as part of the main processor.

Ports

In order to be of any practical value it is normally necessary for a PC to connect to other devices such as printers, modems, and scanners. The original PCs had serial and parallel ports provided by expansion cards. These legacy ports are now largely obsolete, but they can be added to a modern PC (see chapter 7). Parallel and serial ports tend to be awkward to use, and this lead to the development of the USB 1.1 and USB 2.0 ports. These are high-speed and very high-speed serial ports that are largely compatible with each other, but not with ordinary serial ports. After one or two "teething" problems USB ports have now largely taken over from serial and parallel types.

Most of the ports are in a cluster at the rear of a modern PC, and there is usually quite an assortment. In addition to USB and the PS/2 keyboard/ mouse ports, there are often Firewire, Ethernet network, video, and numerous audio ports. Depending on the age of the PC, there might also be a few legacy ports. G.3 in the Colour Gallery shows a typical cluster. The connectors are different colours as most modern PCs use a method of colour coding to help identify the ports. This system has undergone a few changes, and the final version is called PC 2001. The previous version was PC 99, and it is probably better known by this name. These are the colours for each type of port:

Colour	Port
Green	PS/2 mouse
Purple	PS/2 keyboard
Black	USB
Grey	Firewire
Burgundy	Parallel
Teal	RS232C serial
Blue	Analogue video
White	Digital video
Yellow	S-Video or composite video
Pink	Microphone
Light blue	Line audio input
Lime green	Line audio output
Orange	Speaker/sub-woofer
Brown	Line output for left-right speaker
Gold	Game port/MIDI

Soundcards

PCs have a built-in loudspeaker, but this is driven by some very basic hardware that is really intended to do nothing more than produce a few simple "beep" sounds. For anything more than this a proper sound card and a pair of active speakers is needed. Most soundcards do actually have built-in amplifiers, but they only provide low output powers and generally provide quite modest volume levels when used with passive speakers (i.e. speakers that do not have built-in amplifiers). The simplest soundcards only offer synthesised sounds, but these days most also have wavetable synthesis, which is better for music making. This method uses standard analogue synthesis techniques, but the basic sounds are short bursts of recorded instrument sounds rather than simple waveforms from oscillator circuits. This usually gives much more realistic results.

Modern soundcards can typically produce 32 or 64 different sounds at once, and they are capable of reproducing quite complex music sequences. Even the cheapest cards have the ability to record and play back in high quality stereo, and to play back pre-recorded sound samples (.WAV files). There has been a strong trend towards integrated audio systems where the audio circuits are included on the motherboard. Many of these integrated sound facilities are now quite sophisticated, and even the basic ones are adequate for most purposes.

Specification

People who ask for advice about upgrading their PC tend to assume that all PCs are much the same, and that an upgrade for one will be suitable for all other PCs. This is clearly far from the truth. PCs have changed quite quickly and radically in recent years. A good upgrade for one PC might be totally inappropriate for most others. Before you try to upgrade a PC it is essential to find out as much as you can about its specification. You can learn a great deal by simply looking at the ports and connectors on the outside of the computer, and more can be gleaned by looking inside the case. Are there any spare expansion slots, and if so what type or types are these slots?

The manual for the PC or its motherboard should provide plenty of detailed information about compatible processors and memory modules, the BIOS, and just about everything you need to know. It is normal for the BIOS to produce various screens of information just after the computer is started, and these can be useful if information is difficult to obtain. There are system analyser and testing programs available, and these can provide some useful information about the installed hardware. Do not commence upgrading a PC until you are sure of its current configuration, and the suitability of the proposed upgrade components.

Upgrade basics

Ad infinitum

In this chapter some general points will be addressed, so that they only have to be covered here, and not over and over again as they crop up throughout the book. You could skip this chapter and refer back to it each time a relevant reference is encountered in the later chapters. However, I would definitely not recommend doing things this way. Modern computer components are easily damaged and simply taking some components out of their wrapping can be sufficient to ruin them if you do not know what you are doing. Although modern computers are relatively inexpensive, learning from your mistakes could still prove to be a costly business. The information in this first part of this chapter will enable you to avoid costly and unnecessary damage to components.

Chapter 16 deals with upgrading the BIOS, but it also contains useful background information that it is better to learn sooner rather than later. In particular, there is a substantial section dealing with the BIOS settings database and the BIOS Setup program. With more and more aspects of a PC controlled via the BIOS this is no longer an aspect that can be largely ignored when upgrading PCs. A lot of problems can be solved or avoided in the first place if you have a reasonable understanding of the BIOS. It is definitely a good idea to read chapter 12, and the general information provided in chapter 1, before undertaking any significant PC upgrade.

Shocking truth

When dealing with modern electronic components it is not just a matter of handling the components carefully to avoid physical damage. There are hidden dangers that can cause a lot of expensive damage if you do not take suitable precautions. Those readers who are used to dealing with electronic components will no doubt be aware that many modern semiconductors are vulnerable to damage by static electricity, as is any equipment that incorporates these devices. They will also be used to handling static-sensitive components and taking the necessary precautions to protect them from damage. Probably most readers are not familiar with these precautions, and I will therefore outline the basic steps necessary to ensure that no components are accidentally "zapped".

I think it is worth making the point that it does not take a large static charge complete with sparks and "cracking" sounds to damage sensitive electronic components. Large static discharges of that type are sufficient to damage most modern semiconductor components, and not just the more sensitive ones. Many of the components used in computing are so sensitive to static charges that they can be damage by relatively small voltages. In this context "small" still means a potential of perhaps a hundred volts or so, but by static standards this is not particularly large. Charges of this order will not generate noticeable sparks or make your hair stand on end, but they are nevertheless harmful to many electronic components. Hence you can "zap" these components simply by touching them, and in most cases would not be aware that anything had happened.

Health warning

I think it is also worth making the point that it is not just things like the processor and memory modules that are vulnerable. Completed circuit boards such as video and soundcards are often vulnerable to static damage, as is the motherboard itself. In fact most modern expansion cards and all motherboards are vulnerable to damage from static charges. Even components such as the hard disc drive and CD-ROM drive can be damaged by static charges. Anything that contains a static-sensitive component has to be regarded as vulnerable. The case and power supply assembly plus any heatsinks and cooling fans represent the only major components that you can assume to be zap-proof. Everything else should be regarded as potentially at risk and handled accordingly.

When handling any vulnerable computer components you should always keep well away from any known or likely sources of static electricity. These includes such things as computer monitors, television sets, any carpets or furnishings that are known to be prone to static generation, and even any pets that are known to get charged-up fur coats. Also avoid wearing any clothes that are known to give problems with static charges. This seems to be less of a problem than it once was, because

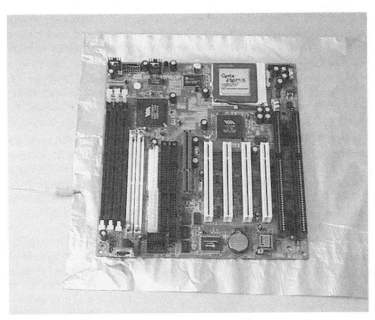

Fig.2.1 An improvised conductive work surface

few clothes these days are made from a cloth that consists entirely of man-made fibres. There is normally a significant content of natural fibres, and this seems to be sufficient to prevent any significant build-up of static charges. However, if you should have any garments that might give problems, make sure that you do not wear them when handling any computer equipment or components.

Anti-static equipment

Electronics and computing professionals often use quite expensive equipment to ensure that static charges are kept at bay. Most of these are not practical propositions for amateur computer enthusiasts or those who only deal with computers professionally on a very part-time basis. If you will only be working on computers from time to time, some very simple anti-static equipment is all that you need to ensure that there are no expensive accidents.

Unless you opt for a massive upgrade it is unlikely that it will be necessary to remove the motherboard from the case. However, if you do replace a motherboard or have to remove the existing one to work on it, make sure that suitable precautions are taken. The motherboard itself is quite expensive, and the potential loss is much greater if it is fitted with memory and (or) a processor. When working on a motherboard it is essential to have some form of conductive worktop that is earthed. These can be purchased from the larger electronic component suppliers, but something as basic as a large sheet of aluminium cooking foil laid out on the workbench will do the job very well (Figure 2.1).

The only slight problem is that some way of earthing the foil must be devised. The method I generally adopt is to connect the foil to the metal chassis of a computer using a crocodile clip lead (Figure 2.2). Crocodile clips are available from electronic component suppliers, as are sets of made-up leads. The ready-made leads are often quite short, but when necessary several can be clipped together to make up a longer lead. Anyway, it should not be difficult to improvise a connection to the foil. The computer that acts as the earth must be plugged into the mains supply so that it is earthed via the mains earth lead. The computer should be switched off, and the supply should also be switched off at the mains socket. The earth lead is never switched, and the case will remain earthed even when it is switched off.

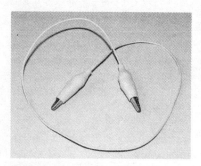

Fig.2.2 A crocodile clip lead

Wristbands

If you wish to make quite sure that your body remains static-free, you can earth yourself to the computer by way of a proper earthing wristband. This is basically just a wristband made from electrically conductive material that connects to the earth via a lead and a high-value resistor. The lead is terminated in a clip that permits easy connection to the chassis of the computer. The resistor does not prevent any static build-up in your body from leaking away to earth, but it will protect you from a significant shock if a fault should result in the earthing point becoming "live". A variation on this system has a special mains plug that enables the wristband to be safely earthed to the mains supply. Earthing

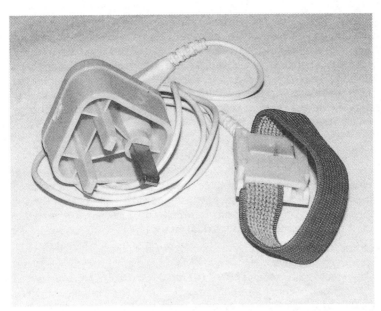

Fig.2.3 An earthing wristband complete with special mains plug

wristbands are available from some of the larger computer component suppliers, and from electronics component retailers.

A typical wristband, complete with lead and special earthing plug, is shown in Figure 2.3. Note that these are sometimes sold together as a kit, but they are also sold as separate items.The one in Figure 2.3 was actually bought as a single item, but it consists of three parts that clip together (see G.4 in the Colour Gallery). Anyway, make sure you know what you are buying before you part with your money. The wristband on its own is about as much good as a monitor without the rest of the PC. It is possible to buy disposable wristband kits, but if you are likely to do a fair amount of PC upgrading from time to time it is probably worthwhile obtaining one of the cheaper non-disposable types. With intermittent use one of these should last many years.

Keeping in touch

If you do not want to go to the expense of buying a wristband, a simple but effective alternative is to touch the conductive worktop or the metal chassis of the computer from time to time. This will leak away any gradual build-up of static electricity before it has time to reach dangerous proportions. Again, the computer must be connected to the mains supply, but it should be switched off and the mains supply should be switched off at the mains outlet. The more frequently you touch the computer or other earthed object the lower the likelihood of static build-up in your body. Before removing any component from its anti-static packing, touch the earthed chassis while holding the component and its packing. While this method is very effective, it is probably worth buying an earthing wristband if you will be handling expensive computer components.

That is really all there is to it. Simply having a large chunk of earthed metal (in the form of the computer case) near the work area helps to discourage the build-up of any static charges in the first place. The few simple precautions outlined previously are then sufficient to ensure that there is no significant risk to the components.

Do not be tempted to simply ignore the dangers of static electricity when handling computer components. When building electronic gadgets I often ignore static precautions, but I am dealing with components that cost a matter of pence each. If one or two of the components should be zapped by a static charge, no great harm is done. The cost would be minimal and I have plenty of spares available. The same is not true when dealing with computer components, some of which could cost in excess of a hundred pounds. Also, the computer would remain out of commission until a suitable replacement spare part was obtained.

Anti-static packing

One final point is that any static sensitive components will be supplied in some form of anti-static packaging. This is usually nothing more than a plastic bag that is made from a special plastic that is slightly conductive. Processors and memory modules are often supplied in something more elaborate, such as conductive plastic clips and boxes. There is quite a range of anti-static packaging currently in use, and Figure 2.4 shows a couple of examples. Some packing effectively short circuits the pins or connectors of the protected components so that no significant voltage can build up between them. Others are designed to electrically insulate the components from the outside world so that stray static charges can not get to them. Both methods should provide complete protection from normal static charges.

Although it is tempting to remove the components from the packing to have a good look at them, try to keep this type of thing to a minimum.

Ideally it should be completely avoided. I think it is worth reiterating the point that due care must be taken when you do remove a component from its packing. Always make sure that both you and the plastic bag or other packing is earthed before the component is removed. As explained previously, simply touching the earthed chassis of a computer while holding the component in its bag should ensure that everything is charge-free. Make sure that you always handle the

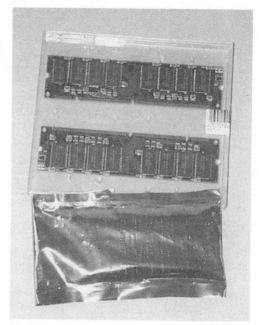

Fig.2.4 Two forms of anti-static packing

components in an environment that is free from any likely sources of static charges. Check for any likely sources of static before you start handling sensitive components. There will then be a minimal risk of any damage occurring. Ideally an earthed wristband should always be worn when touching computer components, even if they will only be handled very briefly.

It is worthwhile keeping some of the anti-static packing that you get with spare parts or components bought for upgrading. Repairing or upgrading a PC often involves partially dismantling the base unit, and it is useful to have some anti-static packing to keep components safe until they are reinstalled in the computer. A few types of anti-static packing are available from some of the larger electronic component retailers incidentally.

Cracking it

It is possible to greatly expand a PC system by adding peripherals to the standard ports, but before too long you will probably need to delve inside

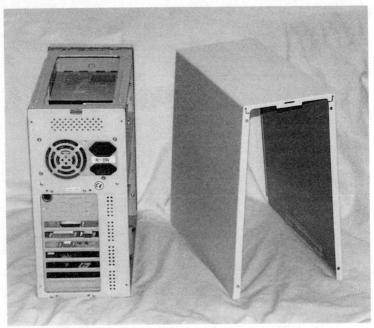

Fig.2.5 An AT case has a one-piece outer casing. PCs of this type are quite old and upgrading them is probably not a practical proposition

to add extra memory, fit an expansion card, or something of this type. Gaining entry to the interior of a PC is straightforward provided it uses a conventional case. Older PCs often have an AT style case, and these almost invariably have the two sides and top panel as a single piece. Four or six screws on the rear of the PC are removed and then the outer casing can be pulled free and completely removed from the chassis (Figure 2.5).

Computers that use an AT case are likely to be pretty old, and are not good candidates for most types of upgrade. For a start, you have to consider whether it is worthwhile spending money on a PC that probably has very little useful life ahead of it. Another consideration is the availability of suitable components for an upgrade. In general, new components are not compatible with older PCs. In most cases it is not possible to fit new components into an old PC due to changes in the interfaces and

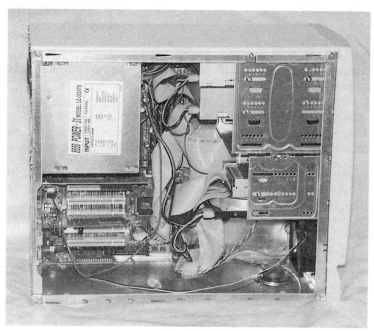

Fig.2.6 An ATX case has removable panels

expansion slots over the years. Suitable driver software is unlikely to be available either. It might be possible to obtain suitable components on the second-hand market. However, this gives you an upgraded but still rather old and out-of-date PC, and is unlikely to be worth the time and money involved. Upgrading AT computers will not be considered further here.

ATX cases

ATX cases look much the same as the AT variety, but in general they are slightly wider (tower cases) or higher (desktop models). Taking tower cases first, the top panel might be removable, but it is usually left in place when working on the interior of the PC. The two side panels are removable, and it is these that give access to the interior of the unit. As viewed from the front, it is usually the left-hand side panel that has to be removed when working on the interior of a PC (Figure 2.6). This gives access to the expansion slots, memory, the cabling, etc. It also gives access to the drives, but in some instances it is necessary to remove the other side panel in order to obtain full access to the drive bays. This is normally only necessary when fitting or removing a drive, and many cases now permit drives to be added or removed with only the right-hand panel in place.

The situation is much the same with desktop cases, but it is the top panel that is removed in order to gain access to the main components. It might be necessary to remove the base panel when dealing with some components. In the world of PCs there is probably no such thing as a true standard, and manufacturers tend to "do their own thing" for the slightest excuse. Cases seem to have more than their fair share of variations with the PC manufacturers trying to make their particular models stand out from the crowd. Consequently, it might be necessary to study the outer casing of your PC very carefully in order to discover how to "crack" it. Some of the desktop cases are the most difficult to deal with.

There can be further complications with the low-profile desktop cases which have insufficient height to accommodate expansion cards. The usual solution is to have a vertical daughterboard that plugs into the motherboard, and the expansion cards then fit horizontally into the daughterboard. In addition to its awkwardness, this system has the drawback that there are usually only two expansion slots. With most of the hardware integrated with the motherboard on modern PCs this is less of a drawback than was once the case. On the other hand, it does limit the upgrade potential of the PC, especially if one slot is already used by (say) a wi-fi adaptor. Low-profile cases are not the only non-standard type in use, and with any of these imaginative cases you have to do some careful investigation in order to get them apart. You then have to do some further delving in order to find where everything is situated inside the case.

Fitting cards

Although there has been a trend towards the use of USB wherever possible for upgrades, some types of expansion still require an expansion card to be fitted inside the case. Physically fitting the card is much the same regardless of whether it is a PCI, PCI Xpress, ISA, AGP, or AMR type. Once the case is open you have an obvious problem in that the expansion slot you wish to use will be blocked by a metal bracket at the rear of the PC's casing. There are three main types of blanking plate.

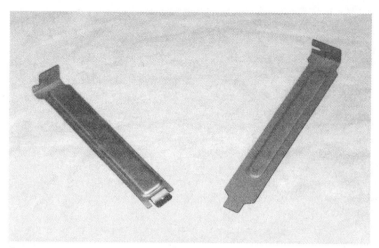

Fig.2.7 Two types of blanking plate

The original type is held in place by a single screw that fixes the bracket to the rear of the case. A bracket of this type is shown on the right in Figure 2.7. If you undo the screw using a largish cross-point screwdriver the bracket should pull free without any difficulty. It is advisable to keep the bracket so the hole in the rear of the case can be blocked up again if you remove the expansion card at some later date. The bracket's fixing screw will be needed to hold the expansion card in place.

Some modern PC cases still use this method of fixing the brackets in place, but it is mainly the more upmarket cases that retain this method. Probably the most popular kind of bracket these days is the type that is semi cut out from the rear of the case. In order to remove one of these it is necessary to twist it to and fro until the thin pieces of metal connecting it to the main casing fatigue and break. Figure 2.8(a) shows the rear of a new ATX case with all of the brackets in place. In Figure 2.8(b) two of the brackets have been twisted round slightly to show how they can be broken away from the main casing. There is little point in keeping this type of bracket since it can not be fitted back in place again. A third method has brackets that clip into the screw holes in the main case. A bracket of this type is shown on the left in Figure 2.7. These can be twisted slightly and pulled free, and the process is reversible. It is therefore worthwhile keeping these brackets as they can be fitted into the case again should the need arise.

Fig.2.8(a) A new case with a full set of blanking plates

Softly, softly

With the metal bracket removed, the expansion card can be taken from its anti-static packing and pushed into position on the motherboard. Some cards and slots fit together quite easily while other combinations are less accommodating. Never try the brute force method of fitting expansion cards into place. Using plenty of force is virtually always the wrong approach when dealing with PCs, but it is certainly asking for trouble when applied to expansion cards. Apart from the risk of damage to the card itself there is also a likelihood of writing off the motherboard.

If a card seems to be reluctant to fit into place, start by checking that the metal bracket is slotting correctly into place between the case and the motherboard. With some PCs the bottom end of the bracket has to be bent away from the circuit board slightly as it otherwise tends to hit the motherboard rather than fitting just behind it. Look carefully at the connector on the card and the expansion slot. It can be quite dim inside a PC, so if necessary, get some additional light inside the PC using something like a spotlamp or a powerful torch.

Fig.2.8(b) The plates can be twisted and eventually broken free

Probably the most common problem is the card being slightly too far forward or back. This is the same problem with the metal bracket, but manifesting itself in a different manner. The bracket is fitting into place correctly, but the rest of the card is then out of alignment. If the misalignment is only slight, you should be able to ease the card backwards or forwards slightly and then into place.

Where there is a large error it will be necessary to form the bracket slightly in order to get the card to fit properly. In one or two cases where all else has failed, slightly loosening the screws that fix the motherboard to the chassis has provided the solution. Presumably in these cases the motherboard has been bolted in place when it is fractionally out of position. Loosening the mounting bolts and then fitting the expansion card shifts it into the correct position. The mounting bolts are then retightened, and fitting further expansion cards should be perfectly straightforward.

Fig.2.9 This expansion card is fully fitted into place

Down and out

Sometimes everything appears to be in position correctly, but when the PC is switched on and booted into Windows there is no response from the card. Windows seems to be oblivious to its presence in the computer. Alternatively, with the new card installed the computer refuses to do anything when it is switched on. It could be that the card is genuinely faulty, but in most cases it is simply that the card has not been pushed down into the expansion slot correctly.

Look inside the computer and check that the card is parallel to the slot and not raised slightly at one end. With the card in the expansion slot at an angle it is possible for the connector on the card to short circuit the terminals on the connector in the expansion slot. This will be detected by the power supply at power-up, and it then refuses to switch on as a safety measure. Hence there is no response from the PC when it is switched on. Getting the card pushed right down into the expansion slot should cure the problem.

Fig.2.10 Here the card has only partially slotted into place

If the computer boots into Windows correctly but ignores the card, the most likely cause is that the card is simply not pushed down into the slot correctly at either end. In consequence, all or most of the terminals on the card's connector are failing to make contact with their counterparts on the expansion slot. Windows fails to recognise the card because it is effectively absent from the PC and is not contactable. Shut down Windows and switch off the computer before trying to rectify the problem.

Look carefully at the card, which should have little or nothing of the connector showing if it is fitted into the expansion slot correctly (Figure 2.9). It is probably not properly inserted into the expansion slot if the copper "fingers" of the edge connector are still clearly visible (Figure 2.10).

Remove the fixing screw so that the card can be manoeuvred easily, and the try gently pushing the card right down into the slot using a rocking motion. Do not force it into position as this could damage the motherboard, and should not be necessary. The front to back alignment is incorrect if the board will not go down into the slot. Correct this problem and it should fit into place without too much difficulty.

Fitting AGP and PCI Xpress cards is a little more involved than the standard PCI variety, because AGP and PCI Xpress slots have a lever that locks the card in place. Where appropriate, it is clearly necessary to ensure that a card is properly locked in place before switching on the computer and trying out the card. AGP and PCI Xpress cards are covered in detail in chapter 6, which deals with video and audio upgrades. It is not a subject that will be considered any further here.

All change

In the event that the card seems to be fitted correctly but it is failing to work properly or stalling the computer at start-up, it is worth trying the card in a different expansion slot. In theory the expansion slots are all the same, but in practice it sometimes happens that a card that fails in one slot works perfectly well when installed in a different one. There is no problem in using a different slot provided the computer actually has a spare slot. If it does not, you could still try swapping the new card with an existing one. Alternatively, try removing the card and reinstalling it. In the case of an AGP slot there will only be one, and removing and reinstalling the card will be the only option. The same is likely to be true for PCI Xpress cards. Many PCs have two of these exapansion slots, but they are often different sizes. The larger one is for a video card and the smaller type is for general expansion.

It is by no means certain why using a card in a different slot will often cure the problem. Perhaps there are minor physical differences between the slots giving better compatibility between some slots and certain cards. Inserting a card into a slot and removing tends to clean the card's connector and the one in the slot, possibly producing more reliable connections between the two. This could explain why removing and reinstalling a card sometimes brings results. Perhaps some cards appear to be properly installed but are not quite into the expansion slot correctly. Removing and reinstalling the card could then result in it fitting that little bit further into place the second time. Whatever the reasons, it does sometimes work, and it is certainly worth a try when dealing with troublesome expansion cards.

Which slot?

I am often asked if it matters which expansion slot is used when adding a new card. Apart from fussy cards that work well in one slot but refuse to work in another, it does not matter which slot is used provided it is the correct type for the card. Some people prefer to use the slots nearest the processor first, working on the basis that inductance and capacitance in the board's copper connecting tracks will have less effect on the slots nearest the processor, giving greater reliability. I do not know of any testing that has proven this theory, but I suppose that working methodically away from the processor is as good a way of doing things as any other.

Switches and jumpers

Although many settings have been transferred to the BIOS over the years, I have yet to encounter a PC that lacks any configuration jumpers or switches. In fact some PCs still have large numbers of them, although in some cases they are optional and the BIOS can be used for most settings if preferred. Anyway, in order to deal with a PC, ancient or modern, it is certainly necessary to understand the use of configuration switches and jumpers. What parameters are likely to be set via switches or jumpers?

With Socket 7 motherboards and some later ones it is necessary to set the correct clock multiplier for the processor. This is less common but not unknown with later boards. With more recent boards it is more likely to be the motherboard's bus frequency that is set via jumpers or switches. The multiplier is usually set automatically so that the processor can not be overclocked by setting a higher than normal multiplier value.

With Socket 7 motherboards it is usually necessary to set the processor core voltage. Conventionally logic circuits operate from a 5-volt supply, but in order to get the highest possible performance it is common practice for other supply voltages to be used in parts of the computer. Memory circuits and some sections of the processor often operate at 3.3 volts, and the main processor circuits often work at a somewhat lower voltage. It is this second voltage, or core voltage that is set via the jumpers or DIP-switches. The instruction manual for the motherboard should give the correct settings for all the usable processors. It is common for the correct core voltage to be marked on the top surface of the processor, particularly with non-Intel devices. If the marked core voltage is different to the one indicated on the chip itself, set up the motherboard to provide the voltage indicated on the chip.

Clear CMOS

There may be other settings that are controlled by jumpers or switches, but these additional parameters vary a lot from one motherboard to another. One virtually standard feature is a jumper that enables the CMOS memory to be disconnected from the backup battery. By default this should be set so the board functions normally, with the backup battery ensuring that the BIOS is free from amnesia, with the correct drive parameters, etc., being used each time the computer is switched on. Setting this jumper to the "off" position for a few minutes wipes the CMOS memory of all its contents. With the jumper restored to the "on" setting the computer is able to function again, but it is a matter of starting "from scratch" with the CMOS memory settings.

In effect, this jumper provides a means of resetting the CMOS memory. This would be probably only be necessary if someone started to use the password facility and then forgot his or her password. The only way of getting the computer to boot if this happens is to clear the current set-up from memory. The next time the computer is started it uses the default settings, which means that it starts up without implementing the password facility. Unless there is a good reason to do so, it is best not to use any BIOS password facility. Note that it is not usually necessary to clear the CMOS memory in this way if you manage to make a complete mess of the BIOS settings. From within the BIOS Setup program it is usually possible to revert to one or two sets of default settings, and then do any necessary "fine tuning". It would only be necessary to clear the CMOS memory if a bad setting was preventing the PC from starting up.

There can be other jumpers or DIP-switches to set such things as the supply voltage for the memory modules, to disable the built-in audio system, and this type of thing. You really have to read the manual for the motherboard to determine what jumpers or DIP-switches have to be set up correctly, if any. As pointed out previously, the modern trend is towards as much as possible being set using auto-detection methods, or via the BIOS Setup program. Older motherboards often have numerous switches or jumpers, but many modern motherboards only have one switch or jumper that can be used to power-down the CMOS memory.

Setting up

Actually setting any jumpers or switches should not give any major problems. There are two types of jumper, which are the straightforward on/off type and the two-way variety. The on/off type has two pins and

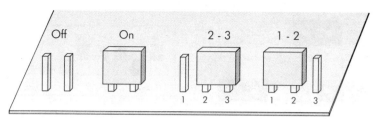

Fig.2.11 The two types of jumper normally used on motherboards

you fit the jumper over the pins to connect them together ("on") or do not fit the jumper at all ("off"). This simple scheme of things is shown in the left-hand section Figure 2.11. It is common practice to fit the jumper on one of the pins to provide the "off" setting. If you should need to change the setting at a later time you then know exactly where to find the jumper. The jumpers are minute and are likely to get lost if you store them somewhere other than on the motherboard.

The second type of jumper block has three pins, and the jumper is used to connect the middle pin to one of the outer pins, as in the right-hand section of Figure 2.11. The jumper is connecting together two pins, as before, and the jumpers are exactly the same whether they are used on a two-pin block or a three-pin type.

DIP-switches are normally in blocks of four or eight switches, but not all the switches in a block will necessarily be utilized. They are a form of slider switch, and are more or less a miniature version of the switches often

Fig.2.12 The "ON" marking on a DIP-switch

used in small electronic gadgets such as cassette recorders and personal stereo units. The block of switches is marked with "on" and (or) "off" legends (Figure 2.12) to make it clear which setting is which.

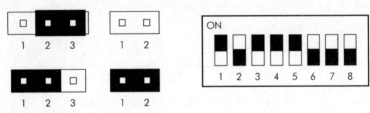

Fig.2.13 Some switch and jumper diagrams are clearer than others

The motherboard's instruction manual normally includes a diagram showing the correct switch or jumper settings for a given processor. There is a slight problem here in that these diagrams are open to misinterpretation. In the two examples of Figure 2.13, which pins do the jumpers connect and which switches are in the "on" position. My guess would be that the black blocks represent the jumpers and the control knobs on the switches, but there is no way of telling for sure without some further assistance.

The manual should provide this assistance in the form of another diagram showing exactly how the switch or jumper setting diagrams should be interpreted. These diagrams will be something like Figure 2.14 and 2.15. Never rely on guesswork when setting jumpers and DIP-switches. Mistakes are unlikely to result in any damage, but it is not worth taking the risk. Carefully study the instruction manual for the motherboard and get things right first time.

PCMCIA/PC Card

The expansion cards used for desktop PCs are too large for use in laptop PCs, and this has led to the development of miniature expansion cards

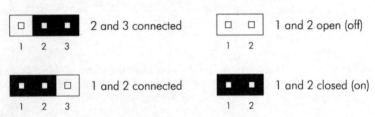

Fig.2.14 An explanatory diagram for jumper settings

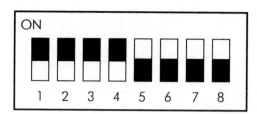

1 to 4 = ON

5 to 7 = OFF

Fig.2.15 An explanatory diagram for DIP-switches

specifically designed for laptop PCs and other portable computing devices. PCMCIA cards are popular form of miniature exapansion card for use in laptops. PCMCIA stands for Personal Computer Memory Card International Association, and it is the type of expansion slot/card used with many laptop PCs. As its name suggests, it was designed as a means of using memory cards with computers. In practice it has only been used to a significant degree with laptop computers and other portable electronic gadgets, and has never been used very much with desktop computers. Also, its use has spread to accommodate a wider range of applications than additional memory. These days PCMCIA cards are used in applications such as wi-fi adaptors, advanced sound systems, and to provide additional ports.

The original PCMCIA name has been largely dropped now. Various alternative names have been used, but PC Card seems to be the one that has gained the most widespread acceptance. Since there are now some alternative types of expansion card, you need to take due care to obtain one of the right type for your laptop.

These days there is often the choice of using a USB port for expansion purposes rather than fitting a PC card. The advantage of the PC card method is that the card fits right into the PC, and effectively becomes part of it. A USB add-on is an

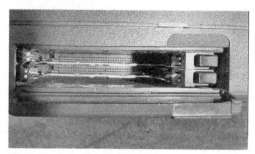

Fig.2.16 A double PCMCIA slot

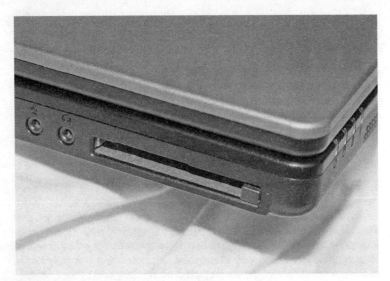

Fig.2.17 An ExpressCard expansion slot

external unit that either connects to the computer via a lead, or plugs straight into the port and protrudes on one side of the laptop. Therefore, a PC card is generally the better choice for a laptop that will be used on the move. It avoids the need to plug anything into the computer and remove it again each time you set up the computer and pack it away again. Using a PC card has little or no advantage where a laptop is used as a home or small office computer.

Most laptops that use this type of expansion have one PC card slot, but a few have two (Figure 2.16). Probably only a fairly small percentage of laptop users ever need even one expansion slot. It is possible to obtain laptops that are equipped with things such as integrated wi-fi adaptors and Firewire ports. It is only necessary to add them via an expansion slot if you buy a laptop that lacks these features initially.

Ideally you should assess your requirements before buying a laptop, and where possible select one that has everything you require built-in. It is then likely that there will be no need for any expansion slots during the working life of the computer. However, there will be at least one slot available to accommodate future developments or changes in your requirements.

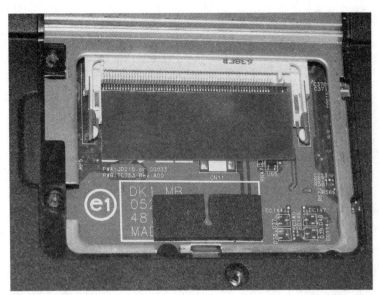

Fig.2.18 A mini PCI expansion slot

ExpressCard

There are alternatives to PC cards, and some manufacturers are now starting to use these instead of PC cards. Whether this is strictly necessary is debatable. Although the PC card system has its origins many years ago and it is getting "a bit long in the tooth", it is nevertheless capable of handling most requirements. It also has the advantage of being well established, which means that it is possible to obtain a wide range of cards that use this technology.

Anyway, it is advisable to check that there is a reasonable range of matching expansion cards available before buying a laptop that has something other than PC card slots. ExpressCard is a new expansion card system that might eventually replace the PC card system. The technology is different, so the two types of card are totally incompatible. Physically, ExpressCards are about half the size of PC cards, and will normally be significantly lighter than PC cards as well. Figure 2.17 shows an ExpressCard slot in a laptop PC.

Mini PCI

As its name suggests, Mini PCI is essentially a smaller version of the normal PCI expansion bus, and many laptop PCs have an expansion slot of this type. As usual with a laptop PC, if the expansion slot is easily accessible, it will be necessary to remove the appropriate cover on the underside of the unit in order to gain access to the Mini PCI expansion slot. Note that Mini PCI expansion slots are sometimes difficult to access, and are positioned underneath the keyboard or something of this nature. Where this is the case it is not a good idea to try accessing it unless you are sure that you have the necessary knowledge to do so. Many laptop PCs are difficult to dismantle, and even more difficult to reassemble!

The slot (Figure 2.18) looks similar to the memory holders that are often fitted to laptop PCs, and the Mini PCI cards look rather like taller versions of laptop memory modules (see G.5 in the Colour Gallery). Removing a Mini PCI card is very easy, and it is just a matter of pulling the arm at each end of the holder outwards. They should be operated simultaneously, and the card will then flip up at a slight angle. It can then be pulled free from the holder. Fitting a card is equally straightforward. Push the card fully into the slot, keeping the card at a slight angle to the base of the computer. Provided the card is fully into the slot, it can then be pressed down into place, and the two arms will lock it in position.

One slight snag with Mini PCI slots is that they are often used to provide part of the computer's basic specification. In particular, many laptop PCs are now supplied with wi-fi connectivity as standard, and the wi-fi facility is often provided by a Mini PCI card. This means that the Mini PCI slot is unusable unless you are prepared to forgo the facility that it is already providing.

Memory
upgrades

Chip memory

With so many modern programs requiring large amounts of memory in
order to work at their best (or to work at all in some cases), it is not
surprising that adding memory is the most popular form of hardware
upgrade. Memory upgrading is a potentially confusing subject, since
there are now several types of memory in common use, and numerous
types have been used over the years. PCs prior to the 80386 processor
had their memory in the form of integrated circuits that plugged into
rows of holders on the motherboard. In some cases there were about
three dozen of these sockets.

Upgrading on-board RAM was a fiddly and time consuming process. If
you ran out of sockets it was possible to increase the RAM further using
expansion cards, but this gave rather poor performance due to the
relatively low operating speed of the ISA expansion bus. Memory
expansion cards are now totally obsolete, but you can probably still obtain
the chips for on-board memory upgrades. However, in a PC context this
type of memory is well and truly obsolete, and it will not be considered
further here.

Memory map

Memory that comes within the normal 640k MS/DOS allocation is usually
termed "base memory". With a modern PC there will be no need to
expand the base memory, as the computer will have been supplied with
the full 640k of RAM as standard. RAM, incidentally, stands for "random
access memory", and is the form of memory used for storing application
programs and data. The contents of the RAM in a PC are lost when the

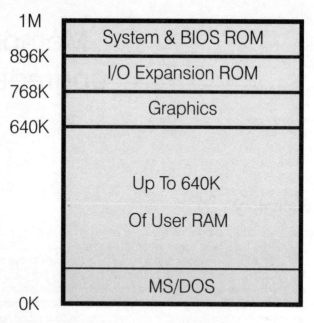

Fig.3.1 The memory map for a PC's base memory

computer is switched off, and it is, for all practical purposes, lost if the computer is reset (whether a hardware or software reset is used). ROM (read only memory) is used for programs that must not be lost when the computer is switched off, which in the case of a PC means its BIOS program. The 8088 series of microprocessors used in the early PCs can address 1 megabyte (1024 kilobytes or 1024k) of memory, but in a PC only 640k of this is allocated to RAM for program and data storage. The rest is set aside for purposes such as the ROM BIOS and the video RAM. Figure 3.1 shows the original memory map for PC.

Modern PC processors can operate in modes that permit large amounts of RAM to be accessed. In the past the maximum RAM limit was usually imposed by the motherboard design rather than the capabilities of the the processor, with an upper limit that was usually around 256 to 1024 megabytes or so. Things have moved on though, with RAM becoming much cheaper, and motherboards have been designed to accommodate more memory as a consequence of this. The maximum memory that can be installed is not much higher though, because the limits do not allow a vast increase. The maximum amount that can be handled by a PC that has a 32-bit processor is 4 gigabytes (4096 megabytes). However, for various reasons it is usual for the maximum amount of physical RAM that can be installed to be somewhat less. For example, the graphics system is sometimes integrated with the motherboard, and it is then normal for it to use the ordinary system memory. In many cases though, a graphics card with its own high-speed memory is used, and this still occupies some of the available address range. Either way, a significant chunk of the 4 gigabyte address space is occupied by the graphics system, leaving less space for normal system memory. In most cases the limit for system memory is 3 gigabytes, but some motherboards have the wherewithall to handle 3.5 gigabytes of RAM.

In practice, even one gigabyte is sufficient to run most operating PCs, the inevitable background tasks that seem to be an essential part of modern computing, and some application programs. This is not to say that things will not run better with more RAM. Probably the most frequently asked of frequently asked PC questions is "how much RAM do I need." This is very much a "how long is a piece of string" style question, and it is entirely dependent on the operating system and applications software that you will be running.

The software manuals should give details of the minimum requirements, but the minimum is the bare minimum needed to run the software at all. Most programs can run in a relatively small amount of RAM by using the hard disc for temporary storage space. This usually works quite well, but gives noticeably slower results than when using RAM as the temporary data store. With complex graphics oriented programs the operating speed can be painfully slow unless the PC is equipped with large amounts of RAM. There will probably be a recommended minimum system to run the software, a typical system, or something of this type. I tend to regard the amount of RAM recommended for a typical system as the minimum that will really be usable in practice.

In the days of Windows 95, 98, and ME, most software would run using 32 megabytes of RAM, but even with these operating systems it was preferable to use upwards of 64 megabytes. The story is very different with Windows XP, where 128 megabytes represents a realistic minimum. At least 256 megabytes of memory is preferable, and I would install at least 512 megabytes in a PC that will run XP. With Windows Vista it is preferable to use a minimum of 512 megabytes, and I would not settle for less than one gigabyte. Some applications require large amounts of memory, and programs that handle photographic images or other large bitmaps are particularly demanding in this respect. Programs that handle video also require large amounts of memory, and probably hard disc space as well.

As an example, when handling large bitmap images in PhotoShop it is recommended that the amount of RAM in the PC should be at least double the size of the bitmap. In order to handle scanned bitmaps of around 25 to 30 megabytes at least 60 megabytes of RAM would therefore be required. With (say) four images of this size loaded into the program, the amount of RAM required would be about four times this figure, or some 240 megabytes. Bear in mind that this is in addition to the RAM required by PhotoShop itself, the operating system, and any other software that is running.

Bear in mind that large amounts of RAM can be needed in order to run several programs at once. In theory you do not need (say) 290 megabytes of RAM to multitask with two programs that require 120 and 170 megabytes of RAM. Somewhat less than 290 megabytes should suffice, because you are only running one copy of the operating system, and the two programs will share some resources. Practical experience would suggest that 290 megabytes would actually represent a realistic minimum in this situation, and with Windows XP or Vista it would probably be necessary to have substantially more than this.

Although memory has been very expensive in the past, it is currently quite cheap and putting large amounts of RAM into a PC is likely to be well worth the modest cost involved. Memory is like money, you know what, and hard disc space: you can never have too much of it. You do not hear people claiming that they have wasted money putting too much memory in their computers, but you do hear people expressing regret for not having specified more RAM when buying their PC. If your PC will take 3 gigabytes or so of RAM, installing the full amount is unlikely to "cost the earth", and doing so will ensure that the computer runs any memory-hungry applications as efficiently as possible.

Note that some operating systems permit the use of more than 4 gigabytes of memory. With some 64-bit versions of Windows for example, as much as 128 gigabytes of memory can be accommodated. This is not to say that the motherboard will be able to take such a large amount of memory. Before trying to install massive amounts of memory it is essential to check the physical limitations of the computer's hardware. If the operating system can accommodate 128 gigabytes of RAM but the motherboard can only use a maximum of 8 gigabytes, the 8 gigabyte limit is the one that matters. The 128 gigabyte limit is purely academic.

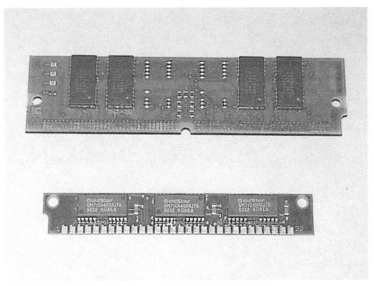

Fig.3.2 A 72-pin SIMM (top) and a 30-pin type (bottom)

SIMMs

Memory in the form of individual chips was replaced by SIMMs (single in-line memory modules). A memory module of this type is a small printed circuit board, which is fitted with miniature DRAM chips of the surface-mount variety. A 30-pin SIMM is shown in Figure 3.2 where it is the smaller of the two memory modules.. This board plugs into a socket on the motherboard, and this set-up is like a sort of miniature version of the standard expansion slot system.

80386 and 80486 based PCs mostly use 30-pin SIMMs. These modules are available with normal eight-bit wide memory, and nine-bit wide memory. It is the nine-bit variety that is needed for most 80386 and 80486 PCs. The additional bit, incidentally, is used for a method of error checking known as parity checking. These modules come in 256k, 1 megabyte, and 4 megabyte varieties, reflecting the type of DRAM chip they use.

These modules are also available in a variety of speed ratings, again reflecting the type of DRAM chip they utilize. From the early days of memory chips to the latest memory modules there has always been RAM of the same general type but with various speed ratings.

Fig.3.3 A 168-pin DIMM (dual in-line memory module)

Consequently, when buying RAM you have to make sure that you obtain the right type and memory of adequate speed rating. With 80386 based PCs the modules normally have to be used in pairs or even in sets of four, but some 80486s can use odd numbers of these modules. There may also be restrictions on using SIMMs of different sizes. In general, later PCs are more accommodating, but it is still advisable to check for memory restrictions before buying any memory modules.

Bigger and better

30-pin SIMMs are now long obsolete, and have not been used in new computers for many years. They were been superseded by 72-pin SIMMs, which provide capacities of more than 4 megabytes per module. 72-pin SIMMs are available in 4, 8, 16, 32, and 64 megabyte versions. Like the 30-pin variety they are available with or without the parity bit. The larger memory module in Figure 3.2 is a 72-pin SIMM. Unlike the 30-pin SIMMs, it is the modules that lack the parity bit that are normally used in PCs. Some motherboards can actually accommodate either type, but in practice the non-parity type are used because they are significantly cheaper.

Two types of memory are available in 72-pin SIMM form. The original modules of this type were fitted with fast page memory (FPM), and this type of memory is based on ordinary DRAM chips. Later 72-pin modules use an alternative form of memory called extended data output (EDO) RAM. This usually gives somewhat faster performance than fast page memory, although the improvement obtained is unlikely to be more than about 10 percent or so. 72-pin memory modules are now obsolete, but you may need to use them if you upgrade the memory of an old PC. Obviously care has to be taken to obtain the right type.

If in doubt, it is a matter of checking the manual for the computer or the motherboard to determine which type or types of memory module are supported. The BIOS usually displays details of the installed memory during the start-up procedure, and programs such as Sisoft's Sandra will supply this information.

SIMMs were superseded by DIMMs (dual in-line memory modules). These look like outsize SIMMs (Figure 3.3), and have 168 terminals. SIMMs operate from a 5 volt supply, but the DIMMs used in PCs operate from 3.3 volts (like the input/output terminals of a Pentium processor of the same period). However, 5 volt DIMMs are produced. Fast page and EDO DIMMs are available, but it is SDRAM (synchronous dynamic random access memory) DIMMs that are normally used in PCs. Many PC motherboards will actually operate with fast page and EDO DIMMs, but as these are more difficult to obtain, slower, and usually more expensive than SDRAM, there would seem to be no point in using them. Buffered and unbuffered SDRAM DIMMs are available, but it is the unbuffered variety that is normally required for use in PCs.

SDRAM DIMMs are available with capacities of 16, 32, 64, and 128 megabytes, but many of the early Pentium motherboards that accept this type of memory are incompatible with the larger sizes. In fact some of the first boards to accept DIMMs will only take the 16-megabyte type.

SDRAM is available in various speeds. For ordinary Socket 7 and Pentium II computers the 12ns variety is sufficient, but the faster 10ns DIMMs are also suitable. PCs that use faster motherboards which operate at 100MHz, such as 350MHz and faster Pentium II systems, require 10ns SDRAM. The modules that use this memory are usually referred to as "PC100" DIMMs in advertisements. Although this type of memory has not been used in new PCs for some time, it is quite likely that this is the type that will be needed if an old PC is upgraded.

Many older motherboards only have sockets for DIMMs, but there are plenty of boards that can take DIMMs or SIMMs. A typical Socket 7 motherboard of this type has sockets for two DIMMs and four 72-pin SIMMs. Some PC upgraders get into difficulty because they assume that it is possible to utilize all six sockets. Using a mixture of DIMMs and SIMMs is not a good idea, and is strictly prohibited with many motherboards. Even where the manufacturer of the motherboard does not ban this practice, I would certainly advise against it. The problem in using a mixture of the two memory types seems to stem from the fact that they operate at different supply voltages rather than any differences in their timing.

Whatever the cause, I have never managed to get satisfactory results when using a mixture of these two types of memory module. If you read the "fine print" in the motherboard's manual you will almost certainly discover that one bank of SIMM sockets is connected to use the same address space as the DIMM sockets. Regardless of any other considerations, it is not possible to use both of these sets of sockets, as there would be a hardware conflict.

Modern memory

As processor speeds have increased it has been necessary for new types of memory to be produced in an attempt to keep pace. 168-pin DIMMs have been used in new PCs until quite recently, but in a faster version. These are known as PC133 DIMMs, and they look much the same as the slower versions. This type of memory is not quite obsolete, but it is now little used in new PCs. The most popular form of memory for recent PCs is the DDR (double data rate) variety.

The "double" part of the name refers to the fact that the memory operates at twice the clock frequency of the motherboard. Clock frequencies of 200 megahertz and 266 megahertz are used with the original versions of DDR memory, and these respectively use motherboard bus frequencies of 100 and 133 megahertz. I think it is fair to say that DDR memory did not give the sort of speed increase that many had hoped for, but it did give a significant improvement. When the price of DDR memory became comparable to the PC100 and PC133 varieties it was inevitable that it would gradually take over.

DDR memory is sold in the form of 184-pin DIMMs (Figure 3.4). From the physical point of view a DDR DIMM is essentially just a slightly scaled-up version of the 168-pin components. The 200 and 233 megahertz DDR modules are sometimes sold as such, but they are more usually called PC1600 and PC2100 modules respectively. The number in each case refers to the bandwidth in megabits per second. The PC1600

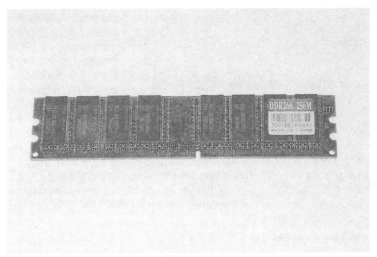

Fig.3.4 This is a 184-pin PC2100 DDR DIMM

modules seem to be relatively difficult to obtain these days, but the faster PC2100 type can be used instead. Things move on, and faster (PC2700 and PC3200) DDR modules are now starting to appear. The PC2700 modules are for use at 333 megahertz and the PC3200 modules are for operation at 400 megahertz. Of course, these are the operating frequencies for the memory modules, and in standard DDR fashion the motherboards operate at half these frequencies.

With DDR memory, and possibly with other types, you may encounter a rating such as "CL3" or "CL2.5". This refers to a memory timing parameter in the BIOS Setup program, where it is usually called something like CAS Latency. A low figure here gives higher performance, but there is no guarantee that "bog standard" memory modules will work reliably with so-called "aggressive" memory timing. If you wish to push the system to its limits it is essential to obtain modules that are guaranteed to operate with a low CAS Latency setting.

RIMMs

There is an alternative form of high-speed memory in the form of RIMMs (Figure 3.5), which are memory modules from Rambus Inc. Each Rambus DRAM (RDRAM) can operate at up to 800 megahertz over a 16-bit wide

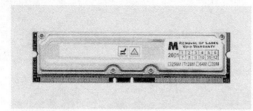

Fig.3.5 A Rambus memory module (RIMM)

channel. RIMMs are often called PC800 modules, with the 800 being derived from the maximum operating frequency. Note that a PC1600 DDR module is not twice as fast as a PC800 RIMM. The 1600 refers to the bit rate, whereas the figure of 800 is the frequency for a 16-bit bus. The PC800 modules should be something like eight times faster than the PC1600 variety, but the difference in overall performance is, of course, very much less than this. The latest RIMMs (PC1066) operate at up to 1066 megahertz.

RDRAM memory is certainly very fast, and it was used with many early Pentium 4 based systems. Its drawback was the very high price tag which added substantially to the cost of the complete computer system. RIMM prices did come down over time, but other types of RAM also became cheaper. Consequently, this type of memory remained relatively expensive, and it is some time since it was used in new designs. A memory upgrade will be relatively expensive if you have a PC that uses RIMMs, and it might prove difficult to track down suitable memory modules.

DDR2 and DDR3

While DDR memory is not yet obsolete, it is not the best that is currently available. Many motherboards are now designed to use an improved version called DDR2. DDR2 modules look very much like the ordinary DDR variety (Figure 3.6), but they are somewhat larger and have 240 terminals. This type of memory is available in various speeds up to about PC6400 (800 megahertz). Fitting DDR2 modules is much the same as fitting the DDR type. DDR2 memory modules are physically incompatible with ordinary DDR sockets, and there is no danger of fitting the wrong type of module to a motherboard. On the other hand, you obviously have to make sure that you order the right type for the particular motherboard you are using.

For the ultimate in performance you need DDR3 memory. This type of memory is not in widespread use at the time of writing, but it seems likely that it will gradually usurp other types of PC memory. A DDR3

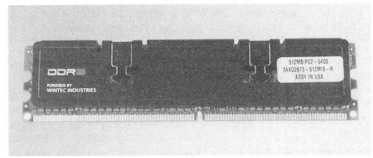

512MB/PC2-5400
3AXQ2675-512MIS-R
ASSY IN USA

DDR2

POWERED BY
WINTEC INDUSTRIES

Fig.3.6 A DDR2 module has obvious similarities with a DDR type

module has obvious similarities with a DDR2 type, but there are significant differences. The DDR3 specification covers speeds from 800 to 1600 megahertz, so it carries on where DDR2 left off, and there are also improvements to the overall design. Although DDR3 memory is in the form of modules having 240 terminals, physically they are slightly different to DDR2 memory modules. These two types of memory are therefore totally incompatible. This makes it impossible to fit DDR2 modules into DDR3 holders, and vice versa.

Other types

The types of memory detailed previously are the ones that have been in common use over the past few years. It is only fair to point out that there are variations such as 200-pin SODIMS and that some PC manufacturers have gone their own way with so-called proprietary memory. The memory chips on these modules are much the same as those on equivalent types of standard memory, but the modules are physically different to the standard types. Of course, a memory module will only work in your PC if it has the right kind of memory chip and it is physically compatible with the memory sockets.

The right memory

When purchasing memory to upgrade a PC it is clearly imperative to proceed carefully, as it would be very easy to buy the wrong type. I think it is fair to say that determining the type of memory needed is usually more difficult than actually fitting the new memory. There is really no alternative to reading the relevant section of the computer's manual, or the manual for the motherboard if that is what was supplied with the PC, to discover what type or types of memory module are usable.

Do not use more than one type of memory. If the PC already has two fast page SIMMs, use two more fast page SIMMs to increase its memory and not a couple of EDO SIMMs. If a motherboard has sockets for (say) four PC133 and two PC2100 memory modules, it is highly unlikely that a mixture of the two types can be used. With very few exceptions, SIMMs must be used in pairs in Pentium PCs, but DIMMs can be used in multiples of one.

It will sometimes be necessary to remove one or more of the existing memory modules in order to increase the memory capacity of the computer. With only a few memory sockets on the motherboard, you can not go on increasing the amount of memory fitted by simply adding more and more memory modules. It therefore pays to think ahead and fit large memory modules, rather than working your way up to high capacity modules, wasting a lot of smaller ones along the way.

Do not jump to conclusions about the maximum memory capability of your PC. Recently I was asked for help by someone with a PC that had 512 megabytes of DDR memory in the form of a single memory module. This left one free memory socket, and the owner of the PC wished to add an extra 256 megabytes via this socket. Although this seemed to be entirely reasonable, a quick inspection of the manual for the motherboard revealed that the maximum memory limit of 512 megabytes had already been reached. Although the PC had a free memory module it was of no practical value. The maximum memory capacity of many older PCs is quite low when compared to the amounts of memory often fitted into modern PCs. A limit of 256 megabytes or less is quite common.

Compatibility

In a similar vein, do not assume that a motherboard is compatible with any memory module that is physically compatible with its memory sockets. As explained previously, the same sockets have been used with different memory types and (or) speeds. Also, the higher capacity modules are sometimes incompatible with certain motherboards. This is usually because the higher capacity modules simply did not exist when these motherboards were designed. The sockets used for memory modules have minor variations that prevent most unsuitable modules from being fitted, but there are some exceptions. Before buying extra memory it is essential that it fully compatible with your PC, and that the PC can actually take additional memory.

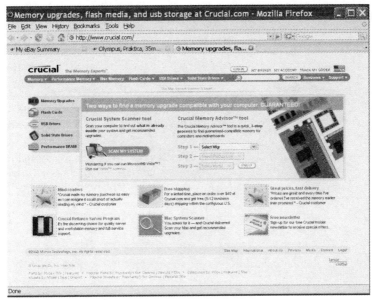

Fig.3.7 The Crucial Memory homepage

If you are not sure of the way in which the memory of your PC is made up, one solution is to simply look inside to see which memory sockets are occupied. This may not be necessary, because the BIOS start-up routine usually produces a screen that gives this sort of information about the system hardware. The BIOS will probably report the amount of memory in each bank of sockets, and the exact type of RAM fitted.

Unfortunately, system testing and analysing programs are not usually very forthcoming with precise information about the memory. The amount of physical memory present will be reported, but it is unlikely that any further information will be given. The BIOS is usually the best source of information. Also look through the information provided with the PC when you bought it. This should include a detailed specification that gives full details of the memory.

It is not possible to work out the best way of expanding the computer's memory unless you know what memory is already fitted. You really need to look at all the possible upgrade options, and cost them. Older types of memory tend to be more expensive than newer types, presumably because the older types of memory module no longer sell in large quantities. If your PC will take a more up-to-date form of memory than

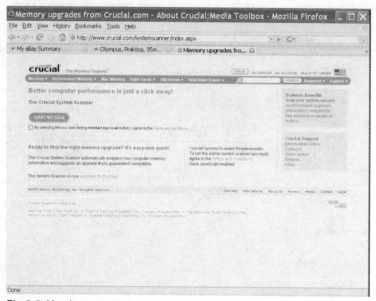

Fig.3.8 You have to agree to the terms and conditions to continue

the type currently fitted, it might actually be cheaper to dump the original memory and start "from scratch". Apart from being cheaper, changing to a more modern form of memory will probably provide a modest increase in performance. Where appropriate, it is certainly worth considering this option.

Online analysis

If you are really not sure about the type of memory fitted to your PC, and how best to upgrade it, there are online resources that can help. In particular, some memory manufacturers have web facilities that, with luck, will sort things out for you. The Crucial Memory web site (www.crucial.com) is probably the best known of these, and one of the available tools is the Memory Advisor. With this you are asked a series of questions that are used to identify your PC, or the motherboard fitted to your PC, and the amount of memory fitted. A list of possible upgrade options is then provided.

This works quite well, but there can be problems with motherboards that can take memory of various types and (or) speeds. The speed of the

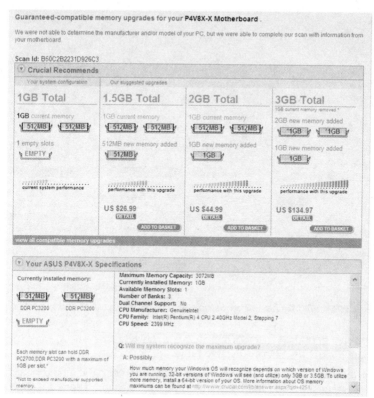

Fig.3.9 The analysis has been completed successfully

memory fitted to the motherboard is often dependent on the clock rate of the processor used. Results might be perfectly satisfactory if you simply use the fastest memory that is appropriate for the motherboard, but reliability is often best if the memory modules have identical ratings. One solution is to simply remove the existing memory modules and fit larger ones that are of exactly the same type and speed.

An alternative approach is offered by another online tool at the Crucial web site, and this is an analysis utility that tries to determine the exact type of memory already fitted to a PC. This can be accessed via the Scan My System button on the home page of the Crucial web site (Figure 3.7). You then have to agree to Crucial's terms and conditions (Figure 3.8) before going to the next stage by operating the Start My Scan button.

Fig.3.10 A DIMM has a polarising key that matches a bar in the socket

A scanner utility is then downloaded and run, and after a short while the scan results are displayed in the browser (Figure 3.9).

In this example the scan utility has correctly identified the motherboard, the processor, and the memory currently installed. There are three

Fig.3.11 There are actually two polarising keys in each DIMM

Fig.3.12 A DIMM fitted into its socket but not yet locked into place

memory slots, which can be used with PC2700 or PC3200 DDR memory modules, and the results correctly indicate that there are currently two PC3200 modules installed. Various options for increasing the amount of memory are provided, with the simplest of these being to add a third 512 megabyte DDR PC3200 module. The most costly is to remove the current modules and replace them with three 1 gigabyte PC3200 modules, giving the maximum for this motherboard, which is 3 gigabytes.

Fitting memories

Fitting numerous RAM chips into their sockets is a tedious task, and it is easy to accidentally buckle one of the pins or fit a chip around the wrong way. Memory modules were produced in an attempt to make fitting and removing memory much easier, and something that practically anyone could undertake. Fitting DIMMs is certainly very easy, and it is impossible to fit them the wrong way round because the circuit board has a polarising "key". This is just an off-centre notch cut in the circuit board that matches

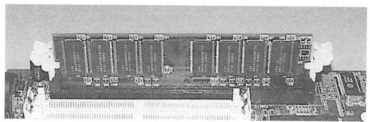

Fig.3.13 Here the DIMM has been fully pushed down into the socket and locked into place. The locking levers have gone right into the cutouts in the module

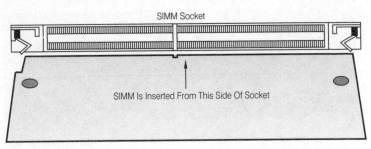

*Fig.3.14 A SIMM is fitted in the socket at an angle and then raised to
a vertical position*

a bar in the DIMM socket (see Figure 3.10). In fact there are two of these
keys (Figure 3.11), and they are apparently in slightly different positions
depending on the supply voltage of the module and the type of RAM
fitted. This should make it impossible to fit a DIMM of the wrong type.

When fitting a DIMM always look for the notch that is well off centre.
This, plus the bar in the socket, makes it clear which way round the
module must be fitted. The module simply drops into place vertically
and as it is pressed down into position the plastic lever at each end of
the socket should start to close up. Pressing both levers into the vertical
position should securely lock the module in place. Of course, the two
levers must be set fully downwards and outwards before you start to
insert the module.

Do not try to fit these modules by simply pressing hard until they click
into place. They will probably fit into place correctly using this method,
but it risks damaging the motherboard. Operating the levers enables
modules to be fully inserted into their sockets without having to exert
much force on the modules and motherboard. Figures 3.12 and 3.13
respectively show a DIMM before and after it has been locked into place.
To remove a DIMM, simply press the two levers outwards as far as they
will go. This should unlock the memory module so that it can be lifted
free of the socket.

Fitting SIMMs

In my opinion at any rate, SIMMs are slightly more awkward to fit.
Fortunately, they are now obsolete and you will only need to deal with
them if you upgrade a PC that is "not as young as it used to be". Although
in theory it is impossible to fit a 72-pin SIMM the wrong way round, in
practice it does happen occasionally. This seems to be due to the rather

Fig.3.15 A SIMM before it has been locked in place

flimsy and slightly too basic SIMM holders used on some motherboards. There is the usual polarising notch in the module and matching bar in the socket, but they are small and only very slightly off-centre. Also, there is one corner of the circuit board missing. The old 30 pin SIMMs seem to be somewhat easier to deal with. They have the missing corner, but not the notch incidentally. These days it is only the 72-pin type that you are likely to encounter.

Fig.3.16 Here the SIMM has been raised to a vertical position and it has locked into place successfully

The method of fitting both types is exactly the same. When fitting SIMMs, orient the motherboard so that the sides of the sockets having the metal clips are facing towards you, and the plain sides are facing away from you (Figure 3.14). Take the first SIMM and fit it into the first socket, which is the one that is furthest away from you, but it must be leaning toward you at about 45 degrees and not fully vertical. Once it is right down into the socket it should lock into place properly if it is raised to the vertical position.

If it refuses to fit into position properly it is almost certainly the wrong way round. If you turn it through 180 degrees and try again it should fit into place correctly. You can then move on to the next socket, and fit the next SIMM in the same way. Figures 3.15 and 3.16 respectively show a SIMM before and after it is locked into position.

Because SIMMs have to be inserted into their sockets at an angle, and the sockets are tightly grouped on the motherboard, you normally have to fit them in the right order. Otherwise you put in one SIMM which then blocks access to the socket for one of the others. You therefore have to work your way along the sockets in a methodical fashion. To remove a SIMM, pull the metal clips at each end of the socket outwards. The SIMM should then slump forwards at about 45 degrees, after which it is easily lifted clear of the holder. SIMMs have to be removed in the opposite order to the one in which they were fitted.

Static

Remember that memory modules are vulnerable to damage by static charges, and can be "zapped" by charges that are too small to produce any noticeable sparks and "cracking" sounds. Apart from processors, memory modules are probably the components that are most vulnerable to static damage. They are normally supplied in some form of anti-static packing, which is most usually in the form of a bag made from conductive plastic. Always leave memory modules or any other static-sensitive components in the protective packing until it is time to fit them into the computer. Observe all the usual anti-static precautions when dealing with memory modules. Some memory modules are quite expensive, so be especially careful with any that fall into this category.

Laptop memory

With early portable PCs it was often necessary to open up the main casing in order to get at the sockets for the memory, and getting into this type of case was often extremely difficult. Getting everything reassembled was practically impossible, and a memory upgrade was not usually something for the user to undertake. Usually the computer had to be sent to a service centre where the upgrade was performed by trained service staff, and the cost of the exercise was usually very high. In fact it tended to be so costly that it was not always a practical proposition. This lack of easy and cheap expansion was not popular with the users of these computers.

Things have moved on, and it is now possible for do-it-yourself memory upgrades to be performed on most laptop PCs. There are usually removable covers on the underside of a laptop PC, and one of these should provide access to the memory modules. Note that this may not always be the case, and that performing a memory upgrade yourself is not really a realistic proposition unless the computer provides easy access to the sockets for the memory modules.

Electronically there is no difference between the memory used in desktop PCs and that used in the notebook and laptop varieties. Memory for portable PCs is usually in the form of memory modules, but these are physically different to those used in desktop PCs. As one would probably expect, the memory modules used in laptop and notebook PCs are significantly smaller than the standard types. Picture G.6 in the Colour Gallery shows a standard 256 megabyte DDR memory module (top), and the equivalent for a Dell laptop PC (bottom).

There is less standardisation of laptop memory modules than is the case for the modules used in desktop PCs, which makes buying suitable components somewhat problematic. It might be possible to obtain suitable modules from the computer's manufacturer, or an authorised agent, service centre, or whatever. Buying the same modules that the manufacturer uses has the obvious advantage of guaranteeing that the memory modules will work properly. The likely drawback is that the cost is almost certain to be relatively high.

The alternative is to buy modules from a specialist supplier of memory for laptop PCs. Components obtained in this way might be the genuine article, as used by the laptop's manufacturer, but many of the memory products obtained in this way are from third-party manufacturers. Components of this type are sometimes referred to as "after-market" products. It does not necessarily follow that these after-market products are substandard, and experience suggests that the vast majority work as well as those from the PC manufacturer's official stockists. Using non-original parts has to be regarded as slightly risky though, and using them might invalidate any manufacturer's warranty. The advantage of after-market components, and the reason for their popularity, is that they are often far cheaper than the official equivalents.

Removal and fitting

Although the memory modules used in laptop PCs look much like ordinary DIMMs, but a bit smaller, the sockets for them in the computer are rather different to the ordinary sockets used in desktop PCs. The exact form of the memory sockets varies somewhat from one make and model of laptop to another, but it is not usually too difficult to determine the way in which the memory modules are removed and fitted. Note that there will usually be only two memory sockets, or possibly even just one of them. Consequently, in order to increase the amount of memory it will often be necessary to remove the existing memory modules and replace them with higher capacity types.

The example shown in G7 in the Colour Gallery shows two memory modules fitted to a Dell laptop PC. Each holder has two small arms, one at each end. In order to release a module it is just a matter of pulling the two arms outwards slightly, which results in the module tipping upwards slightly (see G.8 in the colour gallery). It can then be pulled free of the holder. In G.9 of the Colour Gallery both memory modules have been removed and the computer is ready to receive the new modules.

Fitting a module is just a matter of slotting it into its holder in the raised position, and then pressing it down so that it is flat against the underside of the computer. This should result in the two arms locking it in place. Of course, with the modules stacked one above the other to some extent, the top one must be removed first when taking out the old modules, and the lower one must be fitted first when installing the new modules. The memory modules of laptop PCs do not usually lock into place very firmly, and the fact that everything is necessarily very small probably gives the designers a few problems. However, everything should be held firmly in position when the cover plate is fitted back into place.

4

Processor
upgrades

Problems, problems

On the face of it, upgrading the microprocessor is the ideal way of giving a PC a new lease of life. A new faster processor would give the computer increased speed, enabling it to cope with the increasing demands of modern software. The cost of the upgrade would be quite low compared to the cost of a new PC, and would certainly justify the expense. Upgrading a processor is usually something less than straightforward though, if it is possible at all. Unfortunately, the older your PC the more it would benefit from a processor upgrade, but the lower the chances of it being feasible.

The problem with a processor upgrade is that as newer and better processors are developed, new and improved motherboards are also required. The most obvious problem is that of the processor requiring a faster clock speed than the motherboard can provide. Newly designed motherboards are often capable of going faster than the quickest of the processors available at the time. Although a motherboard is fitted with (say) a 2.0 gigahertz chip, it could be that it will actually work perfectly well with a 2.8 gigahertz type, even if that chip did not exist when the motherboard was made. On the other hand, the motherboard may have been struggling to accommodate the 2.0 gigahertz chip fitted when the PC was made, and there might be no upgrade path.

Even where an upgrade is possible, it will usually be necessary to upgrade the BIOS first, so that the motherboard recognises the new chip and can set the correct operating parameters for it. This process is covered in chapter 12. It is usually necessary to do some investigating at the web site of the relevant motherboard manufacturer in order to discover if there is an upgrade path available. Where there is, the updated BIOS is usually available as a free download from the manufacturer's web site.

In some cases there is no possibility of an upgrade because later processors used a different socket, or a new version of the same socket. A further complication is that AMD and Intel have gone their separate ways, and this means that different motherboards are required for each make of processor. If the existing processor in your PC is an Intel type, then there is no possibility of upgrading to anything other than another Intel chip. Similarly, if your PC currently uses an AMD chip, it is only possible to upgrade to another AMD chip, if an upgrade is actually possible. If you have an early PC that can actually take AMD or Intel processors, then it is far too old to be worth upgrading!

Options

The first task with a processor upgrade is to determine what processor is fitted at present. You will probably know this already if you are dealing with your own PC. When helping others with upgrades I have found that they usually have little knowledge of their PC's specification. The type of processor and its clock frequency are often displayed by the BIOS during the initial start-up period. The PC might have a helpfully label, but labels are not totally reliable because the PC might have been upgraded already. If there is any doubt it is advisable to use some system analysis software to check. This type of software can provide masses of useful facts for a "mystery" computer.

There are numerous analysis programs available, but the most popular is probably Sisoftware Sandra Standard, which is available as a free download on the Internet. The Sisoftware Sandra web site is at:

www.sisoftware.co.uk/sandra

This program is available from several of the large shareware download sites such as www.download.com. Having downloaded, installed and run this program, a window like the one in G.10 of the Colour Gallery is obtained. A number of program modules are available, with each one giving detailed information on an aspect of the PC. In this case it is information on the processor that is required, and this is obtained by double-clicking the Hardware icon. In the next window (see G.11 in the Colour Gallery), double-click the Processors icon, which will produce the information window of Figure 4.1.

In this example an Intel 2.4 gigahertz Pentium 4 processor has been correctly identified. The actual clock frequency of the processor is provided, which in this example is 2.4 gigahertz, and the same as its notional clock rate. In some cases the two will not be the same. This is

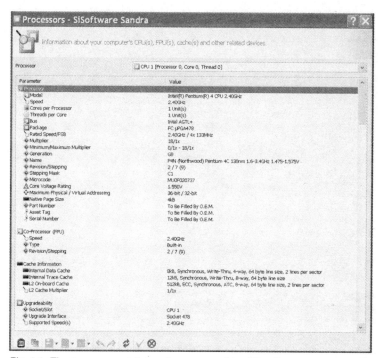

Fig.4.1 The processor information screen identifies the processor and gives its true clock frequency

because the frequency used in the name of the processor is its equivalent in Pentium terms, and not its true clock frequency, which is usually somewhat lower. This only applies to certain non-Intel processors, and due care has to be taken in order to correctly identify these components.

It is possible to get some basic information on a PC using the built-in facilities of Windows. From the Program menu select Accessories, System Tools, and then System Information. A great deal of useful information is available here, but it is usually too vague on the subjects that are of interest in the current context. The clock frequency of the processor and its manufacturer should be identified correctly, but there will probably be little else of use in the current context. For the present purposes it is better to use a program such as Sisoftware Sandra, which will give the more detailed information that is required in this case.

To obtain information on the motherboard using Sisoftware Sandra, close the Processor information window and then double-click the Mainboard

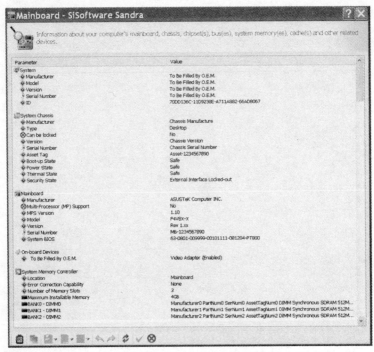

Fig.4.2 The mainboard information screen should name the board's manufacturer and give the model number

Information icon in the main window. This launches a window like the one of Figure 4.2, and this shows a large amount of technical information about the motherboard. In particular, it provides the manufacturer and model number for the motherboard. In this case it is an Asus P4V8X-X

It has to be pointed out that the model number provided by the program can be different to the one used by the manufacturer when marketing the board. This complicates the next step, which is to go to the manufacturer's web site to look for information about the board and the availability of an updated BIOS. Where more than one type number is in use it is likely that the web site will give details for the board under both numbers. An Email to the manufacturer should soon get things sorted out if there is any doubt about the identity of a board. Do not try to update a BIOS unless you are sure that an upgrade is needed, and that the new BIOS is suitable for your motherboard. Loading the wrong BIOS would almost certainly render the board unusable.

Fig.4.3 This motherboard is a Chaintech 5TDM2

The type number of the motherboard plus the BIOS version and date are often shown near the top left-hand corner of the screen during the initial start-up process. It can be difficult to make sense of all the material displayed during start-up, but it is worth noting it all down and looking for a correlation between the type numbers on the manufacturer's web site and the numbers you have noted. There might even be a fancy screen during start-up that gives the name of the manufacturer and the model number.

If all else fails you can try looking on the motherboard itself for the board's name or type number. This might seem to be the obvious approach, but not all motherboards are actually marked with this information. Where it is present the situation will probably be confused by other markings. In the example of Figure 4.3 there is no manufacturer's name on the board, but the logo for Chaintech is present. The board is a 5TDM2, not an M101 or an O30.

A visual inspection of the board will probably reveal the name of the manufacturer and the model number for the board, but it might require a

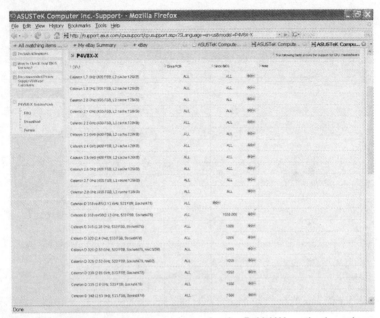

*Fig.4.4 All the compatible processors for the P4V8X-X motherboard are
listed. If a processor is not listed, it can not be used*

certain amount of sleuthing. It is worth looking through the documentation
supplied with the PC. This might include a detailed specification including
details of the motherboard. There could even be a copy of the instruction
manual for the motherboard, which should tell you everything you need
to know.

CPU compatibility

An Internet search engine should soon find the web site for the
motherboard's manufacturer. Having found the site it is then a matter of
looking for information about the CPU compatibility of the motherboard
you are using. Most sites have charts that give information about the
processor compatibility of each motherboard, and the various BIOS
updates that are available. In this example (Figure 4.4) a little searching
of the Asus site located the CPU compatibility page for the P4V8X-X
motherboard. This provides a long list of compatible processors, and
where appropriate it indicates any BIOS update that might be required.

If the processor you wish to use is not in the list of compatible types, then that processor can not be used with the existing motherboard. Either a different processor that is compatible must be selected, or both the motherboard and processor will have to be upgraded.

Remember that where a BIOS upgrade is required, it is essential to perform the upgrade before installing the new processor. It is possible that the computer will work with the new processor fitted, even if the processor is not recognised by the BIOS. The BIOS might resort to default settings that will enable the new processor to function to some extent, but it will probably operate at something less than maximum speed. Admittedly, it should perform well enough to permit the BIOS upgrade to go ahead.

However, it is not a good idea to rely on the BIOS being this accommodating, as you could easily end up having to reinstall the old processor, upgrade the BIOS, and then reinstall the new processor. I think it is worth reiterating the point that it is not a good idea to upgrade the BIOS unless it is really necessary. The small risk involved is pointless unless it is really required for some reason. Leave well alone if the existing BIOS can handle the new processor.

Out with the old

With the new processor selected and any necessary BIOS update successfully installed, it is time to move on to the hardware side of things. Switch off the PC and remove the outer casing so that you have access to the motherboard. There is likely to be a problem with access to the processor, which is often hidden away underneath the power supply. This might not be a problem if the PC has a fairly large case, but it is almost inevitable with the more compact types. It is certainly a problem with the example PC, where the part of the processor's heatsink can just about be seen underneath the power supply (Figure 4.5).

It is impossible to change a processor without good access to the relevant section of the motherboard, so where appropriate the power supply must be dismounted from the case. It should not be necessary to disconnect the supply from the motherboard or any of the drives. There should be good access to the processor if the power supply unit is placed on the drive cage. In this example, removing the power supply gave good all-round access to the processor (Figure 4.6).

Removing the old processor usually presents no problems, but the same is rarely true of its heatsink and fan. The heatsink normally clips onto the

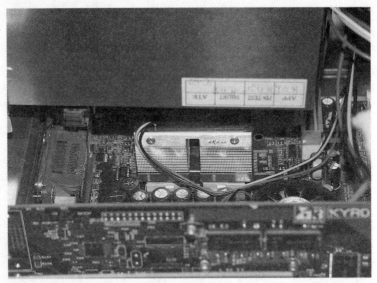

Fig.4.5 This processor is largely obscured by the power supply

Fig.4.6 Access is greatly improved by removing the power supply

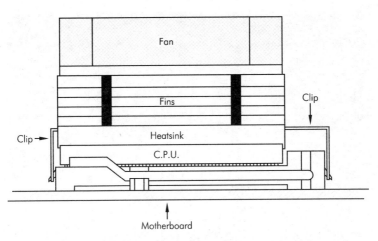

Fig.4.7 The heatsink and fan are clipped onto the processor's socket

socket using the arrangement shown in Figure 4.7. The heatsink must be firmly clipped into place in order to ensure that it operates efficiently. The spring clip that holds it in place is therefore fairly strong. One side of the clip can be pressed down a relatively long way, but there is little movement on the other side. If you are lucky, pushing down on the side that has the greatest movement will result in it unhooking from the socket and the heatsink can then be pulled free.

In most cases it will not be quite as simple as this. Often it is necessary to use a screwdriver to gently lever the clip outwards as it is pushed downwards. This ensures that having been pushed down far enough it then moves out and free of the socket. Some heatsink clips can be very difficult to manoeuvre out of position because the clip is designed to press inwards quite firmly. Presumably it is done this way to make the heatsink easy to fit, with the clip tending to lock into place if it is pressed down far enough. Unfortunately, it makes things much more difficult when trying to remove the heatsink.

With some of them there is a notch in the clip that will take the blade of a medium size screwdriver. With the blade firmly fitted in place it is then quite easy to push downwards and then outwards to get the clip free of the socket. Take due care though. Slipping and gouging the motherboard with the blade of the screwdriver could seriously damage it.

Fig.4.8 The Athlon processor can be seen once the heatsink and fan have been removed

Fig.4.9 Older processors do not have the metal heat pad

Do not get a case of "computer rage" if the heatsink is very reluctant to unclip. Trying to use brute force is a good way of damaging the motherboard and possibly injuring yourself in the process. In cases where the heatsink refuses to unclip there is little option other than removing the motherboard from the case so that you have totally unrestricted access to the heatsink. Try to get a good side-on view so that you can see what is preventing the clip from pulling free. What was previously an unsuccessful struggle can usually be solved in a few seconds once there is better access to the heatsink.

Some advocate removing the motherboard from the case whenever undertaking memory or processor upgrades. The reason for this is that both types of upgrade usually involve pressing down on the motherboard,

causing it to flex slightly. This puts the motherboard at slight risk, but it is unlikely to be damaged unless you adopt a "hammer and tongs" approach. Most motherboards now have provision for extra stand-offs around the processor, which greatly reduces the risk of damage occurring. Removing the motherboard and reinstalling it is a time consuming business, and I suppose that it is not entirely risk-free.

Fig.4.10 A "missing" hole ensures that the processor can only be fitted correctly

It is an approach that I only use where there is no other way of getting adequate access to the motherboard.

With the heatsink removed you should be able to see the processor in the socket (Figure 4.8). The metal pad in the middle is the bit that conducts heat from the processor and into the heatsink. This is a feature of virtually all modern processors, but it is lacking on some older types (Figure 4.9). The four rubber pads are included on many processors, and they help to keep the underside of the heatsink parallel to the top of the processor. The heatsink would operate very inefficiently if it was allowed to keel over slightly. It is unlikely that any damage would occur, because most motherboards have protection circuits that shut down the system if the processor gets too hot. It is best not to put this type of thing to the "acid test" though.

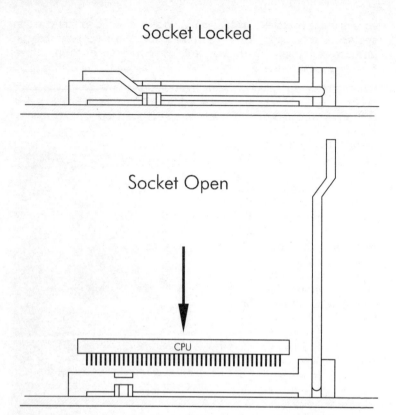

Fig.4.11 The lever is raised to open the socket and lowered to lock it

Orientation

There should be a dot, arrow, or other marking near one corner of the
processor. In the example of Figure 4.8 the top left-hand corner of the
chip's case is missing. On the underside of the processor there is one
pin "missing" in this corner, which matches a missing hole in one corner
of the socket. In Figure 4.10 the absent hole is in the top right-hand
corner of the socket. The point of this is to ensure that the processor
can only be inserted into the socket the right way around. Make a note
of the processor's orientation so that it is quick and easy to fit the
replacement.

The processors in modern PCs are fitted on the board via a form of ZIF (zero insertion force) socket. This simply means that the chip can be dropped into place without having to push it down into the socket. Similarly, the chip can be easily lifted from the socket with no need to prise it free or use any special tools. The socket has a locking

Fig.4.12 *The new Athlon XP processor in its anti-static packing*

mechanism that keeps the processor in place and electrically connected to the motherboard during use. In order to remove the processor it is

Fig.4.13 *The Athlon XP processor installed on the motherboard*

Fig.4.14 A fan fitted with a three-way lead and connector

merely necessary to raise the lever situated at one side of the socket to unlock it, and then lift the processor free. Figure 4.11 shows how this system of locking operates.

Next the new processor (Figure 4.12) is removed from its anti-static packaging and placed in the socket, being careful to get the orientation correct. Make sure that the standard anti-static handling precautions are rigidly observed when dealing with the processors. Put the old processor in the anti-static packing so that it can be stored safely. The new processor should simply fall into place but it might take a certain amount of manoeuvring to get it into just the right position. Lower the locking lever back to its original position once the processor is in position. If the processor will not fall into place, check that its orientation is correct.

If it still fails to drop into place it is likely that one of the pins has become bent out of position. Look closely at all the pins and if necessary use the blade of a small screwdriver to carefully straighten any that are seriously bent out of place. Proceed very careful and gently, because the processor will be a write-off if one of the pins is broken off. Fortunately, the pins on modern processors are quite short and strong, so there should be no problems with bent pins unless the device has been seriously mistreated. Figure 4.13 shows the new AMD XP2000+ processor in place in the example PC.

New heatsink?

Next the heatsink and fan are fitted to the processor's socket. In general, heatsinks have become bigger over the years as more complex processors consume higher power levels and generate more heat. The latest processors actually consume less power than some of their predecessors even though they are more complex and operate at higher clock frequencies. This is apparently due to the use of smaller transistors that give greater speed with reduced power consumption. Even so, it is a good idea not to simply fit the old heatsink and fan onto the new processor.

The safe option is to buy a new heatsink and fan assembly that is properly matched to the new chip. Most

Fig.4.15 This fan taps off power from a 5.25-inch drive power lead

processors are offered in retail boxed and OEM (original equipment manufacturer) versions. The retail boxed version costs more, but it is usually complete with a heatsink and fan that are guaranteed to be up to the task. The heatsink and fan are not included with the OEM version. The retail boxed processor is the safer option, and it is unlikely to cost much more than an OEM chip plus a heatsink and fan bought separately.

There is a potential problem with supplying power to the new fan since there is more than

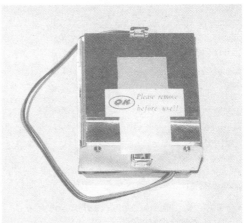

Fig.4.16 The heatsink compound has a protective covering

one way of powering PC cooling fans. The two most common methods are to power the fan from the motherboard via a three-way lead and connector (Figure 4.14), or to tap off power from the power lead for a drive (Figure 4.15). Most of the current fans have the three-way lead and connector for the motherboard. The third wire incidentally, enables the motherboard to monitor the speed of the fan and give a warning if it is too slow or stops.

If the original fan is a type that taps off power from a drive, and there are no fan power connectors on the motherboard, you must be careful to order a new fan that has drive power connectors. Alternatively, it will probably be possible to fit the fan from the old heatsink in place of the fan supplied with the new heatsink.

Heatsink compound

As supplied, the underside of the heatsink will probably look something like the one in Figure 4.16. The paper tear-off strip should be removed prior to fitting the heatsink. Removing it reveals a square of heatsink compound (Figure 4.17) that helps to produce a good thermal contact

between the processor and the heatsink. This pad is not needed for older processors that lack the metal heat conductor on the top, and it will not be present on heatsinks intended for use with these processors.

If the heatsink from the original processor is being used for the new one, any existing pad of heatsink compound will be largely obliterated. The old pad must be

Fig.4.17 Here the heatsink compound has been revealed

carefully cleaned away and then some new heatsink compound must be added in its place. Most of the larger computer component retailers supply at least one grade of heatsink compound. One of the cheaper grades will suffice. The expensive types are intended for use in over-

Fig.4.18 The heatsink and fan in position on the processor

clocking and not for general use. Very little heatsink compound is needed, so one of the small sachets will be more than sufficient. It is also possible to obtain heatsink compound in the form of pads, much like the ones that are supplied ready-fitted to many heatsinks.

The heatsink is fitted in place by first clipping the less springy side of the clip under the lug on the socket. With the heatsink accurately in position on the socket it should then be reasonably easy to press the other side of the clip down and into place. Heatsinks are usually much easier to install than they are to remove. It is advisable to pull firmly on the heatsink to make sure that it is reliably secured to the socket. There could be dire consequences for the processor if the heatsink should come adrift. Figure 4.18 shows the heatsink securely fitted in place in the example PC.

Pentium 4

The method of mounting the heatsink described previously is the one used for most older processors, including those that fit Socket 7, Socket 370, and Socket A boards. There are some processors that use a different

Fig.4.19 A Pentium 4 requires a different heatsink and fan

Fig.4.20 The Pentium 4 processor installed in its socket

Fig.4.21 The heatsink and fan for the 2.4 gigahertz Pentium 4

type of heatsink. The socket for a Pentium 4 processor looks quite conventional (Figure 4.19), and there is the usual lever that is used to lock or release the processor. Figure 4.20 shows the processor fitted into its socket. The processor itself also looks fairly conventional, but it is smaller than previous Pentiums, Athlons, etc. The way in which the heatsink is mounted is very different to the system used for earlier processors. Around the processor there is a black plastic mounting bracket that is used to clip the heatsink in place. This can be seen in Figures 4.19 and 4.20. The heatsink itself (Figure 4.21) is relatively large, and it has two locking levers, one at each end.

Fitting the heatsink onto the motherboard is very easy, and it simply presses down into place on the black plastic mounting bracket. If it is reluctant to fit into place you probably have one or both of the levers in the locked position, and correcting this should enable it to be pressed down into place. The levers are set to the locked position once the

Fig.4.22 The heatsink and fan locked in position

Fig.4.23 One of the locking cams can be seen in front of the fan

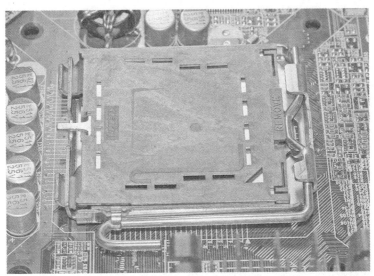

Fig.4.24 Socket 775 has a plastic cover to protect the pins

heatsink has properly clipped into place. The levers operate a cam mechanism that forces the heatsink down onto the processor. Figure 4.22 shows the heatsink locked into place, and one of the cams can be seen in the side-on view of Figure 4.23.

Socket 775

There are new processors appearing all the time, most of which use existing sockets and the normal heatsinks associated with them, or sockets and heatsinks that are used in much the same way as well-established types. However, if you upgrade a recent PC you might encounter processors, sockets, or heatsinks that are rather different to those used in the past. The Intel Socket 775 chips use certainly a slightly unconventional approach, which has the socket in the processor and the pins on the motherboard.

This does not really matter a great deal in practice, and the difference is not obvious when fitting the chip. Something which is obvious, is that the "socket" on the motherboard has a protective cover for the pins (Figure 4.24). This is hinged and can be raised when the locking lever is raised (Figure 4.25). The plastic part of the cover must be removed

Fig.4.25 Here the hinged cover has been raised

Fig.4.26 The plastic cover must be removed

Fig.4.27 Here the processor has been placed in position

Fig 4.28 The cover has been closed and locked in place

Fig.4.29 There are four fasteners on the underside of a Socket 775 heatsink

(Figure 4.26), and this is simply a matter of pressing it out of place. Next the processor is fitted in place (Figure 4.27). Although the standard anti-static handling precautions will be taken when dealing with the processor, it is still advisable to avoid touching the contacts on the underside of this component whenever it is necessary to handle it. Finally, the remaining part of the cover is lowered over the processor and the lever is used to lock the processor and cover in place (Figure 4.28).

The heatsink for a Socket 775 processor is a little unusual, and it has four fasteners on the underside (Figure 4.29) that match up with mounting

Fig.4.30 Each fastener clips into a hole in the motherboard

holes in the motherboard. One of these fixing holes is shown in Figure 4.30. In order to fit the heatsink in place it is just a matter of aligning the four fasteners with the holes in the motherboard, and then pressing down on each of the four "legs" to fit the fasteners into place. A "click" should be heard as each one locks into place. The method usually recommended is to press two diagonally opposite "legs" into place simultaneously, but this can be a bit difficult with some heatsinks. With this type of thing you often have to "play it by ear" and use a little common sense.

Once all four fastenings have been fitted it is advisable to pull on the heatsink to check that it is not loose at one

Fig.4.31 There is a lever on one side of the heatsink

corner. If one of the fasteners fails to lock in place, check its alignment and try again. Note that once in place it is not possible to remove the heatsink simply by pulling it free. There is a slot for a screwdriver at the top of each "leg", and about a quarter of a turn in a counter-clockwise direction should free each one so that the heatsink can be easily lifted from the motherboard.

Socket 939 and AM2

The method of fixing the heatsink to a Socket 939 motherboard is not a great deal different from the Socket A method, but it takes things a stage further. Like Socket 478 motherboards, the Socket 939 variety have a plastic "fence" around the processor, and the heatsink attaches to this rather than to the socket itself. If you refer back to Figure 4.19, the "fence" can be seen around the socket. The two large bolts to either side of the socket are used to securely clamp two plastic clips to the motherboard.

A Socket 939 heatsink fits onto these in much the same way as a Socket A type clips onto its socket. One side of a Socket 939 heatsink has a simple spring-clip. There is a slightly more complex clip on the other side of the heatsink (Figure 4.31), complete with a small plastic lever. Initially though, it fits onto the "fence" in the usual way. Getting the heatsink in position can be a bit awkward. The obvious approach is to fit the simple clip first and then the one with the lever, since the lever makes it easier to get a firm grip on this one. In practice the heatsink often fits into place much easier if the clip with the lever is fitted first.

Once the heatsink is in place it will be a fairly loose fit and will not work efficiently. It is clamped tightly onto the socket and processor by moving the lever down from a vertical position. Note that the lever should be vertical when the heatsink is initially clipped into place. Note also, that the heatsink will only be clamped in place correctly if the lever is lowered in the right direction. There is a thumb-grip moulded into one side of the lever, and this side should be facing upwards once the heatsink is clamped in position

Some Socket 939 heatsinks can be used with AM2 motherboards. However, with the more usual arrangement the heatsink pushes into place on four mounting clips and is then locked in place by a lever. This is essentially the same as the system used for Socket 478 heatsinks.

Currenty there are several different methods of fixing heatsinks in place, and the manufacturers seem to come up with a steadily flow of new types. Retail boxed processors are supplied with an instruction leaflet that explains how the heatsink is fitted in place, so if in doubt you can always refer to this. A heatsink obtained separately from the processor should also be supplied complete with fixing instructions, but some lack worthwhile fitting instructions. Clearly it is essential to be very careful when buying a processor and heatsink separately, as it would be very easy to end up with a heatsink that did not match the fixing method used by the motherboard. Buying a retail boxed processor, complete with heatsink and fan, is a much safer option, and should not be significantly more expensive.

Jumperless

With the heatsink and fan in place it is time to do any reassembly such as refitting the power supply, check that no cables have come adrift, and then try out the new processor. It is assumed here that the motherboard is a so-called "jumperless" type that does not require things such as voltages and clock frequencies to be set via jumpers or switches on the motherboard. With an older motherboard it might be necessary to adjust some settings to produce the right operating conditions for the new processor. The motherboard manufacturer's web site should have details of the correct settings for each processor that the board will accept.

Motherboard
upgrades

Major upgrade?

One reason for the success of PCs is undoubtedly their modular construction, which makes it easy to add new features such as CD writers, or to upgrade existing facilities. If your video card is not up to the latest 3-D games, you can simply remove it and fit the latest high-speed 3-D video card instead. If the hard disc drive no longer has sufficient capacity for the latest mega-powerful software suites, it can be replaced with a higher capacity drive that will provide you with all the storage space you could possibly want.

In theory, you can go on upgrading a PC for ever, keeping it fully up-to-date with all the latest "bells and whistles". In practice there is a limit to the length of time that you can continue with this form of gradual upgrading. Eventually the basic PC becomes so out of date that it can no longer accommodate the latest PC peripherals, etc. This obsolescence occurs due to the changes in the PC interfaces, and there can also be problems with the BIOS when trying to use the latest gadgets in an old PC.

Does this mean that a PC can not go on indefinitely? Not really, it just means that after a number of years a major upgrade will be required in order to keep the computer up to date. This means fitting a new motherboard and processor, and possibly some other components as well such as the memory. This is clearly a major undertaking, and when considering any substantial upgrade you need to ask yourself whether it is really worth upgrading the computer at all. If the answer is yes, you then have to work out exactly what you are going to replace, and what you are going to replace it with.

Deciding whether or not a computer is worth upgrading is to some extent a subjective matter. There is relatively little to be gained in the case of a recent computer that needs a new motherboard to accommodate a more modern processor. Unless you genuinely must have more speed, and even a relatively small increase will suffice, it would be a pointless and costly exercise.

The type of PC that is likely to be a good candidate for a massive upgrade is one that is a few years old. A computer in this category is likely to have drives and other components that are adequate for most puposes, but the processor is will probably be slow by modern standards, and the amount of memory fitted will probably be relatively low. By replacing the motherboard, processor, and memory you are getting rid of the oldest and slowest components in the PC, and the gain in performance should be substantial.

An old PC that is still in its original form or has had little upgrading is a less attractive prospect for a major upgrade. It should actually be possible to bring a computer of this type up to a modern specification, but so much would have to be changed and added that very little of the original PC would remain in the upgraded computer. You would effectively be building a new PC rather than upgrading the old one. It might be better to abandon the original computer and any compromises it might impose, and just build a new PC from scratch.

Potential problems

The normal reason for changing the motherboard is to permit a modern processor to be used. The existing motherboard can not accommodate a processor that is significantly faster than the one already fitted, so a new and more accommodating motherboard is fitted. You need to be aware that one thing can lead to another, and that the new motherboard might impose further changes. The existing memory might be usable with the new motherboard, but it is unlikely to provide optimum performance. It is normal to replace the memory with a type that will give good performance from the new motherboard and processor. With the current low cost of PC memory modules it is a good opportunity to upgrade to a much larger amount of memory.

The case and power supply are a likely cause of problems. The vast majority of recent desktop PCs and probably all new ones use ATX cases and power supplies. However, in the past the AT case and power supply were very popular. If the computer has a conventional mains on/off switch, then it is in an AT case. Performing a major upgrade on an old PC of this type is unlikely to justify the time and effort involved, and building a new PC from scratch would be a more practical approach.

The video adaptor is another possible problem area when undertaking a major upgrade. Anything from the pre-PCI era will not be usable with a modern motherboard. If the existing video card is a PCI type there should be no difficulty in using it in one of the PCI expansion slots of the new motherboard. However, an old PCI video card will not give anything approaching the ulitimate in performance, and might perform quite badly. Due to the switch from AGP to PCI Xpress, using an AGP video card on a new motherboard is unlikely to be possible. Few, if any, modern motherboards have slots for AGP video cards.

Bear in mind that the best video cards of a few years ago are quite slow when compared to most of the cheaper boards that are available today. Discarding the old video adaptor and replacing it with an inexpensive modern type is likely to give a large increase in performance. If you are heavily into any form of graphics application it would almost certainly be worthwhile upgrading to one of the modern high-speed video cards. These can greatly increase the operating speed of many heavyweight graphics applications.

Many modern motherboards have built-in graphics adaptors. It would be unrealistic to expect one of these to give the same level of 3D performance as an expensive graphics card, but they are more than adequate for 2D and some 3D applications. The additional cost of on-board graphics adaptors is minimal these days, making integrated graphics a good choice unless high 3D graphics performance is of paramount importance. With this type of motherboard there is normally the option of switching off the integrated graphics and using a video card, as and when necessary.

There are a couple of potential problem when changing the motherboard, and one of these is reactivation. Windows XP/Vista are famous for requiring activation followed by reactivation if large changes are made to the hardware, but there are other programs that use the same basic method of copy protection. Changing the motherboard and processor is almost certain to trigger the reactivation routines in any software that uses this method.

The monitoring software will detect the change in the type of processor, the change in the serial number of the processor, and the change in the BIOS. Any changes in the audio, video, and network adaptor are also likely to be detected. Various methods of reactivation are used, and in some cases it is just a matter of placing a genuine installation disc in a CD-ROM drive. In other cases it is necessary to reactivate the software online or by making a telephone call to obtain a new activation code.

Onscreen instructions should be provided when reactivation is triggered, and there should be no problem provided you are using legitimate software.

The second, and more serious problem, is that some computers are supplied with a copy of Windows that is tied to that particular make and model of computer. Attempts to use a tied copy of Windows on the wrong make or model of computer will just produce an error message, or the operating system will run, but in such a restricted fashion that it will be of little practical value. Your PC almost certainly has a tied copy of Windows if it was not supplied with a normal Windows installation disc. You probably paid a relatively low price for the operating system, but because of this it is not transferable to another PC. Changing the motherboard produces something that the operating system considers to be a different PC.

The only way around this problem is to buy a new copy of Windows and install everything from scratch once the hardware upgrade has been completed. It is only fair to point out that a massive upgrade, such as changing the motherboard and processor, might require Windows to be reinstalled anyway. The old installation might be able to adjust to the huge changes in the hardware, but this is far from certain. Saving all your data, reinstalling Windows and all your programs, and then reinstating the data is a time consuming business. It is best not to start a major upgrade unless you feel confident about handling this task, and are prepared to put in the necessary time, should a full reinstallation be required.

Risks

Many PC users are understandably rather reluctant to attempt an upgrade that involves changing the motherboard. In truth, it is not really that difficult, but things can go wrong. If you buy a new computer or pay someone to perform a major upgrade for you, presumably you will be covered by some form of guarantee, and the risk will be minimal. When performing an upgrade yourself you are covered to some extent by the guarantees for the new components that are being added. On the other hand, if you make a mess of things and damage one or more of the components, these guarantees will be of no help and you have to take responsibility for this type of thing yourself.

Looking at things realistically, the chances of damaging one of the components are quite small provided you take the necessary anti-static handling precautions and do not go at things like the proverbial "bull in a china shop". PC components are not ultra-delicate, but if you start forcing things into place you may well seriously damage one or more of the parts. The cost of repairing PC components tends to be greater than they are worth, so if something should become damaged it will probably be a write-off. However, provided you proceed carefully and patiently it is highly unlikely that any of the components will come to grief.

It is only fair to point out that even if you get everything just right there is still an outside chance that the finished computer will fail to work absolutely perfectly. PCs are notorious for obscure incompatibility problems, and although it is fair to say that problems of this type are quite rare these days, they remain a real possibility. Most hardware incompatibility problems are actually caused by problems with the driver software rather than any real problems with the hardware. The majority of problems are minor niggles and not major failures. In due course the hardware manufacturers usually make improved drivers available on their web sites.

Standard?

Before starting a major upgrade it is as well to check that the PC is built from standard components. In particular, some of the larger PC manufacturers do not always use standard ATX power supplies and motherboards. If your PC is a non-standard type it could be impossible to upgrade it unless the case and power supply are also replaced. Some manufacturers have their own forms of memory module, but this will not be of importance if the memory is being replaced.

Only proceed with an upgrade if you are sure that your PC is one of the standard types or you are prepared to replace the case and power supply with standard ATX types. You need to choose the motherboard carefully if the case is one of the very small ATX towers, or any other very compact case. Many of these will only take the so-called "micro" format ATX boards, which are much more compact than the standard variety. Even if the case has sufficient space for a full-size motherboard, in practice it might not be usable in the case. Once the board is in place the drives might obscure the memory modules, or there could be insufficient space for the processor's heatsink and fan due to the power supply unit getting in the way. With small ATX cases it is safer to opt for one of the smaller motherboards.

Power supply

It is possible that the upgrade will require the fitting of a new power supply unit. However, any increase in power consumption is likely to be relatively small, and you would be unlucky if it was sufficient to result in the power supply being overloaded. A more likely cause of problems is the power supply not having the right type or types of connector for the motherboard. This is most likely to occur when upgrading a fairly old PC, and when switching from an AMD motherboard to an Intel type or vice versa. In some cases it might be possible to avoid a change of power supply unit by obtaining an adaptor for the existing unit. A new supply will almost certainly be needed if the motherboard has additional supply inputs and the existing supply does not have matching outputs. Anyway, be sure to check for supply incompatibility problems before selecting and buying the new motherboard.

If you are in doubt about the supply requirements of a motherboard, it is often possible to download the motherboard instruction manuals in standard PDF format. Most motherboard manufacturers seem to have this facility. These files can be displayed using the free Acrobat Reader program which is available from www.adobe.com. In addition to specifying things like the supply requirements, the type of memory needed, and the compatible processors, the manual should list the accessories supplied and explain how to install and set up the board. This enables you to check that it precisely meets your requirements, and that there is no aspect of installation that will prove awkward. I never buy a motherboard unless I have seen the manual first. It can avoid some nasty surprises and wasted money.

Nuts and bolts

Once all the parts for the upgrade have been obtained it is time to open up the PC and remove the old motherboard. Ideally you should find a reasonably large and uncluttered table to work on. PCs tend to have more than their fair share of sharp corners and bits of metal that protrude slightly, so protect the top of the table with plenty of newspaper or cloths. The manual for your computer should give details of how to remove the outer casing, but this usually just involves removing three or four screws at the rear of the case. With ATX tower cases the top and sides are separate pieces, and it will probably be necessary to remove both of them in order to remove the motherboard. With a desktop case it is the top and bottom panels that have to be removed.

The panels usually pull backwards and away once the screws at the rear of the case have been removed. With some older PCs the front fascia is also part of the removable outer casing, and with these the outer casing is removed by pulling it forwards and away from the main unit. Cases of this type sometimes have the retaining screws on the underside of the case rather than at the rear. As always with the cases of electronic equipment, it can require some careful investigation in order to find the way in.

Before the motherboard can be removed it must be disconnected from the power supply, loudspeaker, on/off LED, etc. The expansion cards must also be removed, and it might be necessary to remove the power supply as well. The old motherboard can sometimes be removed with the power supply in place, and it might also be possible to slide the new board into place. However, if it is going to be a tight squeeze it is better to remove the power supply. Flexing the new board and trying to slide it past small obstructions gives a good chance of damaging it. Remember that the expansion cards are static-sensitive. Where no suitable anti-static packing is available they can be temporarily stored on a piece of earthed metal foil.

Depending on the type of case involved and the number of drives fitted, it might be necessary to remove one or more of the disc drives in order to permit removal of the motherboard. Where possible, leave the data cables connected to the drives. If the cables are found to seriously impede work on the computer they must be completely disconnected and removed. It is then advisable to make some simple sketches or notes so that there is no difficulty in reconnecting them correctly.

Stand-offs

You may find that removing the old motherboard simply requires five or six screws to be undone, and that the board will then lift clear of the chassis. With most boards though, there will only be one or two screws to remove. The board will still be held in place by a number of plastic stand-offs, but in most cases it can be slid sideways and then clear of the chassis. The plastic stand-offs will still be attached to the motherboard, and must be removed so that they can be used with the new board. This requires the tops of the stand-offs to be squeezed inwards using a pair of pliers and then pulled free of the board (Figure 5.1). If the motherboard can not be slid free from the chassis, you may find that the stand-offs can be released on the underside of the case.

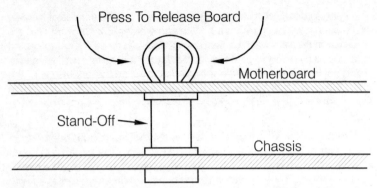

*Fig.5.1 Some plastic stand-offs have to be squeezed to release
the motherboard*

They may fit into the chassis in much the same way that they fit into the
motherboard, or they may be held in place with fixing screws.

The construction of some PC cases is such that it may not be possible to
free the stand-offs from the case. You then have the task of removing
the motherboard with the stand-offs still fixed to the case. This tends to
be rather awkward because the motherboard is likely to be somewhat
inaccessible, and there is also a tendency for one stand-off to slip back
into place while you are freeing the next one. You may need a helper to
hold the board and prevent it from slipping back into place while you
unclip the stand-offs. Alternatively, you could try improvising some simple
wedges to prevent the board from dropping back into place.

Prefabrication

It is advisable to do as much work as possible on the new motherboard
before it is mounted in the case, because it is far more accessible when
it is on the worktop. Usually the processor, heatsink, fan and memory
can be fitted without causing problems later (see G.12 in the Colour
Gallery). The amount of setting up required varies greatly from one board
to another, but with modern boards it is not usually necessary to bother
with any configuration switches or jumpers at all. The correct clock
frequency and processor supply voltages are set using the BIOS Setup
program when the computer is run for the first time. In most cases the
BIOS will automatically detect the processor type and configure the board
accordingly. You only need to intervene if the BIOS makes a mistake or
you wish to use over-clocking techniques in an attempt to improve
performance.

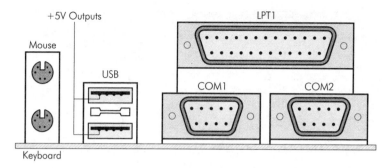

Fig.5.2 The basic port cluster for an ATX motherboard

The instruction manual for the motherboard should give details of any switches or jumpers. Where appropriate, give them the correct settings before fitting the motherboard in the case. It can be very difficult to alter jumper settings once the motherboard is installed, so make quite sure that any jumpers are set prior to installation. It is advisable to fit the microprocessor and memory modules before fitting the motherboard into the case. Fitting memory modules is dealt with in the chapter that covers memory matters, and this aspect of things will not be considered further here. Fitting the processor and heatsink was also covered earlier, and it will not be described again here.

Rebuilding

Once the board has been configured, and the processor and memory modules have been fitted, the motherboard can be mounted on the chassis. There should be no difficulty in using the old fixings with the new board, and fitting the new motherboard is generally easier than removing the old one. There is one potential problem in the form of the various connectors at the rear of the board. These are the connectors for the various ports (mouse, keyboard, USB, etc.), plus those for additional features such as audio inputs and outputs. At one time these ports were in a well standardised layout, but this is no longer the case. A properly standardised layout is not really practical, because the ports included in the cluster vary greatly from one motherboard to another. The original ATX motherboards had just seven ports in the arrangement shown in Figure 5.2. A modern motherboard has far more than this (Figure 5.3), and some of the original ports are no longer included on modern motherboards.

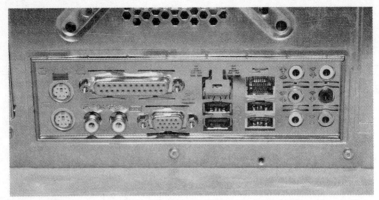

*Fig.5.3 The port cluster for a modern ATX motherboard has numerous
ports, often including video, audio, and network types*

The problem is that the cut-outs in the case are unlikely to match up
properly with the ports fitted on the new motherboard. This will render
many of the ports unusable, if you should actually manage to get the
motherboard correctly into position. In practice it is unlikely that the
motherboard will fit into place properly unless this problem is solved.
One or two alternative plates for the ports (Figure 5.4) are sometimes
included in the bits and pieces supplied with PCs, or a suitable one
might be included with the motherboard. It is then just a matter of fitting
the new plate before installing the motherboard. If all else fails it should
be possible to remove the existing plate and not replace it with anything.
This is not a particularly neat solution, but it will give excellent access to
the ports. It will permit dust to get into the PC, but modern cases are
riddled with ventilation holes so the dust will get in anyway.

Power leads

With the motherboard installed, any drives that were removed to enable
the change of motherboard should be reinstalled in the case, and any
new drives should also be fitted at this stage. If the power supply was
removed it must also be fitted back into place at this stage. It is advisable
to connect the power lead for the motherboard before fitting the power
supply back in place. An ATX power connector can only be fitted the
right way around, but make sure that it is fully pushed down into place.
Any secondary power connector for the motherboard should also be
fitted at this stage.

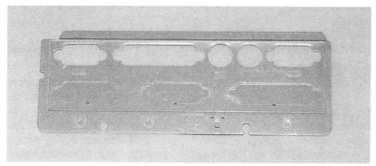

Fig.5.4 An alternative plate to suit some non-standard ATX boards

The next task is to fit the expansion cards, assuming that they are needed in the new PC. It is likely that one or more of the expansion cards used in the original PC will not be needed for the upgraded version. Modern motherboards have all the normal interfaces included on the board, including such things as the serial and parallel ports, the hard and floppy disc interfaces, USB ports, and possibly even LAN or Firewire adaptors. Expansion cards that only duplicate functions provided by the motherboard are not needed in the upgraded PC, and fitting them could prevent the PC from operating properly.

If it is very difficult or impossible to fit the expansion cards in place, the motherboard is probably slightly out of position. Slightly loosen the motherboard's mounting screws, fit one of the cards in place, shifting the motherboard fractionally if necessary, and then tighten the screws again. The manual for the motherboard will include a diagram that identifies the PCI, PCI Xpress, and AGP expansion slots, but there is no risk of fitting a card in the wrong type of slot because they use connectors of different sizes.

Other leads

There are quite a few connecting cables in the average PC, and getting everything connected correctly deters many would-be PC upgraders. Getting everything connected properly is actually much easier than you might expect. Getting the disc drives connected properly is covered in the chapters 8 and 9, and will not be considered further here. The manuals for the motherboard and other components should also have useful diagrams that show the pin numbering for each connector, and indicate how everything fits together.

Fig.5.5 The leads and connectors for the switches, speaker, etc.

There is still plenty to do once the drives have been wired up. Make sure that all the disc drives are wired to the power supply unit. There will be various "flying" leads coming from LEDs, switches, and the loudspeaker mounted on the case (Figure 5.5). There will also be various connectors on the motherboard to accommodate this sort of thing (Figure 5.6). The chances of the facilities offered by the motherboard precisely matching up with those provided by the case are pretty remote. This potential mismatch is not of any great practical importance though.

With these minor functions it is really just a matter of implementing any that are common to both the motherboard and the case, and leaving any others unconnected. This usually means connecting the power on/ off indicator and IDE activity LEDs, the loudspeaker, and the reset switch, and ignoring anything else. The LEDs will only work if they are connected with the right polarity. There may be "+" markings on the leads and the motherboard to indicate the polarity, but these are often missing. Often vague markings or colour coding are used, and neither are likely to be of any real help. Where necessary you can adopt the "suck it and see" method. The LEDs will not light up if they are connected with the wrong polarity, but they will not be damaged either.

The audio output socket of the CD-ROM drive is usually connected to the audio input connector of the sound card, or the motherboard in the case of integrated audio circuits. Audio CDs played in the drive can then be heard through the PC's sound system. There should be at least one audio input connector on the motherboard if it has an integrated audio facility, and most sound cards now have several audio inputs. The existing cable can be used if the original soundcard has been retained.

It is possible that a new cable will be required if a switch is made to integrated audio on the motherboard. Two or three audio connectors have been used in the past, and the existing cable might use one that is now defunct. A suitable cable can be bought from a large computer store or at a computer fair for no more than a few pounds. Of course, if you will only play audio CDs into headphones connected to the CD-ROM drive's headphone socket, or do not intend to use the drive for audio CDs at all, this cable is not required.

Depending on the facilities of the PC, there could be one or two additional cables to connect. Some modems can have additional cables, as can DVD

Fig.5.6 The connector block on the motherboard

decoders and video capture cards. This is just a matter of copying the method of connection used in the original PC. Where the original PC has any unusual features and cabling it is definitely a good idea to make some sketches and notes prior to dismantling it. Rebuilding the PC should then be straightforward. Where appropriate, make sure that you obtain a new motherboard that supports these special features.

Blast-off

With everything installed in the case and the cabling completed, it is time to give everything a final check before reconnecting the monitor, mouse and keyboard, and switching on. At switch-on the computer should go through the usual BIOS start-up routine, but this routine will probably be slightly different to the one performed by the original computer. This is due to the change of BIOS that accompanied the change to a new motherboard.

It is advisable to break into the start-up routine and run the BIOS Setup program before the computer tries to boot-up. A modern BIOS is very good at detecting the hardware present in the computer and adjusting itself accordingly. The user still has to set a few things manually in order to ensure correct operation of the computer. Refer to chapter 12 for an in-depth look at BIOS settings. This aspect of things will not be considered in detail here.

You will need to go into the part of the Setup program that deals with the standard BIOS settings, and here you must set the correct IDE and floppy drive types. If you do not know the correct parameters for the hard disc drive this will probably not matter. The "Auto" option will get the BIOS to read the correct settings from the drive and configure itself correctly. It will probably be possible to set the time and date from the operating system once the computer is fully operational, but while you are in the standard BIOS part of the Setup program you might as well take the opportunity to set these.

Once the standard CMOS settings have been dealt with it is likely that the computer should work quite well. You can alter the defaults for things like the printer port's operating mode, and whether Num Lock is on or off at switch-on, but in most cases the standard CMOS settings are the only ones that you must set up correctly before the computer will work

Auto detection

If you have not changed the hard disc drive, once you have saved and exited from the Setup program the computer will try to boot into Windows. The computer will probably start to boot-up in the usual fashion, but the Plug N Play feature will soon start to detect the hardware changes and load the appropriate drivers. In some cases it may have suitable drivers available already, but you will usually have to put the appropriate drivers disc into the floppy or CD-ROM drive when prompted by the on-screen Windows messages. The new motherboard should have been supplied with a disc containing any drivers needed for its hardware. It may be necessary to use the Windows installation CD-ROM at some stage in the proceedings, so have this disc handy just in case.

Read the installation instructions provided with the various items of hardware that you have bought for the upgraded PC. Most hardware does things in standard Windows fashion, and apart from providing the drivers disc when prompted, you have to do nothing more than sit back and watch while Windows gets on with it. Some hardware requires additional installation though, and there may also be some useful utility software on the discs that has to be installed separately.

On the face of it, there is little hardware that will need new drivers. A change in the video or sound circuits will necessitate new drivers, but one might reasonably expect everything else to work normally. It can therefore be rather puzzling when Windows starts reporting all manner of new hardware, and announces that it is finding and loading new software to support this hardware. In some cases it is simply rediscovering old hardware, and loading drivers that are already there.

Unfortunately, you occasionally end up with a PC that has two sets of drivers, neither of which are working properly. Normally the only solution to this problem is to go into Device Manager and delete both versions of the offending driver. Next exit Windows and re-boot the computer. When the operating system starts to load it should detect the "new" hardware and load the drivers for it. You may not have to provide it with the drivers disc, as it may well find that it already has the necessary files on the hard disc and reinstall them from there.

Port drivers

In addition to drivers for any new expansion cards, Windows will load drivers for new hardware on the motherboard. These drivers accommodate such things as improved hard disc and parallel ports, and the USB ports. The computer will probably re-boot two or three times as part of the installation process, but with luck you should eventually end up with the Windows desktop displayed on the screen, and the computer ready to run your applications.

It is worth going into the Device Manager and checking that none of the hardware entries are marked with the dreaded exclamation marks, which indicate that all is not well. If there is a problem with one or more of the drivers, I usually find that deleting the offending driver or drivers and re-booting the computer clears the problem. During the re-boot the drivers are reinstalled, and they normally reinstall correctly. With an awkward PC it may take several attempts before everything installs correctly, and I assume that in some cases the drivers will only coexist peacefully if they are installed in a certain order.

Problems adjusting

In theory Windows should be able to adjust to suit the new hardware. In practice there is a fair chance that it will refuse to work really well, or at all, with the new hardware. The chances of success can be increased by uninstalling some items of hardware before starting the upgrade. Ideally, anything that will not be used in the upgraded PC should be uninstalled. This prevents confusion after the upgrade has been completed, when Windows expects to find one set of hardware and actually finds a completely different set. In particular, it can be helpful to uninstall the video card and set up Windows for use with a standard video adaptor.

Reinstalling Windows

Even with the right preparations it is possible that Windows will fail to adjust to the new hardware correctly. Reinstalling Windows should clear away any problems. Reinstalling Windows onto a new hard disc drive is covered in chapter 8, and this process will not be considered further here.

Installing Windows from scratch is probably something that most PC users try to avoid, but it has definite advantages. In particular, installing Windows from scratch ensures that the PC has a "clean" installation that will work quickly and efficiently. However, bear in mind that any data on the hard disc will be lost if it is reformatted. Any important data will therefore have to be backed up before the disc is formatted. With Windows reinstalled on the hard disc it will be necessary to reinstall all the applications and restore your data from the backup device. All this is avoided if you salvage the original installation, and get it to work well with the new hardware.

Budget upgrades

Many people own PCs that are too old to be of any real use any more, and are not worthy of an expensive upgrade, but they do not wish to simply dump them on the nearest scrap heap. The rapid rate of change in the PC world does provide an alternative in the form of a budget upgrade. Buying the current technology is not necessarily that expensive, particularly if you opt for something less than the fastest up-to-the-minute components. Buying last year's technology is even cheaper, but last year's technology is still quite fast.

We are now reaching the stage where the ultimate in modern PCs is starting to provide overkill for many applications. Game enthusiasts and those who deal with complex 3D graphics need a very fast computer. For general office applications a fairly modest Pentium PC is usually perfectly adequate, and a computer of this type is even likely to be good enough for things such as 2D computer aided design (CAD) and basic desktop publishing (DTP).

In essence a budget upgrade is not much different to an upgrade to the latest specification. It will be necessary to replace the motherboard, processor, and memory modules. Other components such as the video card and hard disc drive can optionally be changed as well. The difference is that you buy surplus components that are not exactly new, but have probably never been used. The large mail order companies sometimes have sales of surplus stock, but local computer fairs are probably the best source for items of this type. The best buys are often in the form of a motherboard kit. These typically comprise a processor fitted on a suitable motherboard, complete with some memory, and a heatsink.

6

Video and audio

Video card types

On the face of it, upgrading a video card is much like upgrading any other expansion card, but there are actually some important differences. One complication is that several different types of video expansion card have been used over the years, and you must obtain one of the right type or it will not fit into the expansion slot of your PC. Here we will ignore anything prior to cards that fit into ordinary PCI expansion slots. The older types of video card are now long obsolete, and there is no realistic prospect of upgrading a PC of this vintage.

Matters are not much better with PCs that do not have an expansion slot specifically for a video card, and instead just use an ordinary PCI type for the video card. Removing the old card and fitting the new one should be straightforward with a PCI video card, but there is the problem of finding a suitable card. Ordinary PCI versions of modern video cards are something of a rarity, and the speed of a standard PCI interface is inadequate to fully utilize the capabilities of the latest super-fast 3D video cards. While it should be easy enough to obtain a PCI video card, finding one that is significantly better than the one already fitted to the PC could be more difficult.

If the PC has an expansion slot specifically for a video card it is likely to be an AGP type. AGP stands for Accelerated Graphics Port, and a slot of this type provides greater bandwidth than an ordinary PCI type. Matters are complicated by the fact that there are various speeds for AGP slots and cards (1X, 2X, 4X, and 8X). An AGP card should be backwards compatible, and there should be no difficulty in using (say) a 4X card in a 1X or 2X AGP slot. Of course, the card will operate at the slower rate of the slot if this is done. There are still plenty of AGP video cards available, so finding a fast AGP card should not be difficult.

Modern PCs mostly use a 16X PCI Express slot, which is also known as a PCI-E or PCI Xpress. This type of expansion slot offers a higher bandwidth than ordinary PCI or AGP slots. Being a modern interface, there should be plenty of choice if you need to upgrade a computer that uses this type of video card.

Practicalities

Upgrading the video card can produce a massive increase in performance, but only with the right type of software. Programs such as word processors, databases, and photo editors only use the 2D facilities of the video card. The super-fast video cards are really only needed for certain types of 3D graphics, such as those used in games that provide a sort of pseudo-photographic display. A "run of the mill" video card should work perfectly well if you only require 2D or simple 3D graphics, and there will not necessarily be any increase in speed if the computer is upgraded to the latest mega-powerful 3D video card. Integrated graphics are more than adequate for running basic business applications, photo-editors, and other undemanding programs.

There is a lot of processing power on modern graphics cards, and as a result of this they tend to be quite chunky due to the heatsinks and fans required by the graphics chips. This is not just of academic importance, and it does have practical consequences. Some of the more extreme cards are so large that it can be difficult to fit them in some PCs. In fact it can be impossible, and it often means that any expansion slot near the graphics slot has to be left empty. This second point is not usually too restrictive with modern PCs, where little reliance is placed on the PCI expansion slots. It is more likely that they will all be empty rather than none being free. However, it is something that needs to be borne in mind if the PC being upgraded does not have any unused PCI slots. The point about not being able to fit the larger cards at all is a more important one. Before buying a large video card make sure that it will not be blocked by the power supply, the processor and its heatsink, or any other component situated in that part of the computer. Be especially careful if the PC is a compact type that has a crowded interior.

Another point to bear in mind is that a lot of power is going into the graphics card, and that is why it generates so much heat. The heat itself can be problematic, since it is being generated within the case, and will tend to increase the temperature inside the case. It can be necessary to fit one or two additional cooling fans to the case in order to keep the interior temperature down to satisfactory levels. The increased power consumption might be too much for the existing power supply unit, which will then have to be replaced with a more powerful unit.

Of course, this does not apply if the original video card is one that also has a high level of power consumption. The loading on the power supply and the heat generated by the new card will then be much the same as before. The same is not true when upgrading from integrated graphics to a mega-powerful graphics card. The increases in power consumption and heat generation could then be very substantial.

Preliminaries

It is normally necessary to undertake one or two preliminaries before fitting a new video card. In particular, it is usually advisable to go into the Windows Control Panel and uninstall the existing card. Also, if any supporting software was installed with the old video card, this should be uninstalled before fitting the new card. In practice it is more or less standard for at least one utility program to be installed with a video card, and there could be two or more programs of this type. Sometimes the software will have a submenu in the Programs menu, and there might be an Uninstall option here. Otherwise it is a matter of going into the Control Panel and uninstalling the program or programs in the standard Windows fashion. There is a much better chance of the new video being installed without a hitch if any drivers and supporting software for the old card is removed.

Before installing a new video card it is important to at least briefly read through the installation instructions provided with the card. There is a standard way of installing a video card into Windows based PCs, but the card manufacturers do not always adopt the standard approach. In fact it seems to be quite normal for manufacturers to "do their own thing", and not just with video cards. It is important to closely follow the manufacturer's

Fig.6.1 A notch in the front of an AGP card enables it to be locked in place

Fig.6.2 The locking lever on an AGP expansion slot

installation instructions even if they are at odds with the normal way of doing things.

Try to do things using the standard method is unlikely to work with driver software that has been designed to handle things in a different way. You tend to keep going round in circles with the hardware never being installed properly. Having produced an inoperative installation it can then be difficult to get everything cleared from Windows so that the installation can be started from scratch. Getting it right first time can save a great deal of frustration and wasted time.

AGP and PCI Express

Fitting AGP and PCI Express cards is slightly different to fitting a PCI type. There is a locking lever at the front of the expansion slot, and the locking mechanism is much like the one used on memory sockets. Unlike a memory socket, the locking mechanism is only included at one end of the connector. It is quite common for expansion cards to ride up slightly at the front when the mounting bolt is tightened. The connector of an

Fig.6.3 An AGP card locked into position in the expansion slot

AGP or 16X PCI Express card has so many terminals in such a small space that even a small degree of tilt can prevent it from connecting to the motherboard properly. The purpose of the locking mechanism is to ensure that the card can not ride up slightly at the front.

Any modern AGP card should have a cut-out in the front edge of the connector to take the locking mechanism (Figure 6.1 and G.13 in the Colour Gallery). Initially the locking lever on the AGP slot should be in the open (down) position, as in Figure 6.2. When the card is pushed into its expansion slot the lever should automatically move up and into place (Figure 6.3), but if necessary it can be given a little manual assistance. Essentially the same system is used for 16X PCI Express cards. Be aware that some motherboard manufacturers use their own methods for clipping video cards in place. Consult the motherboard's instruction manual if the video slot seems to have a non-standard locking mechanism. Make sure that the locking mechanism is fully released before trying to remove a video card.

Note that some motherboards can be rather fussy about the video cards that they will work with reliably. In particular, some motherboards lack proper compatibility with some 2x/4x AGP boards. The problem seems to stem from the fact that 2x operation uses higher signal voltages than 4x operation, but some video boards do not adjust to low voltage operation in the 4x mode. If you are using a motherboard of this type there will probably be a warning sticker on the AGP slot itself as well as warnings in the instruction manual. Make sure that the video card is a compatible type if you use one of these boards, since a mistake could result in damage to the motherboard. Any reasonably modern AGP motherboard should support 8x operation, and there should be no problem using any AGP card.

Settings

Once the new video card is installed and operating properly it is possible that it will be necessary to alter some settings. Video cards are often supplied with a utility program that enables various settings to be altered, and where possible, it will probably be better to use this software rather than the built-in facilities of Windows. If no control software is provided, or you prefer to alter the settings directly in Windows, it is a matter of first going to the Windows Control Panel. With the Class View selected, double-click the Display icon and then operate the Settings tab in the new window that appears.

This will produce a window something like G.14 in the Colour Gallery. The slider control is used to set the required display resolution, which will normally be the native resolution if an LCD monitor is used. In other words, the maximum resoloution that the monitor can handle. The monitor should be able to handle a useful range of lower resolutions, but these involve compromises that are unlikely to produce optimum display clarity. Only use a lower resolution if it is really necessary to do so.

It is also possible to alter the colour-depth, which is the range of colours that the display can use. Bear in mind that using a display mode that can handle many millions of colours will not necessarily produce a display that looks significantly better than one that can only produce a few hundred thousand colours. On the other hand, having a massive colour-depth uses up extra video memory and generally slows things down. It is advisable to try reduced colour-depth if using a massive number of colours produces slow, jerky, and unrealistic results with some software. For the same reason, it can sometimes be advantageous to use reduced screen resolution.

Analogue/digital

Not so long ago, the first decision that had to be made when selecting a new monitor was choosing between a conventional CRT (cathode ray tube) monitor and a flat panel LCD (liquid crystal display) type. These days there are few CRT monitors available, and an LCD monitor tends to be the automatic choice. The problems with the early LCD monitors have been largely overcome by modern technology, and they have few real drawbacks. They do have real advantages though, such as perfect geometry, the ability to fit into restricted spaces, and much lower running costs.

The choice that has to be made when choosing a modern monitor is deciding between an analogue connection and a digital type. CRT monitors are analogue in nature, and require analogue signals from the video card. LCD monitors are digital, but many have standard analogue inputs like those of CRT monitors. Some internal electronics are used to convert the analogue input signal into digital types that can be used to drive the monitor. This is doing things the hard way though, and it is better to have a digital output on the video card and a matching digital input on the monitor so that any digital-to-analogue and analogue-to-digital conversions are avoided.

When buying a new monitor is it essential to check the type or types of video output available from the video card. It is likely that there will only be an analogue output with an older PC or one that has integrated graphics. The monitor must then be a type that has an analogue input. Due to the way the taxation and system of import duties operates, analogue monitors are often cheaper than equivalent digital types, even though their internal electronics is presumably similar. If there is a digital output on the video card, even if there is an analogue type as well, it is probably better to opt for a digital monitor. This should give better picture quality, although the difference in quality between the two types of connection is usually something less than obvious. In some cases it seems to be practically non-existent.

The connector used for analogue video outputs is a form of 15-pin D connector, and it is the one on the left in G.15 of the Colour Gallery. The digital output uses a more complex form of D connector, and this is the one on the right in G.15 of the Colour Gallery. This type of output is often referred to as a DVI (digital video interface) type. There will sometimes be other connectors on the video card, and these are inputs and outputs intended for use with television sets, digital camcorders, and other items of audio-visual equipment.

Audio

These days most computers have motherboards that include integrated audio circuits, and in many cases the built-in audio adaptor is quite advanced. Some PCs have simple stereo outputs, but it now seems to be the norm to have some form of surround sound capability as standard. The advanced capabilities of the original audio circuits usually render it unnecessary to upgrade. Indeed, the only upgrades are to highly advanced audio cards for games use or the production of electronic music. Anything less is unlikely to represent a real step up from the built-in circuits.

If you need to upgrade to an upmarket audio card, in most cases it will just be a standard PCI card that is installed in the normal way. While it is not essential to remove any existing audio card, or disable the integrated audio system, there is usually no point in having the existing audio system operate alongside the new system. This just wastes system resources and becomes a potential source of confusion. It is usually possible to switch off integrated audio systems, and this is sometimes achieved via a switch or jumper on the motherboard. However, it is more usual for this feature to be controlled via the BIOS Setup program.

Some audio cards come complete with a control panel that fits into an externally accessible 3.5-inch or 5.25-inch drive bay. This approach has the advantage of making the controls and sockets easily accessible at the front of the PC instead of being tucked away at the rear where they are difficult to get at. A cable or set of cables is used to connect the soundcard to the control panel.

These days there are some very sophisticated PC audio systems that connect to the PC via a USB port. An advantage of external units is that the controls and sockets are fitted on the external unit, which can be positioned where they are easily accessed. There can be problems with the noise performance of internal soundcards being compromised by the large amounts of electrical noise generated by the computer. This problem is not avoided by having the sound circuits in an external USB device, but in practice an external device often has superior performance in this respect. Anyway, it is worth investigating external sound systems if you are interested in an up-market sound system for your PC.

Adding ports

Legacy ports

While it is not inconceivable that a computer could be put to good use without the aid of printers, modems, and other peripheral devices, few people can utilize one in this way. Unless you are using a computer for an application where there will be no need to produce any hard copy, or transfer data via means other than swapping floppy discs, at least one parallel, serial, or USB port will be required. Until recently it was normal for PCs have two serial ports and one parallel port, with the necessary hardware (including the connectors) fitted on the motherboard. The serial ports are being phased out, and they are now something of a rarity on new PCs. Parallel ports are going the same way, and are now absent on many new PCs. Parallel and serial ports have not been a standard feature of laptop PCs for some time now.

The reason for their demise is that both types of interface are slow and lacking in versatility by current standards. Using them was not always straightforward, and could be decidedly awkward at times. Newer types of computer interface are definitely an improvement on the older types, but this is "cold comfort" if you have a peripheral device that only has a serial or parallel port, and your new PC has neither of these so-called "legacy" ports. Fortunately, and as explained later in this chapter, there is an easy and inexpensive solution if you really must have a serial or parallel port on a modern PC.

USB

Modern PCs have lost the old serial and parallel ports, but they have gained two or more USB ports. The standard arrangement is to have at least two USB connectors included on the motherboard together with the other standard ports, plus some additional USB ports on a bracket at the rear of the PC. In fact many PCs have the additional ports on the front panel, often behind some sort of hinged or sliding cover. This feature is useful if you will use the ports with peripherals like mice and digital cameras.

Although USB ports have been around for some time, and modern motherboards support several of them, at first they were little used in practice. This was due to a lack of proper support from the Windows operating system of the day, which was Windows 95. This problem was rectified with the release of Windows 98, and USB has played an increasingly important role in the PC world since then. USB is a form of serial interface, but it is much faster than a conventional RS232C serial port. An ordinary PC serial port can, at best, operate up to about 115000 bits per second, whereas a USB 1.1 port can operate at more than 10 million bits per second, and a USB 2.0 type can operate at up to 480 million bits per second in short bursts. Another advantage of a USB port is its ability to operate with more than peripheral device.

USB (universal serial bus) was designed to address the problems with the existing computer interfaces used with Macintosh computers and PCs. A lack of proper standardisation caused problems with most of these interfaces, but particularly problematic with the SCSI and RS232C varieties. A parallel system such as SCSI offers very high data transfer rates, but the cables tend to be bulky and expensive. A high-speed serial port offers reasonably fast data transfers, and can use relatively simple and inexpensive cables. A serial system was therefore adopted, and after a few "teething" problems USB 1.1 was launched, and finally worked properly.

USB 1.1 has a maximum data transfer rate of 12 megabits per second, but this is not quite as good as it seems because any one device in the system can only utilise half of the bandwidth. Even so, data can be uploaded or downloaded at a rate of over 600,000 bytes per second, which is sufficient for most purposes. After a slow start, USB is now the standard way of connecting a computer to most types of peripheral. In order to broaden the usefulness of USB ports, version 2.0 was devised and it is now the standard form of USB port. The speed of USB 2.0 is more than adequate for virtually all peripherals, including fast disc drives and video devices. It is backward compatible with USB 1.1, and devices that do not require high-speed connections often have a USB 1.1 interface. A USB 3.0 interface is planned, but has not been finalised at the time of writing this piece. It will be about ten times faster than USB 2.0, but few practical applications will noticeably benefit from such a high transfer rate.

USB advantages

USB was designed to have advantages over the alternative types of port, and it has been successful to a high degree. These are the main advantages:

Built-in

USB has the advantage of being built-in to a PC, unlike the main alternatives of SCSI and Firewire. Apart from the greater convenience, this avoids the cost of an expansion card, and the problems that can arise when trying to install the card.

Speed

Like an RS232C interface, a USB type provides two-way operation, but with much faster transfer rates. A modern parallel port can provide fast two-way operation, but requires the use of bulky and expensive cables.

Expandability

PC parallel and serial ports are only intended for use with one device per port. With the aid of switching units it is possible to use more than one device on each port, but only in a relatively crude and inconvenient fashion. USB is designed to handle numerous devices, and in theory at any rate, up to 127 peripherals can be connected to a PC via this interface.

Power

A few serial and parallel ports have power supply outputs, but this is not a standard feature and it is something that is not supported by PC versions of these ports. A USB port has a +5-volt supply output, and a version 1.1 port can supply up to 0.5 amps. This works out at only 2.5 watts, and large peripherals still require their own power supply. However, it is sufficient for smaller devices, such as joysticks and modems. USB 2.0 ports can supply 2 amps, which works out at up to 10 watts of power. This is still not very high, but it is adequate for many broadband modems, some disc drives, etc.

Plug and Play

USB properly supports the Windows Plug and Play feature. With some of the more simple devices, Windows will detect their presence at boot-up and automatically load the necessary device driver. It is necessary to go through the usual installation process when dealing with units that are more complex. A disc containing the device drivers should then be supplied with the peripheral. Either way, the new device should always be detected properly provided there are no hardware faults. Using other ports, Plug and Play tends to be a bit iffy, or even non-existent.

Standardised

The slow speed of an ordinary serial port is a major drawback, but the lack of standardisation and built-in complexities make it difficult to use. There can be problems when using a serial interface with a modem, but the likelihood of problems are many times greater when it is used for other peripherals. In fairness, the RS232C standard was only designed for use with communications devices such as modems, and it was never intended for printers, etc. A USB port is suitable for non-technical users because it requires no setting up of baud rates or word formats. All data is handled using the same system.

Simple cables

A USB link uses a four-way cable, and two of the wires carry the ground and +5-volt connections. The other two wires form what is termed a "twisted pair", and they carry the data. There are no handshake lines to deal with, and it should never be necessary to make a custom cable. The complexities of a USB link are handled in the software rather than by having numerous connections between the two units. For example, a system of addressing is used so that the computer can send data to the appropriate device when there are two or more peripherals connected to the same USB port. A system of coding is used so that the peripherals treat received data in the correct way. This complexity is handled by the device drivers and the firmware in the peripherals. Users just plug everything in, load the device drivers where appropriate, and then start using the equipment.

Plugging/unplugging

Connecting any device to a computer while either of the units is switched on is not normally to be recommended. Disconnecting devices under the same circumstances is usually discouraged as well. There is a real risk of damage to the computer and the peripheral if you simply plug in and unplug things as the fancy takes you. However, USB is designed for connection and disconnection "on the fly", thus removing the need to switch everything off before adding a USB device to or removing it from the system.

Conflicts

USB makes it easy for peripherals to share system resources. In theory at any rate, it is possible to add dozens of peripherals to the USB ports without any risk of problems with hardware conflicts.

USB 2.0

Although USB 1.1 has many advantages over the older PC interfaces, it is still not fast enough for some applications. In particular, downloading large amounts of video information in real-time is beyond USB 1.1 unless the resolution and quality are quite low. Even downloading high resolution still images can be time consuming using an ordinary USB interface. The speed of external USB drives such as CD-RW types is relatively low due to the limitations of ordinary USB ports.

USB 2.0 ports operate properly with USB 1.1 equipment, but only at the normal data transfer rate. In theory anyway, faster overall operation can be obtained when using several USB 1.1 devices with a USB 2.0 port. Note that connecting a USB 2.0 device to a USB 1.1 port is not permitted. When a USB 2.0 port is used with USB 2.0 equipment the data transfer rate is very high at a theoretical maximum of 480 megabits per second. This equates to something in the region of 50 megabytes per second, which is fast enough for video, fast external drives, or practically any current application. In practice such a high data transfer rate might not be achieved, and it is probably beyond the capabilities of many PCs. It still provides much greater speed than USB 1.1 though, and opens up new possibilities.

The maximum number of devices per port remains the same at 127, but with USB 1.1 this figure was rather theoretical. The relatively limited bandwidth of the system made it impossible to use the full number of peripherals. It is unlikely that USB 2.0 could actually handle 127 devices properly, but its wider bandwidth means that the realistic maximum number is raised to something close to this figure. USB 2.0 should certainly be able to handle more devices than most users will ever need to connect to their PC.

USB hubs

If your PC already has a couple of USB ports and you wish to add some more, it is not necessary to add a USB card to the PC. In fact this is definitely not the way to go about things. It is possible to use the chain

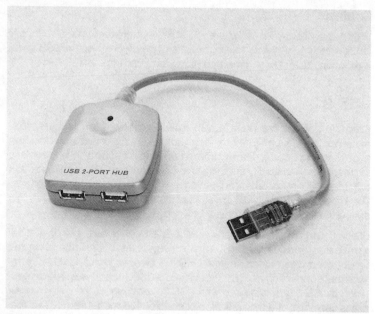

Fig.7.1 A simple twin port USB hub

method of connection with USB peripherals, where each device has a USB output that can be connected to the next device in the chain. This approach never seemed to catch on, and I have yet to encounter a USB device having an output port.

The usual way of using more than one device per USB port is to use a device called a hub. This is a box having two or more USB ports on the front, and a cable at the rear that connects to a USB port on the PC. The simplest USB hubs are non-powered devices that have two ports (Figure 7.1 and G.16 in the Colour Gallery). With most PCs the USB ports are in the cluster of connectors at the rear of the PC where they are difficult to get at. Some PCs have one or two more USB ports in a concealed compartment on the front panel. This is a more convenient place when the ports are used with gadgets such as USB microphones and pointing devices. It is now quite common for monitors to have a built-in USB hub that also gives easy access to two or more ports. If your system lacks these facilities, a simple two-port hub is useful if you need a couple of easily accessible USB ports.

The larger USB hubs have four or more ports and have their own power supply. The USB hubs built into monitors are normally of this type. The practical significance of the hub being powered is that the full 0.5 or 2.0 amps of current should be available from each port. With a non-powered hub only 0.5 or 2.0 amps can be drawn in total, since that is all that is available from the PC port to which the hub is connected. Trying to draw too much current produces an on-screen error message, and the device or devices concerned will fail to work.

In order to be certain of satisfactory results, only one device that draws power from the USB port should be used with this type of hub. In practice, it is likely that there will be no problem if two low-power devices are used, such as a USB mouse and a microphone. However, there is no guarantee that both devices will work with a non-powered hub. Note that the hub should be of the same type (USB 1.1 or 2.0) as the port it is driven from.

USB cards

There are two reasons for using an expansion card to add USB ports to a PC. One is simply that the PC does not have any built-in USB ports, and a hub is not an option. Some older PCs do actually have the necessary hardware on the motherboard, but were not supplied with the connectors to permit the hardware to be connected to the outside world. This may seem to be a strange state of affairs, but the USB hardware was around for a year or two before proper support was available from the operating system. PC manufacturers were reluctant to sell PCs complete with ports that were not fully operational. Hence the hardware on the motherboard was not made available to users.

All that is needed to get these ports working is a metal blanking plate fitted with the appropriate connectors and leads. A spare expansion slot is needed so that an existing blanking plate can be removed and the new one can be added. The leads from the new blanking plate are connected to the USB ports on the motherboard.

In practice there is a major complication in that each motherboard manufacturer tended to use a different connector on the motherboard, or the same connector wired in a different manner. This is a viable way of adding USB ports if a suitable blanking plate assembly can be obtained, but it is easy to end up buying the wrong thing. The odd economics of the electronics industry mean that it is unlikely to cost much more to use a USB expansion card instead. This is the safer method, since it is guaranteed to work.

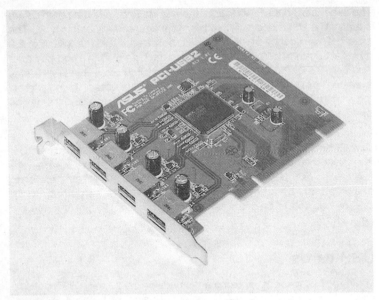

Fig.7.2 This USB 2.0 expansion card provides four ports

USB 2.0 cards

The second reason for adding a USB expansion card, and the more likely one these days, is that you need to use USB 2.0 peripherals with a PC that only has USB 1.1 ports. Modern PCs have USB 2.0 ports. but older PCs predate USB 2.0 and therefore have USB 1.1 ports. Fortunately, USB 2.0 cards are not very expensive, so abandoning the built-in ports will not cost the proverbial "arm and leg". The fact that most USB 2.0 cards have at least four ports, like the one shown in Figure 7.2, makes this upgrade more attractive. Most PCs only have two built-in USB 1.1 ports. Remember that the new USB 2.0 ports are fully compatible with USB 1.1 peripherals, so any existing peripherals should work at least as well with the new ports.

A USB expansion card is usually in the form of a small PCI card that is added in the usual way. The new card might work with the existing ports enabled, but before fitting the new card it is advisable to go into the BIOS Setup program and disable the USB hardware on the motherboard. The Plug and Play feature will operate when the PC is booted into Windows with the new card installed. It is advisable to carefully read

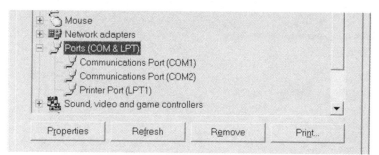

Fig.7.3 Each category can be expanded in standard Explorer fashion

through the installation instructions supplied with the card, as some cards have to be installed in Windows without using the Plug and Play facility. Also, the installation method tends to vary somewhat from one version of Windows to another. Any necessary software drivers should be supplied with the card.

Note that USB ports can not be used with Windows 95 or earlier versions or Windows. Support for USB 2.0 is built into Windows XP but it is not supported by earlier versions of Windows such as Windows 98 and NT. This does not mean that USB 2.0 cards are unusable with Windows 98, etc., but it does mean that third-party software is needed in order to get the card working properly. This should all be taken care of by the driver software supplied with the card, but with a USB 2.0 card it is best to check that it is usable with the appropriate version of Windows prior to buying it.

Device Manager

Before testing the new card it is advisable to go to Device Manager and check that the driver software has installed correctly. In fact it is a good idea to check the drivers have been installed properly for any new hardware. In

Fig.7.4 Launching the Control Panel in Windows XP

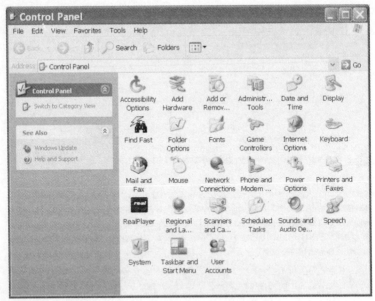

Fig.7.5 The Windows XP version of the Control Panel

Windows 98 and ME the first step is to launch the Control Panel by going to the Start menu and selecting Settings followed by Control Panel. Double-clicking the System icon brings up the System Properties window, and operating the Device Manager tab produces a screen that shows various hardware categories. In standard Explorer fashion, the categories can be expanded by left-clicking on the "+" symbols (Figure 7.3).

In Windows XP and Vista the Control Panel can be accessed direct from the Start menu (Figure 7.4). It looks much the same as the Windows 98/ME version if the "classic" view is used (Figure 7.5). Double-clicking the System icon produces the System Properties window (Figure 7.6). Next the Hardware tab is operated, and in the new version of the System Properties window (Figure 7.7) the Device Manager button is operated. This launches the Control Panel (Figure 7.8), which looks similar to the Windows 98/ME version.

In this example there is a yellow question mark against the Other Devices entry, which has automatically expanded to show the device that is giving the problem. This is a USB controller. Yellow question marks and exclamation marks are used by Device Manager to indicate that there is

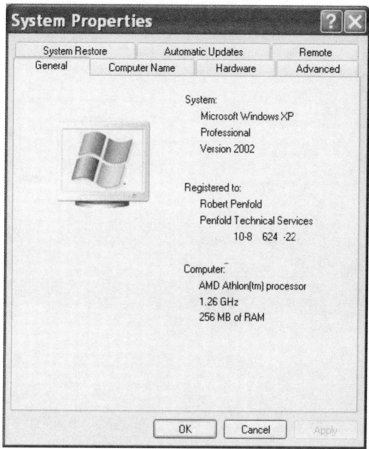

Fig.7.6 Operating the Hardware tab is the next step

a possible problem or that something seems to be seriously amiss. Fortunately, in this case the suspected problem is caused by the USB ports on the motherboard that have been disabled in the BIOS. The drivers are still present, and Windows is puzzled by the lack of hardware for these drivers.

The computer should still work properly, but it is best to tidy things up by removing any drivers for hardware that has been removed or switched off. This is just a matter of right-clicking on the relevant entry and selecting

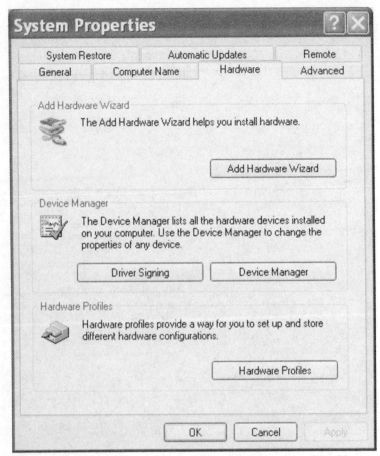

Fig.7.7 Finally, operating the Device Manager button launches this utility program

Delete from the popup menu (Figure 7.9). Note that it is not possible to remove a complete category in this way, and that only individual device entries can be deleted. However, a category will be automatically deleted once it no longer contains any entries. No problems remain once the offending device driver has been deleted (Figure 7.10). The entry for the new USB 2.0 card is the one at the bottom of the list.

Adding ports 7

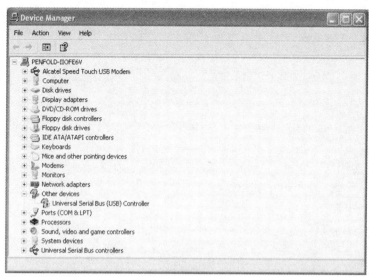

Figure 7.8 The question mark indicates a problem with the
corresponding piece of hardware

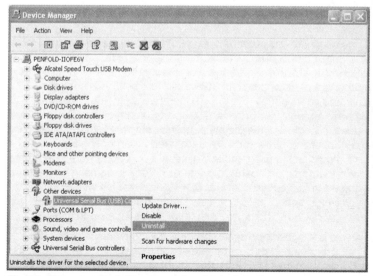

Fig.7.9 The unwanted drivers can be deleted via the popup menu

123

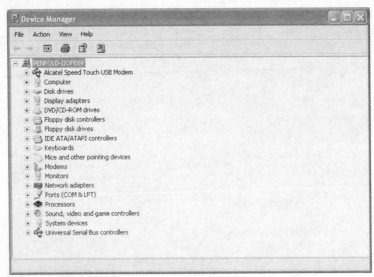

Fig.7.10 The unwanted drivers have been removed and there are no further problems reported

SCSI and Firewire

Some scanners and other devices interface to the computer via a SCSI port (small computers systems interface and pronounced "scuzzy"), which is a form of high-speed bi-directional parallel port. A few motherboards have a built-in SCSI interface, but this is something of a rarity and no longer seems to be a feature of new PCs. There are PCI expansion cards that provide SCSI ports, and many peripherals that require this type of interface are supplied complete with a suitable card and connecting cable (or they are offered as an optional extra). The card should be supplied with any necessary driver software to integrate it with the common operating systems. SCSI is sometimes used for high performance hard disc and CD-ROM drives, but with modern PCs having high speed (UDMA33, etc.) hard disc interfaces built-in, it is probably not worth bothering with SCSI drives for a stand-alone PC.

Firewire is a high-speed serial link, similar in some respects to USB 2.0. It has a maximum data transfer rate of 400 megabits per second, so it is not quite as fast as USB 2.0. Whether it actually manages to produce faster data transfers in a real world situation is another matter. It has been used for up-market scanners and digital cameras, but it is mainly

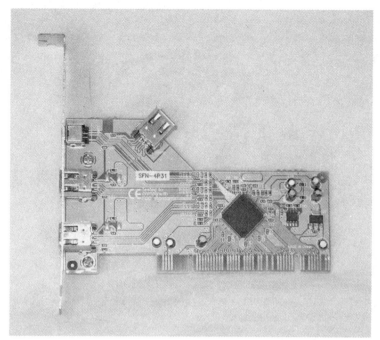

Fig.7.11 This PCI expansion card provides two Firewire ports

used with digital camcorders. It is so well established in this field that it is unlikely to be displaced by USB 2.0 in the near future.

Many PCs now have one or two built-in Firewire ports. Firewire ports are easily added to a PC that does not have any built-in ports of this type, and it is just a matter of adding a Firewire PCI expansion card (Figure 7.11). This card provides two Firewire ports. One is the standard 6-pin type, and the other is of the smaller 4-pin variety. The only significant difference between the two types is that the larger 6-pin port has a supply output that is absent on the 4-pin type. Consequently, a device that is powered from a Firewire port must be used with a 6-pin type.

Adding legacy ports

As pointed out previously, there can be problems if you have hardware that requires a legacy port but your new PC only has USB ports. Very few peripheral devices that require serial or parallel ports have been

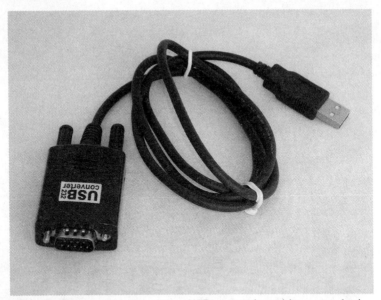

Fig.7.12 This adaptor plugs into a USB port and provides a standard RS232C serial port

produced in recent years, so it is likely that any legacy port hardware that you own will be quite old. The most practical solution might be to simply discard the old hardware and buy a modern equivalent that uses a USB port. Of course, if the piece of hardware is something that would be expensive to replace, such as an upmarket graphics tablet, it is worth trying an alternative approach.

It is possible to add serial and parallel ports to a modern PC, and there are two basic methods. The most simple is to use a USB adaptor, and both serial and parallel port adaptors are available at very low prices. A USB to serial port adaptor is shown in Figure 7.12. It looks rather like a computer lead, but there is some sophisticated electronics in the serial port connector.

Using an adaptor of this type is very simple, and in most cases it is just a matter of plugging the adaptor into a USB port and waiting while Windows detects the new hardware and loads the driver software for it. Older versions of Windows lack built-in drivers for USB adaptors, but suitable software is usually supplied with the adaptor. It is normally necessary to know the port number for a serial or parallel port, so that you can set up application software to use the right port. Serial ports are COM1, COM2,

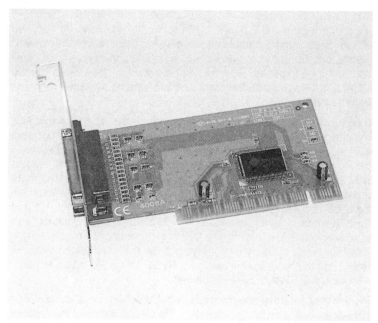

Fig.7.13 A PCI parallel port card

etc., and parallel ports are LPT1, LPT2, etc. Unfortunately, the port numbering is sometimes a little odd, and the adaptor will not necessarly be LPT1 or COM1, as appropriate. Windows is just as likely to designate the new port something like LPT3 or COM4. It is best to go into Device Manager and check the number given to the new port.

The alternative to using a USB adaptor is to fit a serial or parallel port PCI expansion card. The card shown in Figure 7.13 is a PCI parallel port card. Using an internal PCI card is perhaps a neater solution than using an external USB adaptor, but it is likely to be more expensive, and does require the computer's case to be opened. The USB approach is the more popular one these days.

It should be borne in mind that built-in serial and parallel ports are somewhat different to those provided by PCI cards and USB adaptors. The PCI bus is really a form of input/output port, and devices on the PCI bus can not fit into the computer's input/output map, which is the way that built-in ports are interfaced to the processor. The same is also true of ports that are provided via a USB adaptor. On the face of it, this is unimportant because PCI port cards and USB adaptors are supplied with discs containing suitable device drivers. This enables Windows to use the add-on port much as if it was a conventional type at the usual input/output addresses. Provided all the software does things "by the book" and only contacts the ports via the operating system, everything should work fine.

Unfortunately, real-world software does not always do things this way, and it might try to directly control the port's hardware. This will not work at all, because the port's hardware will not be at the usual addresses in the input/output map. It can only be accessed indirectly via the PCI bus or USB port, using relatively complex routines. In general, the more common peripherals such as printers and modems are contacted via the usual channels and should not give any problems with a PCI port card. Many devices are less accommodating though, and parallel port scanners and Zip drives mostly use the direct access method. It is therefore better to use the more "run of the mill" devices on PCI port cards, and the more specialised peripherals on the PC's built-in ports. With luck, this will avoid any problems.

The expansion card or adaptor might be supplied with a software solution in the form of a remapping program. This tries to intercept instructions that are directed at the standard port addresses. It then substitutes an appropriate routine to drive the PCI card or USB adaptor. There is no guarantee that this type of thing will work properly, but it usually works well enough. Unfortunately, remapping utilities seem to be something of a rarity these days, and are not often supplied with PCI port cards or USB adaptors. Getting "awkward" serial or parallel port peripherals to work properly with a modern PC might not be a practical proposition.

Ethernet port

Most modern PCs, whether of the desktop or laptop variety, usually have an Ethernet networking port as standard. Where this port is absent it can be added using the normal expansion methods. In the case of a desktop PC it is probably best to opt for a PCI expansion card, and a typical Ethernet PCI card is shown in G.17 of the Colour Gallery. There are usually two indicator lights on the rear of the card, and and these are present on the card shown here. One light switches on whenever the port is connected to a network. The other one lights up when the port is sending or receiving data.

8

Hard and
floppy drives

Floppy drives

For a stand-alone PC at least one disc drive is an essential feature,
because the operating system is loaded from a disc drive and is not
built-in. While in theory a single floppy drive will suffice, these days the
single floppy approach is only used for troubleshooting. For normal use
the minimum requirement is a fairly large hard disc, a CD-ROM or DVD
drive. Most software will actually run quite happily without a CD-ROM or
DVD drive, but software is mainly distributed on CD-ROMs and DVDs,
and without a suitable drive there is no way of installing it onto the hard
disc drive. A CD-ROM or DVD drive is normally needed in order to install
the operating system.

Those dealing with large amounts of data will almost certainly require
some form of interchangeable disc drive having a high capacity, such as
a CD-RW type. However, some users still require a humble floppy disc
drive even if their PC has a CD/DVD writer, Zip drive, Flash drive, or
whatever. It is essential in order to install or reinstall older versions of
Windows, such as Windows ME. The computer has to be booted from a
floppy disc and then installed from the CD-ROM, making the floppy disc
drive non-optional. The installation CD or DVD is a bootable type with
later versions of Windows, making the floppy disc non-essential.

It is for this reason that most new PCs no longer have a floppy disc drive
as standard. It can still be useful to have a floppy drive available, and it
can be helpful when trying to diagnose problems with a faulty PC or one
that has been infected with some form of malicious software. It is also
more than a little useful if you still have large amounts of data stored on
floppy discs. However, most users can get by quite happily without one,
so there is no point in having it as part of the standard specification.

It still seems to be the norm for motherboards to be equipped with a
floppy drive interface, and a floppy disc drive will often be available as

an optional extra. It can also be added afterwards provided the motherboard has the appropriate interface and the case has a suitable drive bay. Do not overlook the availability of external floppy disc drives that connect to a USB port. These enable the computer to read from and write to floppy discs, and avoid the complications of installing a convention floppy drive. USB floppy drives are often quite inexpensive, and have the advantage of being usable with any PC that has a USB port. They are easily switched from one PC to another.

Types

There are five types of floppy disc drive used with PCs, and these are listed below. All five types use both sides of the disc incidentally.

3.5-inch, 80 track, 720k capacity

3.5-inch, 80 track, 1.44M capacity

3.5-inch 2.88M capacity

5.25-inch, 40 track, 360k capacity

5.25-inch, 80 track, 1.2M capacity

The data on a floppy disc drive is stored magnetically on the metal oxide coating. This is much the same as the way in which an audio signal is recorded onto the tape in an ordinary compact cassette. In the case of a floppy disc though, the data is recorded onto a number of concentric tracks, or "cylinders" as they are sometimes termed. Each track is divided into a number of sectors, and there are nine sectors per track for a 5.25-inch 360k disc for example.

Originally the 5.25-inch 360k drives were used on PCs, PC XTs, and compatibles, while the 5.25-inch 1.2M type were used on ATs and compatibles. 3.5-inch drives have been adopted as the industry standard, and 3.5-inch 1.44M drives have gradually take over from the 5.25-inch variety. Even the 3.5-inch 720k type is now obsolete. 1.2M 5.25-inch drives are still available, but they are increasingly difficult to track down. It is unlikely that they are still in production, so those that are available must be either old stock or second-hand.

At one time it was common for PCs to have a 1.44M 3.5-inch drive and a 5.25-inch 1.2M drive. The former is used to read and write new data discs, with the latter providing compatibility with the numerous 5.25-inch discs that many users (particularly business users) still possessed. Of course, 5.25-inch discs can have their contents copied onto 3.5-inch discs, but this is time consuming and expensive if you have large numbers of old discs. Hence many users simply opted for the two-disc system. With 5.25-inch drives now well and truly obsolete it is a good idea to copy any 5.25-inch discs onto CD-ROMs, if you can find an old PC that has the drives needed to handle handle this task. Alternatively, you might be able to find an old 5.25-inch drive and install it in a modern computer so that old discs can be copied onto CD-ROMs or DVDs. 3.5-inch floppy discs are virtually obsolete, so it is also a good idea to copy their contents to a more modern storage medium.

It is only fair to point out that many old floppy discs have not stood the test of time. I recently tried to copy the data from a number of old floppy discs. About one third of them were unreadable, and most of those were in such a poor state that they could not even be reformatted properly. Also bear in mind that much of the data stored on old floppy discs is in obsolete formats. In some cases it is possible to convert old data into a modern format, and some modern programs can read data in old formats. It is not always possible to utilise old data in a worthwhile fashion though, and it is prudent to check the usability of the data before spendng a lot of time and money trying to retrieve it from old discs.

The 2.88M disc drives were designed to replace the 1.44M drives as the standard for new PCs. With PCs tending to produce ever-larger files there is a definite advantage in the higher capacity of a 2.88M drive. Despite this, 2.88M drives have remained something of a rarity, and they never replaced 1.44 megabyte drives. The high initial price and a reputation for poor reliability certainly hindered the progress of the 2.88M drives. Consumer resistance to yet another change in the standard floppy disc format probably played its part as well. Another factor is that 2.88 megabytes was not much data by the standards of that time, and is next to nothing by current standrds. My digital camera can produce about 14 megabytes of data each time I take a photograph!

Extra floppy

The first point to bear in mind when adding a disc drive to a PC is that it must be of a type that is supported by the BIOS. Also, it must be a type that the computer's floppy disc controller can handle. There should be no difficulty when adding any standard size drive to a modern PC, since the BIOS and built-in floppy controller will almost certainly support all five types. If you need to add a 5.25-inch drive so that old discs can be copied, then this should be possible. As always though, it is best to check and not jump to conclusions. The manual for the computer or its motherboard might have the information you require, but it is easy to go

Fig.8.1 A 3.5-inch format (Zip) drive fitted in a 5.25-inch bay adaptor

into the BIOS and cycle through the floppy disc options. Actually finding a working 5.25-inch drive to install is likely to be the main problem.

Of course, before fitting a floppy drive you must ensure that the computer's case can accommodate it. Obviously there is no problem if you are simply replacing a faulty drive, as it is then just a matter of removing the old drive and bolting the new drive in its place. These days it is more likely that you will be trying to fit a new drive into a PC that came without a floppy drive. In order to do this you need a free drive bay of the correct size, and with a floppy drive it must be an open type that gives access to the front of the drive. Many modern PC cases have one free 3.5-inch drive bay that meets this requirement, and with older types there will probably be two or more of these bays. There is a potential solution if only an open 5.25-inch bay is available, but you require a 3.5-inch type. It is possible to obtain an adaptor that permits a 3.5-inch drive to be used in a 5.25-inch bay (Figure 8.1). An adaptor of this type should be usable with any 3.5-inch drive and not just with floppy drives. It is actually a Zip drive that is fitted in the adaptor shown in Figure 8.1.

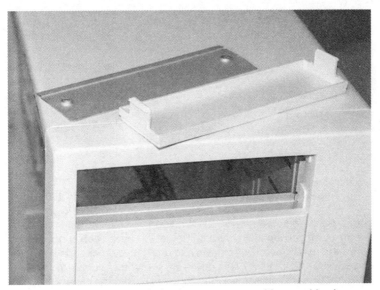

Fig.8.2 The metal plate and plastic cover removed from a drive bay

There are two basic tasks to complete when fitting a floppy disc drive.
The first is to get it physically fixed in place, and the second is to get it
connected to the controller correctly. There are plastic covers over the
external drive bays, and these must be removed at the positions where
drives are to be fitted. These are easily pushed out from the rear, but
there will probably be a slight snag here in the form of a metal plate
behind each plastic cover. These plates are partially cut from the case,
and must be removed from any bays where externally accessible drives
will be fitted. They can usually be left in place where other drives, such
as the hard drive or drives, will be fitted.

These plates are removed in the same way as other blanking plates in
the case. Unclip the plastic cover first. There are usually a couple of
holes in the metal plate so that you can push out the plastic cover from
the rear by poking a screwdriver through one of these holes. With a bit
of pushing and shoving it should be possible to turn the plate through
about 30 degrees or so, although it can take a while to get the blanking
plate completely free. You can then get hold of one edge, and with a bit
of waggling the plate should soon break away from the case. With a few
cases the plates are held in place by screws, so check this point before
you try the flexing method. With the plate and plastic cover removed

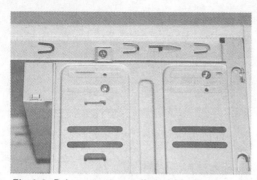

(Figure 8.2) the bay is ready for the drive to be fitted.

With modern PCs the disc drives normally fit directly into the drive bays, and are then fixed in place using two screws each side. Figure 8.3 shows the drive bay and fixing screws for a 5.25-inch drive, but the same method is used for

Fig.8.3 Drives are normally held in place by two screws each side

both types. The screws fit into the threaded holes in the side panels of the drives. If you are lucky, your computer will have been supplied with some additional drive fixing screws and one or two other odds and ends of hardware. Alternatively, disc drives are sometimes supplied complete with a set of four fixing screws, but this is not usually the case with floppy drives.

If not, it could be difficult to locate a source of suitable screws, but your local computer store might be able to help. It is important that these screws are quite short. There is otherwise a risk of them penetrating too far into the drive and causing damage. This will not be a problem if you use screws specifically intended for mounting drives, but could be if you have to improvise with whatever you can obtain. Screws longer than 10 millimetres should certainly not be used. Provided you have the correct fixing screws, fixing a drive into this type of computer is unlikely to give any real difficulties.

Early PCs used a somewhat different method of drive fixing. Two plastic guide-rails were required, and these were bolted one per side onto the drive. This assembly was then slid into place in one of the drive bays, and the rails were bolted to the drive bay. This method is now long obsolete, but some recent PC cases use an updated version of the guide-rail idea. The general scheme of things is to have a guide-rail fitted to one side of the drive (Figure 8.4), and it is usually held in place via a wire clip. This side of the drive is not bolted into place and is only supported by the guide-rail. The other side is held in place by two screws in the normal fashion.

As viewed from the front of the PC, it is the right-hand side of the drive that is fitted with the guide-rail. I assume that the idea is to avoid using

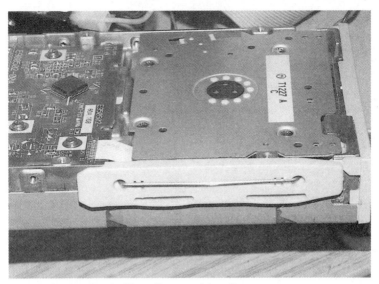

Fig.8.4 A drive fitted with a clip-on guide-rail

fixing screws on the right-hand side of the drive, which is usually less accessible than the left-hand side. In fact I have encountered PCs where it is only possible to access these screws by removing the motherboard. Some spare guide-rails should have been supplied with your PC if it uses this method of fixing, and it will not be possible to fit an additional drive properly without one. The guide-rails are normally used for the 3.5-inch bays with the 5.25-inch types having mounting screws both sides, but there could be some exceptions.

Connections

You must also connect the power supply to the disc drive. Modern PC power supplies have about five or six leads and connectors for disc drives. Simply connect the plug on any spare lead to the power socket on the disc drive. This is a properly polarised plug, and it is impossible to connect it to the drive the wrong way round. With old PCs there may not be a spare disc drive power cable. You will then need to obtain an adaptor which takes one of the drive power leads and splits it to permit connection to two drives.

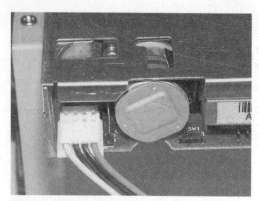

*Fig.8.5 A 3.5-inch power connector
           fitted correctly*

Note that there are two sizes of power connector. The larger type is used for 5.25-inch floppy drives, CD-ROM drives, and most hard disc drives. A miniature version of this power connector is used for 3.5-inch floppy drives. However, if a 3.5-inch drive is fitted in a chassis to permit it to fit into a 5.25-inch bay, this might include an adaptor that enables the drive to be connected to a standard (full size) disc drive connector. If there is a spare power cable but it is the wrong size, obtain an adaptor lead to convert it to the correct type of connector, or use one of the splitter cables mentioned previously.

The 5.25-inch power connectors tend to be rather stiff but are otherwise reasonably foolproof. The 3.5-inch variety fit into place much more easily and are supposedly polarised. In practice the connectors on the drives are sometimes very basic and permit the power leads to be connected incorrectly. The slightly concave side of the connector faces towards the connector on the drive. Another potential problem is that the lead can sometimes be connected one set of pins along from the correct position, so check carefully to ensure that the two connectors are properly aligned. With the lead connected properly you should have something like Figure 8.5, with no power pins visible on either side of the connector. Getting the power lead connected incorrectly can "blow" the drive, so check that this connector is fitted correctly.

Floppy cables

The standard PC floppy disc drive cable consists of a length of 34-way ribbon cable, which is fitted with 34-way edge connectors and IDC connectors at the floppy drive end. 3.5-inch floppy drives require the IDC connectors, and 5.25-inch types connect to the edge connectors. The connector at the controller end is not totally standardised, but anything other than an "antique" PC will require a 34-way IDC connector. Most cables are for twin drives, and therefore have two sets of drive

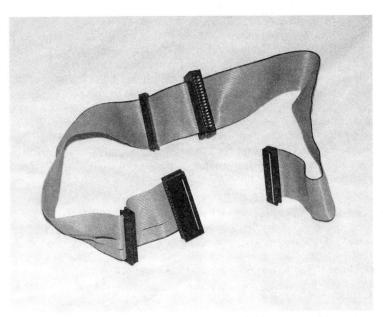

Fig.8.6 A floppy drive cable having two sets of drive connectors

connectors. This makes like easier when adding a second drive, because you can normally use the existing cable. Figure 8.6 shows a standard floppy drive data cable, complete with two pairs of drive connectors. Note that modern floppy cables often lack the edge connectors and are only suitable for use with 3.5-inch drives. A full floppy cable will be needed if you wish to add a 5.25-inch floppy drive.

In a standard floppy drive set-up, the two connectors would be wired in exactly the same way. Pin 1 at the controller would connect to pin 1 of both drives, pin 2 would connect to both of the pin 2s, and so on. The two drives do not operate in unison, and both try to operate as drive A, because there are jumpers on the drives which are set to make one operate as drive A, and the other operate as drive B. Provided one drive is set as drive A and the other is set as drive B there will be no conflicts. The jumper blocks are normally a set of four pairs of terminals marked something like "DS0", "DS1", "DS2", and "DS3" (or possibly something like "DS1" to "DS4"). The instruction manual for the disc drive (in the unlikely event of you being able to obtain it) will make it clear which of the many jumper blocks are the ones for drive selection. Drive A has the jumper lead on "DS0", while drive B has it on "DS1".

Things could actually be set up in this fashion in a PC, but it is not the standard way of doing things. Instead, both drives are set as drive B by having the jumper lead placed on "DS1". The so-called "twist" in the cable between the two drive connectors then reverses some of the connections to one drive, making it operate as drive B. This may seem to be an unusual way of doing things, but there is apparently a good reason for it. If you obtain a PC disc drive, whether for use as a replacement for a worn out drive A, or as a newly added drive B, the same drive configured in exactly the same way will do the job. This avoids the need for dealers to stock two different types of drive, which in reality is exactly the same type of drive with a slightly different configuration.

For the DIY PC upgrader it makes life easier in that any drive sold for use in a PC should work perfectly without the need to alter any of the configuration jumpers. In fact many 3.5-inch drives are manufactured specifically for use in PCs, and do not actually have any configuration jumpers. Of course, if you buy a drive that is not specifically for use in a PC, it might not be set up correctly for operation in a PC. The elusive instruction booklet for the disc drive is then more than a little useful. Since a new 3.5-inch floppy drive for a PC only costs a few pounds there is little point buying one that is not intended for use in a PC.

The computer will still work if you get the connections to two floppy drives swapped over, but the one you required as drive A: will be drive B:, and vice versa. The connector at the end of the cable couples to drive A, while the other one connects to drive B. Figure 8.7 shows this general scheme of things. When adding a drive to an older PC you might find that the cable only has edge connectors for the drives, but that the new drive requires an IDC connector. A suitable edge connector to IDC adaptor could be impossible to obtain these days, and there will probably be no alternative to buying a new floppy drive cable. Unless you are upgrading a really old PC you are unlikely to encounter this problem.

Getting the floppy drive cable connected to the new drive should be straightforward, because the two connectors should be polarised, so that they can not be fitted the wrong way round. The necessary "key" is just a small metal rod on the edge connector, which fits into a slot in the connector on the drive. A lump and a slot on IDC connectors serve the same function. Unfortunately, the polarising "keys" are sometimes missing. Another unhelpful variation is the floppy drive that has the polarising on both the top and bottom edges of the connector.

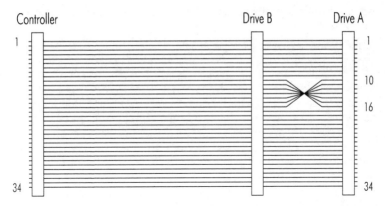

Fig.8.7 The arrangement used for a PC floppy drive cable

You should find that the connector numbers, or some of them, are marked onto the connector on the disc drive and on the motherboard. Incidentally, on modern computers the floppy drive controller is invariably part of the motherboard. The numbers might also be marked on the drive lead connectors, and a coloured lead (as opposed to the grey of all the others) on the cable itself should denote the pin 1 end of the lead/connector. Of course, pin 1 of the floppy drive controller couples to pin 1 of the drive's connector.

Termination resistors

In the past every disc drive had a set of eight termination resistors. These connected to certain inputs of the drive, and tied them to the +5 volt supply rail. They are termed "pull-up" resistors. However many disc drives are used, only one set of termination resistors should be present. It is only the drive at the end of the cable that should have these resistors. Therefore, if you fit a second drive to a PC, as it will fit mid-cable, it will not require its termination resistors. These resistors are normally in the form of a single component, rather than eight individual resistors. They will be mounted in a socket of some kind, and this will often be of the standard 16-pin d.i.l. integrated circuit type. A socket of this type has two rows of eight terminals 0.3 inches apart. The resistor pack itself will probably be in the form of a black plastic component having two rows of eight pins. The resistors have a value of 220 ohms, and so the component will be marked something like "220R", plus some other characters in most cases.

Some drives have a s.i.l. (single in-line) resistor pack. These have nine pins in a single row, usually with 0.1-inch pin spacing. Like the d.i.l. resistor packs, they are mounted in a socket so that they can be easily removed. In fact the s.i.l. variety are generally more easily removed than the d.i.l. type. With any d.i.l. component it is a good idea to use a screwdriver to carefully prise it free from the socket. Keep the termination resistor pack safe somewhere in case it should be needed at some later time. In fact you should always keep anything removed from the computer when performing upgrades. You never know when these odds and ends will be needed again.

It is only fair to point out that many modern floppy drives do not have removable termination resistors. If you install a 5.25-inch drive it will probably have them, but I have not encountered termination resistors on 3.5-inch drives for quite some time. With drives that lack these resistors you simply connect them up to the motherboard and hope they work (which they invariably seem to).

Having installed an additional floppy drive it is likely that the PC will simply ignore it when the computer is booted into Windows. This happens because the existing BIOS setting will be for no drive B. Consequently the BIOS ignores the new drive, as does the operating system. The new drive will only work straight away if the BIOS detects the new drive and alters the relevant setting itself. Assuming this does not happen; you must go into the BIOS Setup program and make the change yourself. The floppy drive settings are usually in the Standard CMOS section of the program. It is just a matter of working through the options for drive B until the appropriate drive type is found.

Hard discs

A hard disc is very much like an ordinary floppy type, but in a highly refined form. In fact modern hard disc drives are so highly refined that they manage to cram incredible amounts of data onto a small disc. The disc itself is a permanent part of the drive, and is not interchangeable like floppy discs (hence the alternative name of "fixed" disc). The disc is made of metal and is rigid (hence the "hard" disc name). The disc spins at a much higher rate that is about ten or more times faster than the rotation speed of a floppy disc. Furthermore, it rotates continuously, not just when data must be accessed.

This is an important factor, since one of the main advantages of a hard disc is the speed with which data can be accessed. Having to wait for the disc to build up speed and settle down at the right speed would slow down disc accesses by an unacceptable degree. In fact the high rotation speed would result in accesses to a hard disc actually being slower than those to a floppy disc. A slight drawback of this continuous rotation is that computers equipped with hard discs are notoriously noisy! The high rotation speed of the disc aids rapid data transfers. Data can typically be read from disc in less than a tenth of the time that a floppy disc would take to handle the same amount of data. In fact modern hard drives are probably several hundred times faster than floppy drives.

Although the disc of a hard disc drive is not changeable, it has a very high capacity so that it can accommodate large amounts of data and several large applications programs if necessary. This is achieved by having what are typically many hundreds of cylinders (tracks) with numerous sectors per cylinder. Early hard discs had capacities of about 10 to 20 megabytes, but the lowest capacity currently offered by most suppliers is 10 or 20 gigabytes (1000 megabytes). Hard discs having capacities in excess of 100 gigabytes are quite commonplace. In most cases the "disc" is actually two, three, or four discs mounted one above the other on a common spindle. This enables around three to eight record/playback heads and sides of the disc to be used, giving higher capacities than could be handled using a single disc.

An important point that has to be made right from the start is that hard discs are highly intricate and quite delicate pieces of equipment. Modern hard drives are somewhat tougher than the early units, most of which had warning notices stating that the mildest of jolts could damage the drive. Even so, they must be treated with due respect, and protected from excessive jolts and vibration if they are to provide long and trouble-free service. You are unlikely to damage a modern hard disc drive simply by picking up the computer in which it is fitted, and carrying it across to the other side of the room. On the other hand, dropping a hard drive or the computer in which it is fitted could well result in serious damage to the hard disc drive.

Hard disc units are hermetically sealed so that dust can not enter. This is crucial, due to the high rotation speed of the disc. Apparently, the heads are aerodynamic types, which glide just above the surface of the disc, never actually coming into contact with it. If the two should come into contact, even via an intervening speck of dust, the result could easily be severe damage to the surface of the disc, and possibly to the head as well. Never open up a hard disc drive if you ever intend to use it again!

Interfaces

Adding a hard disc drive to a PC breaks down into four basic tasks. First the configuration jumpers must be checked and altered if they are not appropriate for your set-up. Then the drive must be bolted in place inside the computer. Next it is connected to the power supply and a suitable hard disc controller. Finally, it must be formatted and made ready for use with the operating system. Note that the configuration jumpers are not normally used with modern drives that have a SATA interface of some kind, making it a three-stage process with drives of this type.

Usually the operating system will be installed on the hard disc so that the computer boots-up from the hard disc at switch-on. Of course, this is not necessary when adding an extra hard disc rather than swapping the existing disc for a higher capacity type. Assuming the original disc has one partition (drive C), the new one will become drive D and any others such as CD-RW drives will move up by one letter. However, it is not always as simple as that, and the new hard disc drive could have a much higher drive letter if the main drive is divided into several partitions, each with its own drive letter. Things like Flash memory card readers can also result in the new drive becoming something like drive G rather than drive D. As we shall see shortly, formatting and making a hard disc ready for use is a slightly more complex business than formatting a floppy disc.

If a second IDE hard disc is installed it will usually be the slave device on the primary IDE channel, with the original (boot) hard drive as the master device on this channel. The new disc drive will be the master on the primary IDE channel if the original drive is being replaced with a higher capacity type. The various configuration options are covered later in this chapter, but whether it is a master or slave device, the drive should be correctly configured before it is mounted in the case. The configuration jumpers are usually inaccessible once the drive has been installed. These days there is almost invariably a configuration chart on the drive itself, so determining the correct jumper settings should be straightforward.

Physically installing a hard disc is much the same as installing a floppy disc. All PC floppy disc drives, with the possible exceptions of some very early types, are of the half height variety. The same is true for PC hard disc drives. Their storage capacities have increased hugely over the years, but the drive units are physically smaller than the early units. In addition to half height drives there are now some "slimline" third height types as well. Anyway, a PC drive bay should be more than ample for any modern hard disc units that are designed for use with PCs. Whether drives are full, half, or third height, they are installed in exactly the same way. As there is no disc swapping with a hard disc drive, it does not need to be mounted in a drive bay that has an open front. In fact the convention is for hard disc drives to be mounted out of sight in an internal drive bay. Any indicator lights on the drive will not be visible in normal use.

A variety of hard disc controllers have been used in the past, but there are now only two types in common use. These are the IDE (parallel) type, and the SATA variety, which is essentially a high-speed serial version of the IDE interface. The trend is for PCs to use SATA hard disc drives, with the normal IDE type only being used for other types of drive, such as CD-ROM and DVD drives. Of course, when upgrading a PC that is a few years old it is quite possible that it will only have IDE ports, and any additional or upgraded drives will then have to be of this type.

The parallel IDE has developed over the years, and a range of "turbo" varsions have been produced. The first of these was the UDMA33 type. This method of hard disc interfacing is basically just connecting the drive direct onto the ISA expansion bus, or in the case of the UDMA33 interface, onto the faster PCI expansion bus. The hard disc controller is contained within the drive. The UDMA33 interface was replaced by the UDMA66 type, followed by the UDMA100 and UDMA133 types.

There is full compatibility between the oldest version of the IDE interface and the modern varieties. Even the oldest of IDE hard disc drives should work perfectly well if it is connected to a modern IDE interface such as a UDMA133 type. Similarly, a modern UDMA133 disc drive should work perfectly well if it is used as a replacement or upgrade drive in a computer that has an old IDE or EIDE hard disc interface. Of course, in order to gain the faster transfer rates of (say) a UDMA100 drive it must be used in a PC that has a UDMA100 or later interface. Using an old drive on a UDMA133 interface will not give an increase in performance either, but the drive will still work as a standard IDE type. In order to get a UDMA133 drive to operate at full speed the PC must have a UDMA133 interface, suitable BIOS support, and an operating system equipped with a suitable hard disc driver. The speed at which the hard drive operates is determined by the oldest and slowest part of the hard disc subsystem.

Connections

With a PC that has no SATA ports there will be at least two IDE ports on the motherboard. Connections from the controller to the hard disc drive are made via a 40-way ribbon cable, and most IDE cables have provision

Fig.8.8 These two IDE data cables look similar, but the one on the right has 80 wires and is suitable for UDMA66 and faster drives. The one on the left has 40 wires

for two IDE devices. Note that drives having UDMA66 or later versions of the IDE interface require a special cable having 80 leads (Figure 8.8) in order to exploit the higher data transfer rates supported by these interfaces. Using a 40-way cable effectively downgrades these drives to UDMA33 operation.

With two drives per IDE port and two ports on the motherboard, up to four IDE devices can be accommodated. Most PCs only have a single hard disc drive, but the IDE ports can also be used for CD-ROM drives, CD writers, and high capacity drives that have removable media such as Zip drives. It is therefore conceivable that all four IDE channels could be used, but two or three are usually sufficient. Unlike PC floppy drives, a twist in the cable is not used to determine which drive is the master IDE device and which is the slave type. Instead, configuration jumpers on the drives are used to set each IDE device as a master or a slave. There might only be the master and slave options, but there is often a third option that is called something like "cable select". This seems to be non-essential in a PC context and should be ignored.

With some IDE devices, but mainly hard disc drives, there are two master options. One of these is used where the drive is the only device connected to that IDE interface, and the other is used where there is a slave device as well. The convention is for the boot drive to be the master device on the first IDE interface, although it will probably be possible to boot from the hard drive if it is used on one of other IDE channels. If you do not wish to boot from a hard drive it can certainly be used on any available IDE channel, as can CD-ROM drives and CD writers.

However, it is important to bear in mind that an IDE interface can not operate as (say) a UDMA133 type when it is accessing a hard disc drive and a UDMA33 type when it is controlling the data flow to a CD-ROM drive. The interface will operate at a speed that suits the slowest device it is controlling. It is therefore best to keep the hard disc drive or drives on one IDE interface and connect CD-ROM drives, etc., to the other. This lets the hard disc operate at maximum speed, or as close to maximum speed as the interface can manage. Of course, with an old motherboard the IDE interfaces might not support any "turbo" modes anyway, and this gives greater choice over the channelling of the drives.

Connectors

The IDC connectors used for IDE data cables are polarised, and in theory can not be connected the wrong way round. In practice the connectors on the motherboard are simplified versions which allow the cable to be connected either way round. Also, the connectors on the cable sometimes lack the polarising "key" which ensures that they can not be connected the wrong way round. You then have to look carefully at the circuit boards, drives, and instruction manuals to find pin one on the IDE port and the drives. You then just follow the convention of making sure that the red lead of the cable connects to pin one of both the IDE port and drive connectors.

SATA connections

Practically all new computers now include a relatively new type of disc interface called Serial ATA. This is essentially a serial version of the standard IDE disc interface, but with a maximum speed of 150 megabytes per second. It is sometimes referred to as an ATA 150 interface. Clearly a serial ATA interface is not much faster than a UDMA 133 IDE interface, and many real-world hard disc drives do not really utilize the speed available from either type of interface. There is also an improved serial

Fig.8.9 A group of four serial ATA ports on a motherboard. A serial
ATA port can only be used with a single drive.

ATA interface, which is called serial ATA 2. It can accommodate a
maximum transfer rate of 300 megabytes per second, and is backwards
compatible with standard ATA devices. Serial ATA 3 is now coming along,
but this is also backwards compatible with earlier versions of the serial
ATA interface.

The real advantage of a serial ATA interface is that the cabling is much
easier to deal with. Far fewer connecting wires are needed with a serial
interface, and this is reflected in the size of the connectors on the
motherboard. Figure 8.9 shows a group of four serial ATA ports on a
motherboard. In order to give a sense of scale, Figure 8.10 shows a
zoomed-out view that includes a floppy disc port and a UDMA 133 type
near the bottom left-hand corner. Perhaps of greater importance than
the smaller size of the connectors, the serial cables can be much thinner.
A serial ATA data cable is shown in Figure 8.11, and Figure 8.12 shows
both types of cable.

A slight problem with the wide ribbon cables normally used for parallel
disc interfaces is that they tend to hinder the flow of air inside the PC.

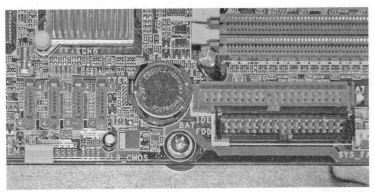

Fig.8.10 The serial ATA ports on the left are much smaller than the IDE and floppy ports on the right

This in turn tends to reduce the efficiency of the cooling system and raises the temperature inside the case. It is possible to obtain round versions of parallel IDE cables (see G.18 in the Colour Gallery), but these are even less flexible than the type that uses ribbon cable, and can be

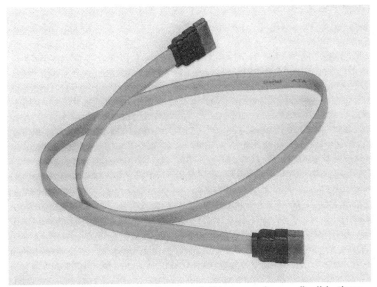

Fig.8.11 A serial ATA cable. It is much thinner and more flexible than an IDE cable

147

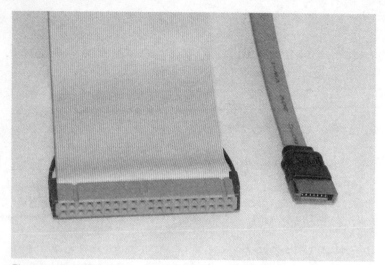

Fig.8.12 An IDE cable on the left and a serial ATA type on the right

awkward to use. Serial ATA cables are relatively flexible, easy to use, and do not significantly hinder the flow of air through the case.

One relative weakness of the serial ATA approach is that each port can only be used with one drive, whereas each IDE port can be used with two drives. However, there are usually at least two serial ATA ports on a motherboard that supports this type of interface, plus one or two ordinary IDE ports. This is sufficient for a total of four or six drives, and is perfectly adequate for most purposes. Having one drive per port has the advantage of avoiding the need for configuration jumpers to set the drive as a primary or slave device. Serial ATA drives do sometimes have configuration jumpers, but this is where the drive does not automatically set itself to suit the particular version of the serial ATA interface in use. Instead, it must be configured for the correct version using the jumpers.

The only other common form of hard disc interface is the SCSI (small computer systems interface) type. This is actually a general-purpose interface that can be used wherever high-speed data transfers are required. It is not just used for internal devices such as hard discs and CD-ROM drives, and is often used with scanners and other external peripherals. Up to eight devices can be connected in chain fashion to a SCSI interface. SCSI hard disc drives have never been very popular amongst PC users, and have mainly been used in network servers rather than stand-alone PCs. The speed advantage of SCSI hard discs has

G.1 A PS/2 mouse connector

G.2 The Abit AV8 is a full-size ATX motherboard

i

G.3 This Motherboard has an impressive range of built-in ports, including optical audio ports

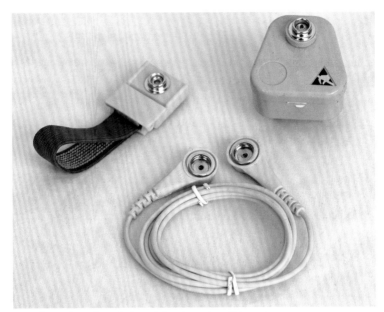

G.4 An anti-static wristband, lead, and earthing plug

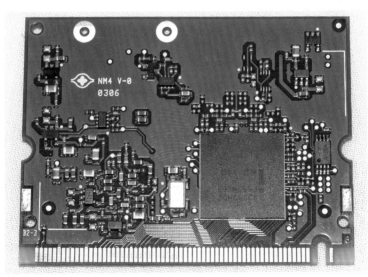

G.5 This Mini PCI card is a wi-fi adaptor

G.6 A laptop memory module (bottom) is shorter than a standard
desktop PC type (top)

G.7 Two memory modules fitted in their holders

G.8 One of the modules has been released from its holder

G.9 Empty holders, ready for the new modules to be fitted

The Colour Gallery

G.10 The initial window of the Sandra analysis program

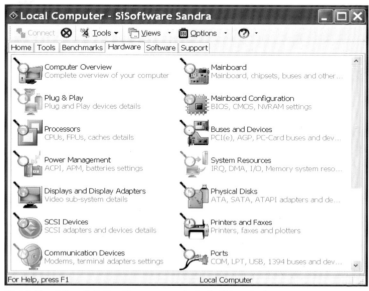

G.11 Double-click the Processors icon in this window

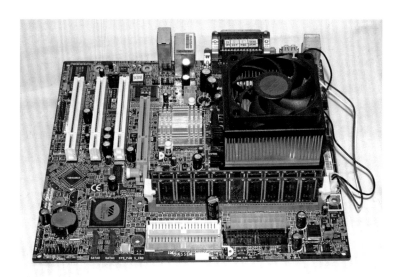

G.12 *The processor, heatsink, fan, and memory have been fitted on the motherboard*

G.13 *The notch at the front of the connector is used to lock ADP and PCI Express cards into their expansion slots*

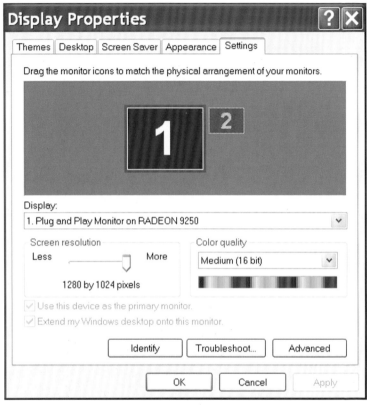

G.14 The Display Properties window

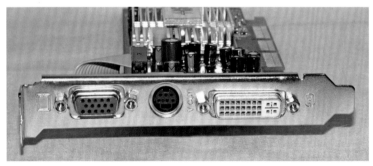

G.15 Analogue and digital outputs are on the left and right respectively

G.16 A simple USB hub that has four ports

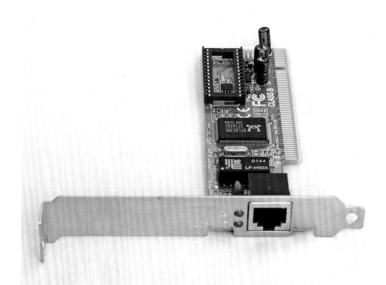

G.17 A PCI expansion card that provides an Ethernet network port

G.18 A round version of an IDE data cable gives better ventilation within the computer's case

G.19 Enter a name for the computer in the textbox

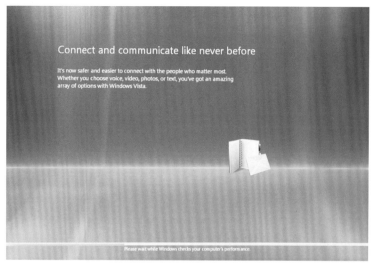

G.20 This is one of a series of information screens

G.21 The Vista start-up screen has been reached

G.22 A hard disc drive for use in a laptop PC

G.23 The connector on a 2.5-inch drive looks similar to that of a 3.5-inch type, but it is different. A 2.5-inch drive does not have a separate power connector

G.24 The CD/DVD drives used in laptops are surprisingly small

G.25 This pen drive has a capacity of 1 gigabyte

G.26 The pen drive has a standard USB connector

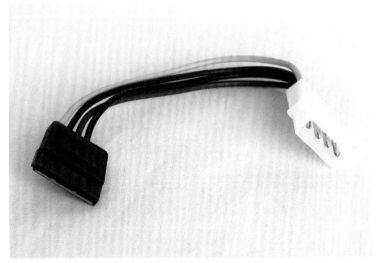

G.27 An adaptor to enable an SATA drive to be used with a PC power
supply unit that only has the older type of drive connector

G.28 A USB modem provides an easy introduction to broadband

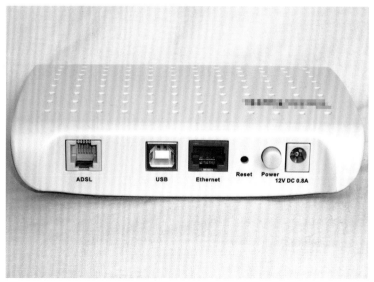

G.29 This broadband modem has Ethernet and USB inputs

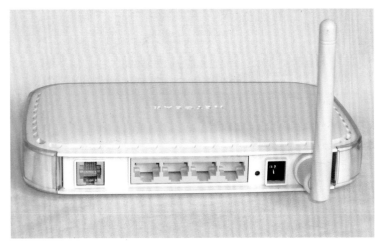

G.30 This combined medem and router has four Ethernet sockets

G.31 A combined router, modem, and wi-fi access point

been largely eroded by the faster IDE and SATA interfaces, and the substantial additional cost does not seem to be justified for most stand-alone PCs.

BIOS

Once you have configured the jumpers on the hard drive, mounted it in the case, and connected it to the controller and the power supply, it is time to switch on and try it out. However, there is still a fair amount of work to do before the computer will boot from the hard drive. The first step is to go into the BIOS Setup program and enter the appropriate parameters for the particular drive you are using. The BIOS Setup program is covered in detail in chapter 12, so refer to this chapter if you are unsure about configuring the BIOS to operate with a new hard disc. The settings for the hard disc are normally in the Standard CMOS section of the BIOS.

When using a high capacity drive in an old PC there can be problems due to the BIOS not supporting disc capacities of more than 528 megabytes. This does not mean that a hard disc having a capacity of more than 528 megabytes is unusable with a computer of this type, but it does mean that it can only use the first 528 megabytes of its capacity. If you set drive parameters that give a higher capacity the BIOS will not accept them. There are actually ways around the 528-megabyte limit, and some hard drives are provided with utility software that can handle this problem. However, there is no guarantee that this type of quick fix will not produce problems in use.

Fitting a more modern BIOS or (where possible) upgrading the program in the existing BIOS ROMs is a better solution, but is often impractical. Finding a more modern BIOS that is compatible with the motherboard is likely to be problematic, and could also be quite costly. It would probably be more cost effective to undertake a major upgrade, including the replacement of the motherboard with a modern type having a BIOS that properly supports modern high capacity drives. Fortunately, there can be few PCs still in use that have this BIOS limitation, so it is unlikely that you will encounter it.

Windows XP

Windows XP is easier to install than Windows 95/98/ME, and there is no need to format the hard disc drive when installing Windows XP. This can be done during the installation process. In fact the partitioning of the

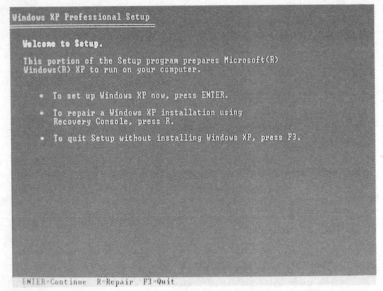

Fig.8.13 The opening screen of the Windows XP Setup program

disc can also be handled by the installation program, so FDISK is not needed either. The Windows XP installation CD-ROM is a bootable type, so it is possible to boot from the CD-ROM straight into the Setup program. No floppy boot disc is required.

The first step is to boot from the installation CD-ROM, and this might require changes to the BIOS settings. The BIOS must be set to boot from the CD-ROM drive before it tries to boot from the hard disc. It is unlikely that the computer will attempt to boot from the CD-ROM drive if the priorities are the other way around, and it will certainly not do so unless the CD-ROM is set as one of the boot devices. If all is well, a message will appear on the screen indicating that any key must be operated in order to boot from the CD-ROM drive. This message appears quite briefly, so be ready to press one of the keys. The computer will try to boot from the hard disc if you "miss the boat". It will then be necessary to restart the computer and try again.

After various files have been loaded from the CD-ROM, things should come to a halt with the screen of Figure 8.13. The Setup program is needed to install Windows XP, so press the Enter (Return) key. The Next screen (Figure 8.14) is the usual licence agreement, and the F8 key is

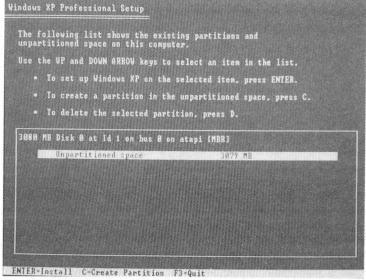

Fig.8.14 You must agree to the conditions in order to proceed

Fig.8.15 There are a few options for the "raw" disc space

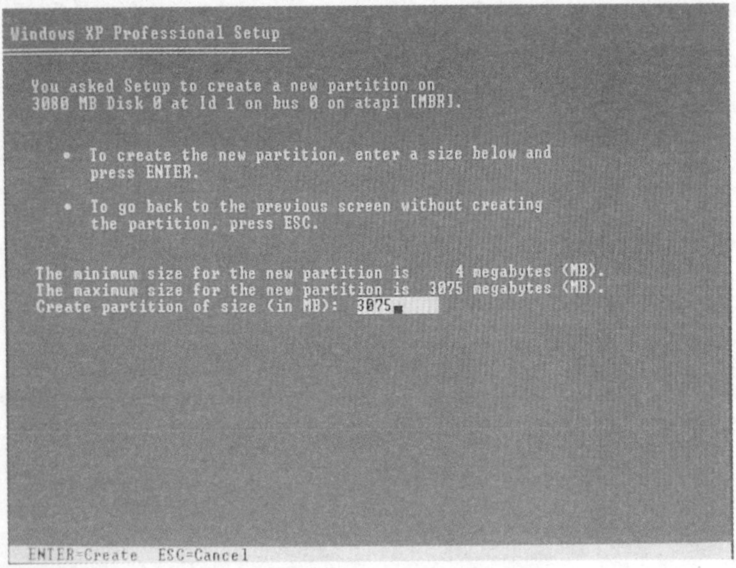

Fig.8.16 The first task is to produce a new partition

pressed in order to agree with the licensing terms.   Note that Windows XP can not be installed unless you do agree to the licensing conditions. Things should now move on to a screen like the one of Figure 8.15 where there is sometimes the option of repairing any existing installation or installing Windows XP from scratch.   In this case there is no existing installation, so you are presented with various options for the "raw" hard disc space.

The first task is to produce a new partition by operating the C key, which produces the screen of Figure 8.16.   By default the Setup program will use the whole disc as a single partition, but you can enter a smaller size if desired.   The remaining space can then be partitioned using the same method used to produce the first partition.   Here we will keep things simple and settle for a single partition equal to the full capacity of the disc.   This is achieved by pressing the Return (Enter) key, which brings up the screen of Figure 8.17.   Operate the Return key again, which will produce the new partition and install Windows XP onto it.

This moves things on to the screen of Figure 8.18 where the desired file system is selected.   Unless there is a good reason to use the FAT or FAT32 file system, such as compatibility with another file system, choose

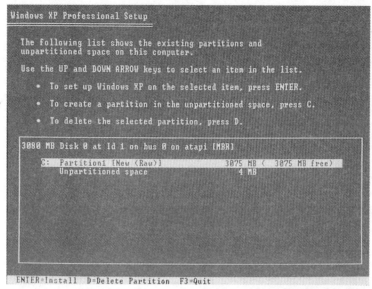

Fig.8.17 Press Return to create the partition and install Windows on it

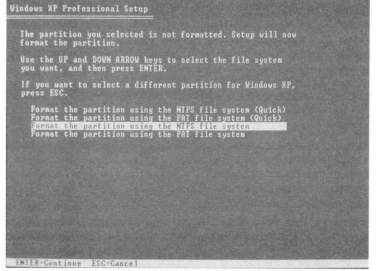

Fig.8.18 NTFS is the file system normally used with Windows XP

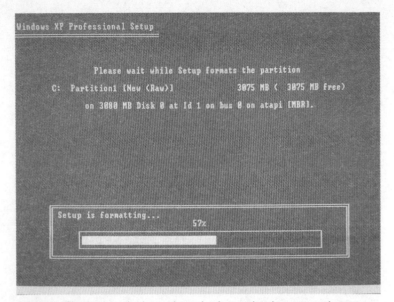

Fig.8.19 The bargraph shows how the formatting is progressing

the NTFS option. This file system makes the best use of Windows XP's capabilities. Having selected the required file system, press the Return key to go ahead and format the partition. This brings up the screen of Figure 8.19, complete with the usual bargraph to show how far the formatting has progressed.

Once the partition has been created and formatted, the Setup program will start copying files to the hard disc (Figure 8.20). Once this stage has been completed you are prompted to restart the computer (Figure 8.21), but this will happen in a few seconds if you do not respond. Having rebooted, the computer will go into the initial screen of the Setup program (Figure 8.22), and installation then carries on in normal Windows fashion.

XP second drive

Windows XP has been designed as an MS/DOS-free zone, and it is not necessary to use the MS/DOS FDISK and FORMAT programs when a second hard disc is added to a Windows XP system. I suppose that these programs could be used, but it would definitely be doing things the hard way. There is a built-in program that greatly simplifies the

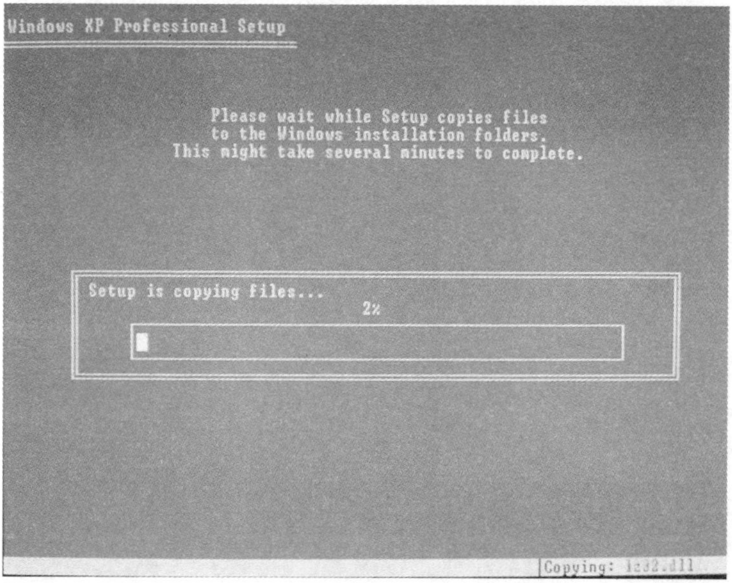

Fig.8.20 With the formatting completed, files are copied to the disc

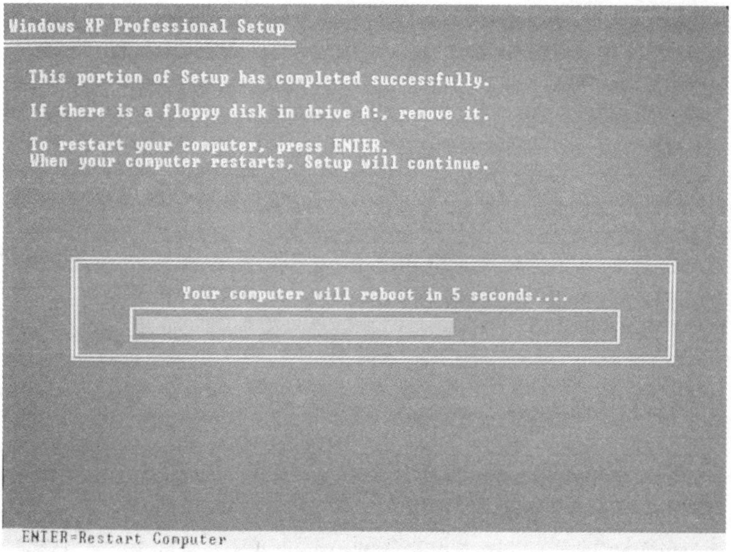

Fig.8.21 Restart the computer once the copying has been completed

8 Hard and floppy drives

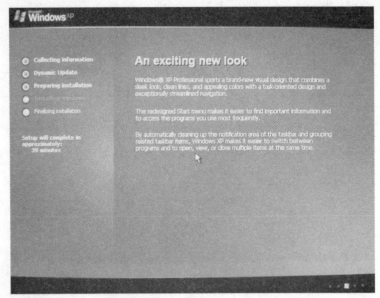

Fig.8.22 Once restarted, Windows XP is installed on the disc

partitioning and formatting of hard drives. This program can be run by going to the Windows Control Panel and double-clicking the Administrative Tools icon. This produces a window like the one of Figure 8.23, and double-clicking the Computer Management icon produces the new window of Figure 8.24. Several utilities are available from the Computer Management window, but the one required in this case is Disk Management. Left-clicking this entry in the left-hand panel changes the window to look something like Figure 8.25.

Details of the boot drive are given at the top of the right-hand panel. The bottom section gives details of both drives, and the new drive is Disk 1. This is described as "Unallocated", which means that it is not partitioned or formatted at this stage. The black line to the right of the Disk 1 label and icon also indicates that it is not partitioned. To partition the disc, right-click on the black line and then select the New Partition option from the popup menu. This launches the New Partition Wizard (Figure 8.26). Windows XP can use two types of disc, which are the basic and dynamic varieties. The New Partition Wizard only handles basic discs, and these use conventional partitions that are essentially the same as those used by MS-DOS and earlier versions of Windows. For most purposes a basic disc is perfectly adequate.

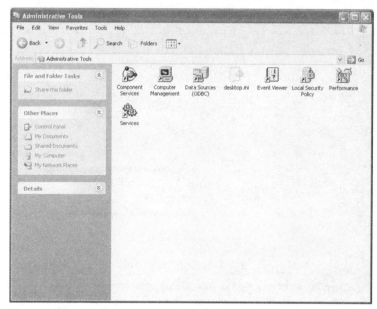

Fig.8.23 The Administrative Tools window

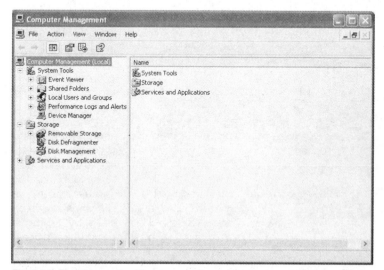

Fig.8.24 The Computer Management screen offers a range of options

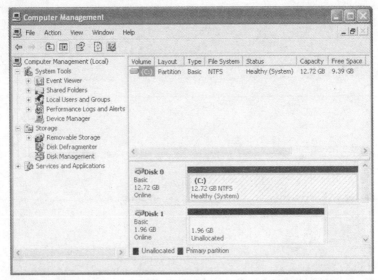

Fig.8.25 The window with the Disk Management facility selected

Operate the Next button to move on with the partitioning, and a window like the one in Figure 8.27 should appear. Either an extended or a primary partition can be selected using the radio buttons, and in this case it is a

Fig.8.26 The opening screen of the New Partition Wizard

primary partition that is needed. The size of the partition is selected at the next window (Figure 8.28), and the maximum and minimum usable sizes are indicated. All the available disc space will be used by default, but a different size can be used by typing a value (in megabytes) into the textbox. Operating the Next

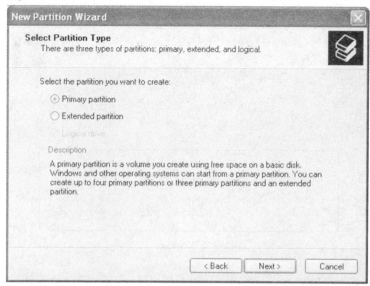

Fig.8.27 Use this window to select the partition type

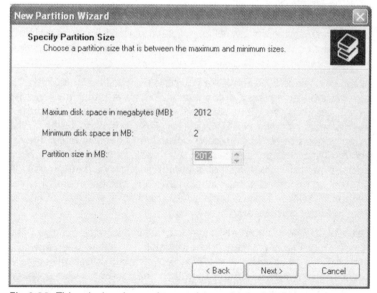

Fig.8.28 This window is used to set the partition size (in megabytes)

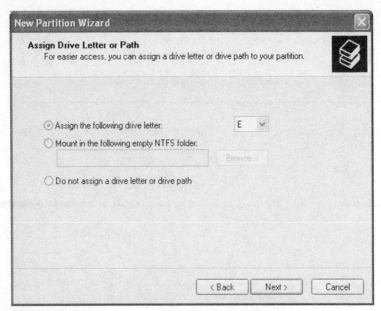

Fig.8.29 Here a drive letter is assigned to the new partition

button brings up the window of Figure 8.29 where a drive letter is assigned to the new partition. Unless there is a good reason to do otherwise, simply accept the default drive letter.

At the next window (Figure 8.30) you have the choice of formatting the new partition or leaving it unformatted. Since the partition will not be usable until it is formatted, accept the formatting option. One of the menus offers a choice of FAT, FAT32, or NTFS formatting. Settle for the default option of NTFS formatting unless you need compatibility with another Windows operating system. Also settle for the default allocation unit size, which will be one that is appropriate for the partition size. A different name for the drive, such as "Backup", can be entered into the textbox if desired. Tick the appropriate checkbox if you wish to enable file and folder compression.

Left-click the Next button when you are satisfied with the settings. The next window (Figure 8.31) lists all the parameters that have been selected, and provides an opportunity to change your mind or correct mistakes. If necessary, use the Back button to return to earlier windows and change some of the settings. Operate the Finish button if all the settings are correct. The partition will then be created, and it will appear as a blue

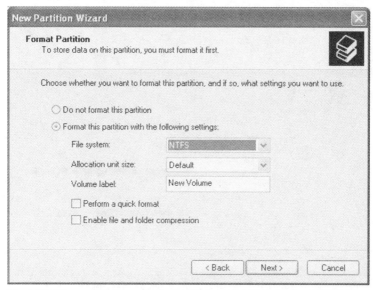

Fig.8.30 The partition can be formatted as an NTFS, FAT, or FAT32 type

Fig.8.31 This window lists the parameters that have been selected

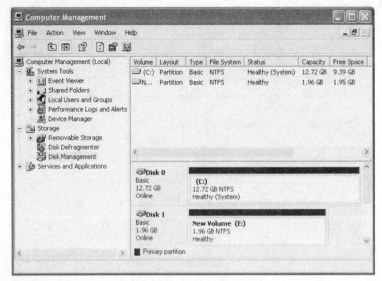

Fig.8.32 The Disk Management window shows the new partition

line in the Disk Management window. It will then be formatted, and this may take half an hour or more for a large partition. The area below the blue line indicates how far the formatting process has progressed. Eventually the formatting will be completed, and the Disk Management window will show the new disc as containing a primary partition using the appropriate file system (Figure 8.32). Once the formatting has been completed, files on the main drive can be copied to the new partition using the Cut and Paste facilities of Windows Explorer.

If space has been left for a further partition on the disc, right-click on the black section of the line that represents the vacant disc space. Then select the New Partition option from the popup menu, and go through the whole partitioning and formatting process again. A maximum of four primary partitions can be used on each physical disc.

Installing Vista

Installing Windows Vista on a new hard disc drive is similar to the Windows XP installation process, and it is installed from a bootable DVD. Note that the methods described here are only applicable if you have the

Fig.8.33 Use this window to select the correct language settings

standard Windows Vista installation disc. If your PC was not supplied with a standard installation disc it probably came complete with a recovery disc that makes it easy to return to a basic Windows installation. With a PC of this type you should consult the instruction manual, and this should give concise information about reinstalling Windows. In most cases it is essentially just a matter of booting from a DVD and letting the recovery program get on with reinstallation.

Booting from DVD

The first step is to boot from the installation DVD. The BIOS must be set to boot from the DVD drive before it tries to boot from the hard disc. It is unlikely that the computer will attempt to boot from the DVD drive if the priorities are the other way around, and it will certainly not do so unless the DVD is set as one of the boot devices. If all is well, a message will appear on the screen indicating that any key must be operated in order to boot from the DVD drive. This message appears quite briefly, so be ready to press one of the keys. The computer will try to boot from the

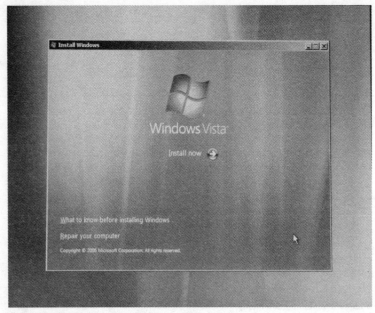

Fig.8.34 Select the Install Now option

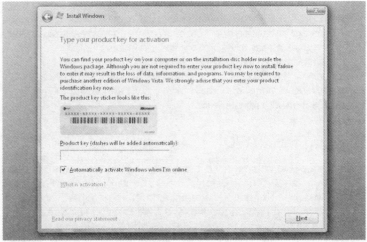

Fig.8.35 It is advisable to take this opportunity of entering your product
code

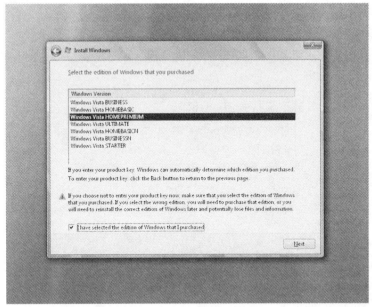

*Fig.8.36 Be careful to select the version of Vista that you have
purchased*

hard disc if you "miss the boat". It will then be necessary to restart the
computer and try again.

After various files have been loaded from the DVD, things should come
to a halt with the screen of Figure 8.33. Here you use the three menus to
set the installation language, the time and currency format, and the
keyboard language or type. For a UK user these are normally set at
English, English (United Kingdom), and United Kingdom respectively.
Operating the Next button moves things on to the screen of Figure 8.34,
where the "Install now" option should be selected. At the following screen
(Figure 8.35) you have the option of entering your product key. It is not
essential to do so at this stage, but it is definitely a good idea to do so.
With a reinstallation it is also a good idea to opt for automatic activation
by leaving the checkbox ticked.

If a screen like the one in Figure 8.36 appears, use the list to select the
version of Vista that you have purchased, and then tick the checkbox.
The Next screen (Figure 8.37) is the usual licence agreement, and you
have to tick the checkbox in order to agree with the licensing terms.

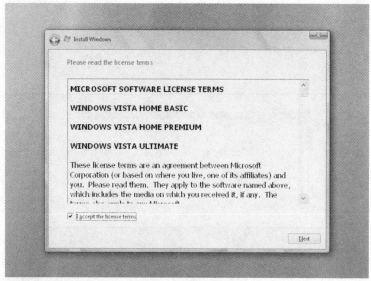

Fig.8.37 You must agree to the terms in order to proceed

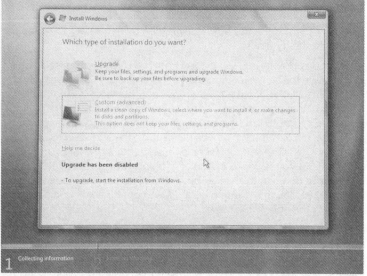

Fig.8.38 Choose the Custom (advanced) option at this window

Fig.8.39 Select the drive that will be used for the installation

Note that Windows Vista can not be installed unless you do agree to the licensing conditions. At the next screen (Figure 8.38) you supposedly have the choice of upgrading an existing Windows installation or installing a fresh one, but the upgrade option is unlikely to be active. This does not matter, because it is the "Custom (advanced)" option that is required in this case.

The available disc drives are listed at the next screen (Figure 8.39), where you select the drive that will be used for the Windows Vista installation. In this example it will be installed on Disk 0 Partition 1, but there is an obvious problem in that an existing installation is present here. This will not occur if you are using a new and totally blank disc. There will usually be an existing installation if you are using a pre-owned disc, installing Vista on top of a previous installation that went awry, or upgrading by installing Vista over an existing installation that is being abandoned. One option is to go ahead and install the fresh copy of Vista on this partition, but this will produce the warning message of Figure 8.40. This explains that the files associated with the existing Windows installation will be

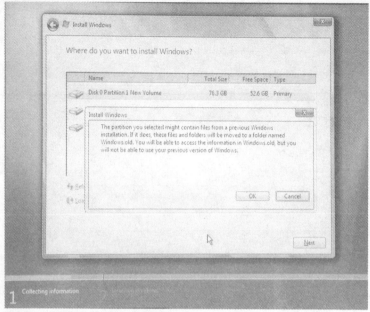

Fig.8.40 The old installation will be saved, but will not be used

moved to a folder called Windows.old, but the old version of Windows and the installed programs will not be usable.

You might prefer to do things this way provided the hard disc drive is large enough to take the old files and the new installation. Unwanted files can be deleted once the new installation is in place and fully operational. However, we will assume here that the "clean sweep" approach will be taken, and that there will be a fresh installation on a blank partition. Of course, any data on the disc will be erased when Vista is installed, so any important data on the disc must be backed up prior to installing Vista.

Formatting

The Vista installation program includes a facility for formatting partitions, making it easy to wipe the boot partition of all existing files and folders. These facilities are accessed by operating the "Drive options (advanced)" link, which changes the screen to look like Figure 8.41. Where

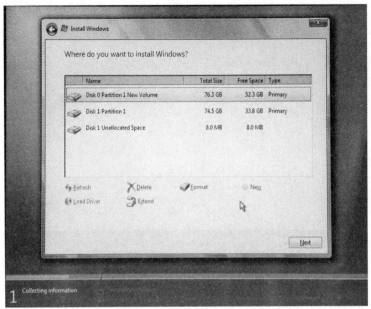

Fig.8.41 The advanced drive options have been activated

appropriate, make sure that the correct drive/partition is selected in the upper panel, and then operate the Format button in the lower section of the screen. This will produce a warning message (Figure 8.42), which explains that all the files in the partition will be deleted when it is partitioned. This is, of course, exactly what is required in this case, but bear in mind that any data on the partition that has not been backed up will almost certainly be lost for ever once the formatting has started.

Operate the Next button once the partition has been formatted, and the installation of Windows Vista will then commence. The screen will change to show a list of tasks, and each one will be ticked as it is completed (Figure 8.43). Installation of a modern operating system takes a fair amount of time, so be prepared to wait several minutes while various tasks are performed. The computer will be restarted at least once during installation, and it is important that it is allowed to boot from the hard disc drive when this happens. Do not get it to boot from the installation DVD, or you will just end up going through the same steps over and over again with installation never being completed. The message of Figure

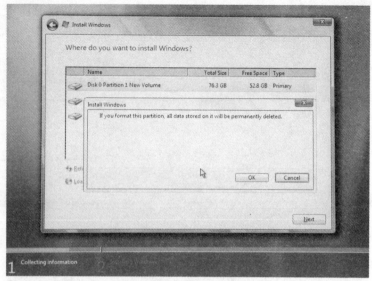

Fig.8.42 All the files on the drive will be deleted if it is formatted

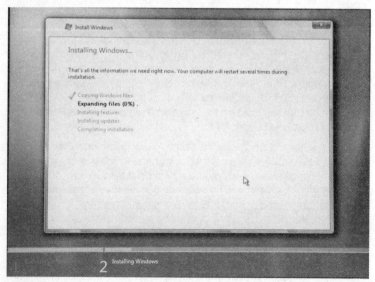

Fig.8.43 Each stage of installation is ticked as it is completed

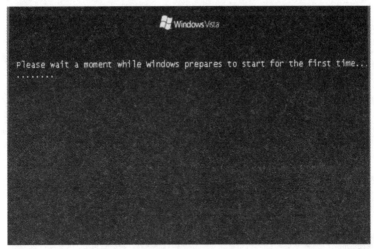

Fig.8.44 The computer will reboot at least once

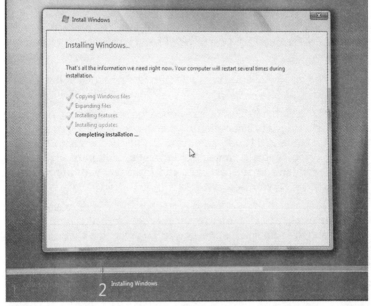

Fig.8.45 Installation has resumed and is nearing completion

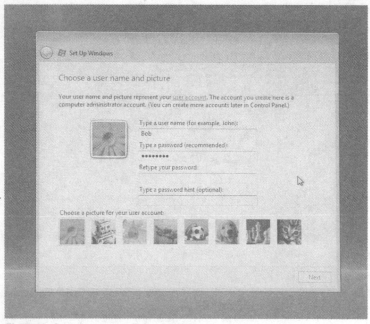

Fig.8.46 Supply a name for your account

8.44 will be displayed if the computer reboots correctly from the hard disc drive.

The screen of Figure 8.45 will appear once the computer has rebooted, and the final stages of installation will then be completed. Although the installation process is largely automatic, it is still necessary for the user to enter some simple information. When the screen of Figure 8.46 appears, you have to select a picture to represent your account, and supply a name for your account.

It is not essential to use password protection, but it is probably best to do so. As usual, you will have to enter your choice of password into one textbox and then confirm that it is correct by entering it again in another textbox. An optional hint can be entered in another textbox, and the hint should be something that will help you to remember the password if you should happen to forget it. Bear in mind that you will be locked out of your account if you forget your password and do not manage to remember it.

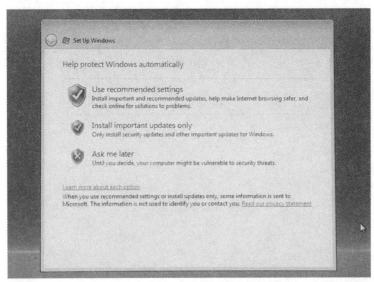

Fig.8.47 The screen is used to control automatic updates

The next screen (See G.19 in the Colour Gallery)) is used to enter a
name for the computer, or the default name can be used. Do not confuse
the account name and the computer name. The name for the computer
is the one that will be used to identify it if the computer is connected to a
network. This name must therefore be different to the names used for
any other computers on the network. It does not matter too much what
name is used if the computer will not be used as part of a network. The
account name given at the previous screen is the one used for your
account on the computer. Other accounts can be added once Vista is
installed and running properly, but this is not mandatory. The general
idea is to have a different account for each user, so there is usually no
point in having more than one account if there is only one user.

This screen is also used to select a background design for the Windows
desktop. The first design in the row of thumbnail images will be used if
you do not select one. Of course, the desktop's background is easily
changed to just about anything you like once Vista has been installed,
so it does not matter too much which design is chosen at this stage.
There are three options at the following screen (Figure 8.47), which is
where you select to have recommended updates installed, important
updates, or neither at this stage. It is probably best to opt for at least

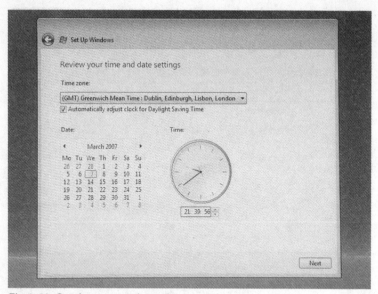

Fig.8.48 Set the correct time, date, and time zone

important updates to be installed, but the automatic update settings can be altered once Vista is installed, so there is no need to make a final decision at this stage.

The next screen (Figure 8.48) allows the time, date, and time zone to be altered, if necessary. The existing settings will probably be correct, but this screen provides an opportunity to check that the time setting is accurate, and to make any necessary adjustments. Tick the checkbox if you wish to have Vista automatically adjust the system clock for daylight saving. Things then move on to the screen of Figure 8.49 where you select Home, Business, or Public Location, depending on where the computer will mainly be used.

This completes the setting up procedure, which will be confirmed by the screen of Figure 8.50. Operating the Start button results in a series of information screens appearing, such as the example of G.20 in the Colour Gallery, while the installation is finalised. The usual log-on screen (Figure 8.51) will then appear if you opted to use a password. Log-on in the usual way, and the Windows Vista desktop (see G.21 in the Colour Gallery)) should then be obtained. The desktop will appear straight away if no password was entered during the setting up procedure. Of course,

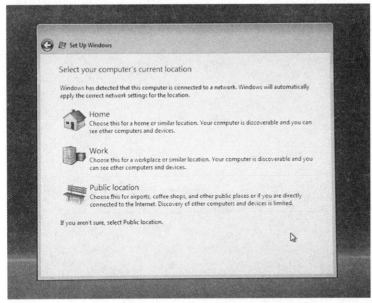

Fig.8.49 Choose whether the PC will be used at a home, work, or public location

Fig.8.50 This screen indicates that the setting up has been completed successfully

Fig.8.51 Log on to the system in the usual way

it is just the bare desktop that is obtained when Vista is reinstalled from scratch. In order to get things back into full working order it is necessary to reinstall all the application software, reinstate any customisation of the Windows environment, restore your data files, etc.

From scratch

In this demonstration of installing Windows Vista the hard disc drive was already partitioned and formatted, making it slightly easier to install the operating system. If you use a brand new hard disc drive it will have the low level formatting performed at the factory, but it is unlikely that it will be supplied with any existing partitions or high level formatting already carried out for you. Apart from the low level formatting the disc will be blank, and the user has to add the required partitions and type of formatting. It will also be necessary to repartition and format the disc if you wish to start from scratch with a disc that has already been partitioned and formatted Either way it is not difficult since the necessary utilities are built into the Windows Vista installation program.

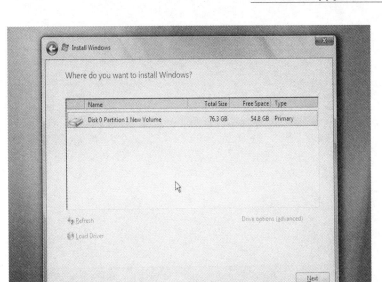

Fig.8.52 In this example there is only one partition which must be reformatted

The installation process is exactly the same as the method described previously, but only until the screen of Figure 8.45 is reached. If there is an existing partition that you wish to remove or reuse from scratch, the screen will look something like Figure 8.52. In order to remove this partition it is a matter of first activating the "Drive options (advanced)" link, which produces a screen like the one in Figure 8.53. There are two ways of dealing with the existing partition, and the format option will suffice if you intend to reuse the existing partition, with no changes being made to the disc's partitioning. Make sure that the correct partition is selected in the upper part of the window if there is more than one listed here. Reformatting a partition will erase any existing data that it contains, and a message to this effect will appear when the Format option is selected (Figure 8.54). Operate the Yes button if you are sure that you wish to proceed. Once the formatting has been completed you are taken

8 Hard and floppy drives

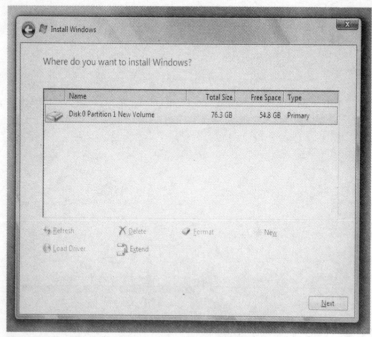

Fig.8.53 Activate the Format link to format the selected partition

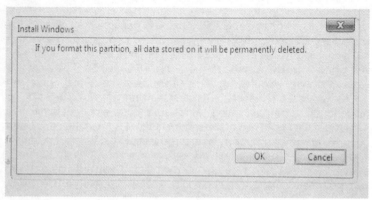

Fig.8.54 All files in the selected partition will be deleted

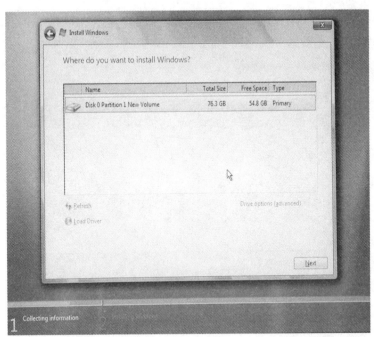

Fig.8.55 Things look much the same as before back at the main screen

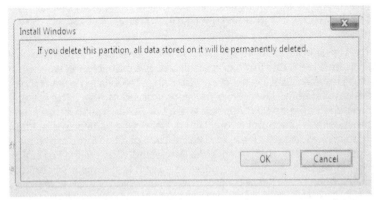

Fig.8.56 You are warned that any data in the selected partition will be erased

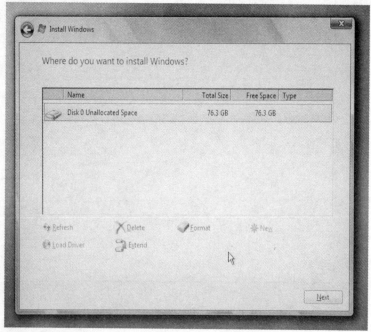

Fig.8.57 The disc is now "Unallocated Space"

back to the main screen, which will look much the same as before (Figure 8.55). However, the disc is now partitioned and formatted, but is otherwise empty.

The Delete option is used if you would like to effectively start with a new and totally blank disc that has no partitions. It is probably only worthwhile using this method if it is necessary to change the existing partitioning of the disc, such as having two partitions instead of one. The warning message of Figure 8.56 appears when the Delete option is used, and this message simply points out that any data in the partition will be lost if you proceed. Again, if there is more than one partition listed on the main screen, make sure that the right one is selected. Operate the Yes button if all is well and you wish to proceed. Back at the main screen, the deleted partition will now be shown as "Unallocated Space" (see Figure 8.57). This is where things start if you use a new disc that has no existing partitioning.

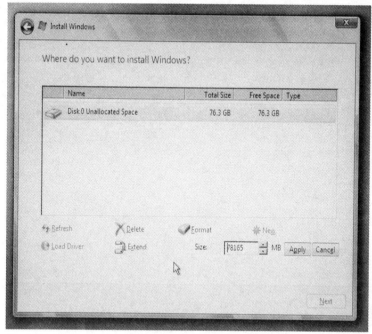

Fig.8.58 By default, one large partition will be produced

Partitioning

In order to use the disc it must have at least one partition, and the partition or partitions must be formatted. The first task is to create the required partition or partitions. In this example two partitions will be used, but regardless of the number of partitions, the first step is to operate the New link in the bottom of section of the window. The screen then changes, with a textbox appearing in the lower section of the screen (Figures

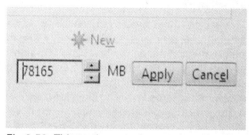

Fig.8.59 This textbox can be used to alter the partition's size

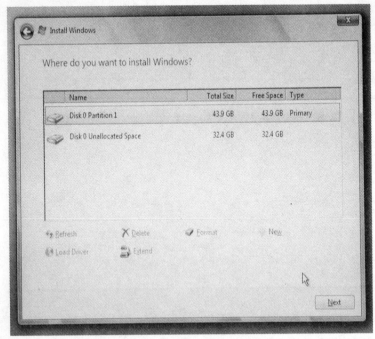

Fig.8.60 The new partition has been added successfully, but there is still some unallocated disc space

8.58 and 8.59). Simply leave this unchanged if you wish to have a single partition on the disc that is as large as possible. If more than one partition is required, enter the size required for the first one. The size of the partition is specified in megabytes, and there are 1024 megabytes per gigabyte. In this example I specified a size of 45000 megabytes, which is just under 44 gigabytes.

This partition was created successfully (Figure 8.60), leaving a large amount of unallocated disc space for a second partition. The second partition is produced by selecting the unallocated disc space and repeating the procedure (Figure 8.61). It is not essential to accept the default size and use all the space for a single partition. As before, a smaller size can be specified leaving space for a third partition. Dividing a disc into three separate partitions can have advantages, but bear in mind that it can also be inefficient and inconvenient in some circumstances. Do not partition a disc in this way just for the sake of it.

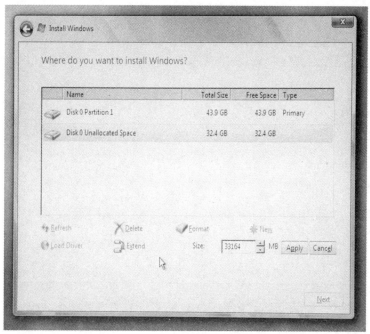

Fig.8.61 As before, the size of the partition can be specified

Only do so if you have a good reason to do so. In this example I settled for two partitions that were produced without any problems (Figure 8.62).

The disc now has two partitions, but they are not usable until they have been formatted. Start by selecting the first partition and operating the Format link. This will produce a warning message (Figure 8.63) pointing out that any data on the partition will be erased by the formatting, but in this case there is no data to lose. However, make sure that the right partition is selected in cases where there is a partition that contains data. Having formatted the first partition, repeat the process to format any other new partitions. Things do not look any different back at the main window (Figure 8.64), but the disc is now ready for the Windows installation to proceed. Operating the Next button moves things on to the beginning of the installation process (Figure 8.65), and from here everything progresses in the manner described previously.

With Windows installed it is a good idea to use Windows Explorer to check that any extra partitions are present and correct. In this example

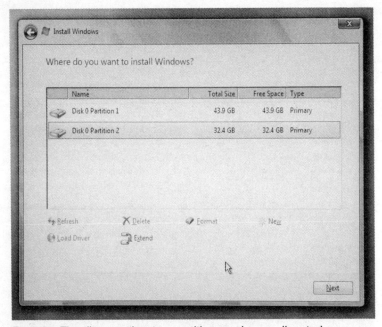

Fig.8.62 *The disc now has two partitions and no unallocated space*

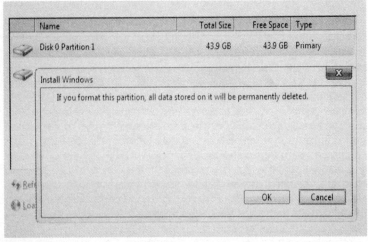

Fig.8.63 *Using the Format option produces a warning message*

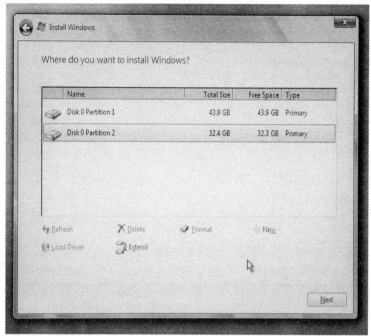

*Fig.8.64 The main window looks much the same as before, but both
partitions have been formatted*

both partitions are present (Figure 8.66). Partition 1 is Disc C in Windows,
and it contains the Windows Vista installation. Partition 2 is drive D, and
as yet contains no data. Writing a few test files to this disc should confirm
that it is functioning correctly. It is worth noting that Windows Vista has
facilities for partitioning and formatting hard disc drives, so it is only
necessary to produce one partition during the installation process. If
preferred, any others can be added once Windows has been installed.

Laptop hard disc

Modern 3.5-inch hard disc drives are quite compact, but are still too
large for use in laptop PCs. They also tend to have quite high power
consumptions, and would run down the average laptop battery in a short
space of time. As one would probably expect, the hard disc drives used

8 Hard and floppy drives

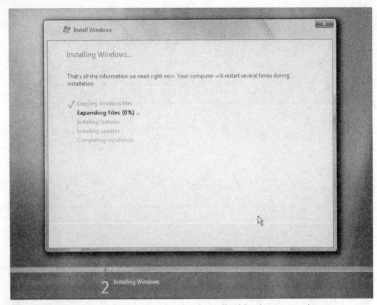

Fig.8.65 Windows Vista can now be installed in the normal way

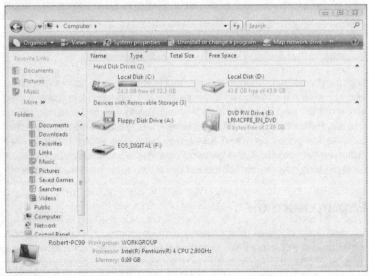

Fig.8.66 Partitions 1 and 2 are drives C and D in Windows

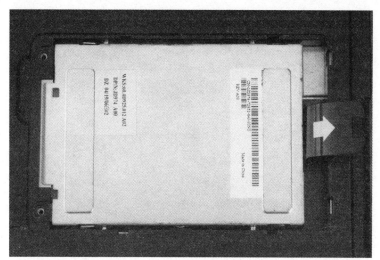

Fig.8.67 The hard disc drive with the cover and two fixing screws removed

in laptop PCs are special miniature units that have relatively low levels of power consumption. Some of these disc drives, particularly in the really small portable PCs, are totally non-standard and can not be upgraded by the user. It should be possible to upgrade the hard disc yourself provided your laptop has a standard 2.5-inch hard drive, like the unit shown in G.22 and G.23 of the Colour Gallery. In fact it will probably be easier than upgrading the hard disc drive of a desktop PC.

Before starting work on a laptop PC it is a good idea to check that it is not connected to its charger/mains supply adaptor, and that the battery is removed. The normal anti-static handling precautions should be observed while removing the old disc and installing the new one. Bear in mind that upgrading the hard disc drive yourself might invalidate any remaining warranty from the manufacturer, but your statutory rights will not be altered.

The first task is to remove the cover on the base of the computer that covers the hard disc drive. An information sheet that identifies the various covers on base should have been supplied with the computer, or this information should be included in the instruction manual. It will probably be necessary to remove two or more small screws in order to remove the panel. The screws used with laptops tend to be much smaller than those used with desktop PCs, and a tiny cross-point screwdriver will be

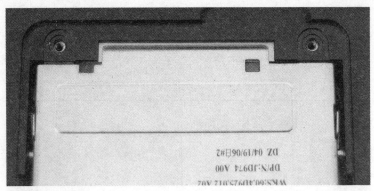

Fig.8.68 A close-up view showing the holes for the two fixing screws

needed for this task. A set of "jewellers" screwdrivers is useful when working on laptop PCs.

You should see something like Figure 8.67 when the panel covering the hard disc drive is removed. A 2.5-inch drive is held in place by two small screws. These have already been removed in Figure 8.67, leaving two empty holes which can be seen near the extreme left-hand side of the photograph. A closer view is shown in Figure 8.68. It is easy to remove the drive once these screws have been removed. In this case there is a tab on the drive, and it is just a matter of pulling this tab in the direction indicated by the arrow. This disconnects the drive from a connector that is similar to the type used with 3.5-inch hard disc drives. Figure 8.69 shows the drive bay with the drive removed, and Figure 8.70 shows a close-up of the connector.

Fitting the new drive is just a matter of reversing the process used to remove the old drive. Place it into the drive bay with the correct orientation, slide it into place, fit the two fixing screws, and then replace the cover. Note that, like desktop PCs, serial and parallel interface drives are used with the laptop variety. You therefore have to be careful to obtain an upgrade drive that is the same type as the old unit. Also, 2.5-inch drives are available in more than one height. With any laptop upgrade it is a good idea to obtain the new part or parts from a specialist supplier of laptop components. They can often advise whether a given component is suitable for a particular make and model of computer, which can avoid expensive mistakes. Of course, once the new drive is installed it will be necessary to do the partitioning, formatting, installation of the operating system, etc., in the usual way.

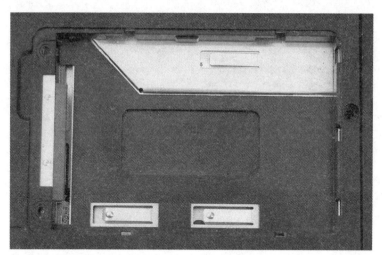

Fig.8.69 The drive bay with the drive removed

Second drive

Laptop PC designers have a tough time finding space for one hard drive, so it is unrealistic to expect any provision for fitting a second internal drive. However, provided your laptop has a USB or Firewire port it should be possible to fit an external hard drive. Drives of this type were very expensive at one time, but even some of the higher capacity units can now be obtained at very reasonable prices. They are very popular, and offer a good alternative to upgrading the internal hard drive to one of higher capacity.

Leaving the original hard drive in place and using an external unit to give increased capacity avoids the problem of reinstalling the operating system and transferring all your data to the new drive. With an external drive it is basically just a matter of plugging it in whenever large amounts of data must be stored, or you need to read data from the drive. It does not have to be permanently connected to the computer. Things on the built-in drive can be left just as they were.

While using an external drive is less convenient than using internal storage, it has a huge advantage. An external drive can be used with any PC that has a suitable port, which probably means it can be used with any PC you own, any PC at your place of work, or any PC belonging to friends and family. An external drive can therefore be used for

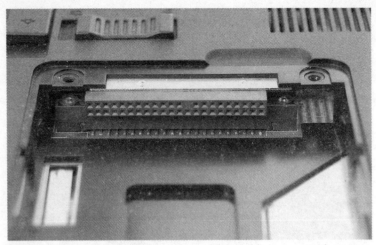

Fig.8.70 The connector for the drive, which in this case must be a type that has a parallel interface

transferring data from one computer to another, or for sharing data such as family photographs or home movies. External drives are not just for use with portable PCs, and they are equally useful with desktop PCs.

Ideally a Firewire or USB 2.0 interface should be used with an external drive, as these provide sufficient speed for rapid data transfers. USB 1.1 ports are much slower, and loading or writing (say) a gigabyte of data via this type of interface would take something like 10 to 20 minutes. Using a USB 2.0 port or a Firewire type it would take well under a tenth of this time. Any modern desktop or laptop PC will have either Firewire or USB 2.0 ports, but with older types it may be necessary to make do with the more pedestrian data transfer rates of USB 1.1 ports.

Note that some external drives are powered from the host computer while others have their own power source, which could be a rechargeable battery, but is more likely to be a mains adaptor. Having the drive powered from the computer is the more convenient method, but in the case of a laptop PC it will result in the battery life being significantly reduced. Some laptop PCs might not be able to provide sufficient power to operate the drive properly. Using a mains adaptor for the drive gives the inconvenience of an additional cable, and the drive will only be usable when a suitable power socket is available. On the other hand, a drive of this type should work with any PC that has a port of the appropriate type, and it will not reduce the battery life of a laptop PC.

9

CD-ROM and
DVD drives

The rest

The previous chapter covered floppy and hard disc drives, but there are
now several other types of internal drive for PCs, including CD-ROMs,
CD-ROM writers, DVD drives, and various types of removable hard disc
drive. Installing one of these is very much like installing a hard disc
drive, and the new drive will normally interface to one of the IDE or serial
ATA ports. There are a few exceptions, such as drives which use a SCSI
interface card, or their own dedicated interface card. However, these
are now something of a rarity and will not be considered here.

Replacement drive

Physically installing the drive is usually straightforward with CD-ROM
and DVD drives. If you are replacing an existing unit, start by removing
the appropriate panels of the case in oder to gain full access to the drive,
and then remove its fixing screws. There will usually be four of these,
with two used on each side of the drive. Also disconnect the cables, and
there could be as many as three of these (the data, power, and audio
cables). It should then be possible to slide the old drive forwards and
out of the case. Where appropriate, check that the jumper settings on
the new drive match those of the old unit. Jumper settings are considered
in more detail later.

It is then just a matter of going through a reverse process to fit the new
drive. Leave the fixing bolts slightly loose at first so that the drive can be
moved backwards and forwards to get its front facia accurately aligned
with the front of the case. Then tighten the bolts, being careful not to
shift the drive out of position. It has been assumed here that the old and
new drives have the same type of interface. Obviously a new data cable
will be required if there is a switch from an IDE interface to a serial ATA

type. A suitable cable should be included with the drive if it is obtained as a retail boxed unit, but this is not always the case. Data cables are not normally supplied with "bare" drives. Consequently, you might have to purchase a separate data cable. Of course, using a drive that has a serial ATA interface is only possible if your PC has a spare port of the appropriate type. Older PCs do not have serial ATA ports at all, and with modern PCs there might be just two of them, with at least one of these already occupied by a hard disc drive. Confirm the suitability of your PC before buying a serial ATA drive.

Additional Drive

A suitable drive bay is required if the new drive is in addition to the existing drives rather than replacing one of them. Bear in mind that a DVD writer should be able to read and write CD-ROMs as well, so the existing drive can be removed when upgrading from some form of CD-ROM drive to a DVD writer. Of course, it is not essential to remove the existing drive if the PC has the wherewithal to accommodate the old and new drives. Indeed, it could be advantageous to have the two drives installed. For example, copying CD data discs is easier when it is possible to copy from one drive to another.

A 5.25-inch drive bay is required for CD and DVD drives, and the bay must be a type that provides front access to the drive. In practice it seems to be the norm for all 5.25-inch drive bays to provide front access to the drive, so this should not be a problem. With many tower and midi tower cases you could well have three or four bays to choose from. Computer drives tend to get quite hot, so there is something to be said for keeping them well apart rather than grouping them together in adjacent drive bays. There will be a metal plate and a plastic cover that must be removed from the bay before the drive can be fitted (see the previous chapter).

5.25-inch drives normally have eight mounting holes, with four in each side plate (Figure 9.1). However, two mounting bolts each side are sufficient to hold one of these drives securely in place. Four mounting bolts are usually supplied with retail boxed drives, but you may be supplied with no accessories if you obtain a "bare" drive. In general, it is well worth paying a little extra in order to obtain a retail version of a drive, which will usually be supplied with fixing screws, one or two leads, and probably some useful software as well. If you obtain a "bare" drive, it is possible that some suitable mounting bolts will be found in the bits and

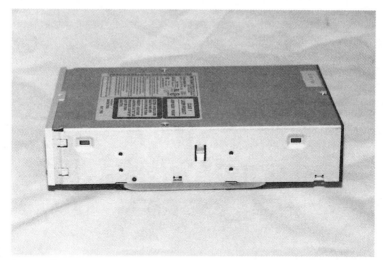

Fig.9.1 There are four mounting holes in each side of a 5.25-inch drive

pieces supplied with the computer. Failing that, it should be possible to obtain suitable bolts from your local computer store or computer fair.

Connections

It is just a matter of connecting the drive to a spare port of the appropriate type if the new drive has a serial ATA interface. A suitable data cable might be supplied with the drive, but if not, any computer store should be able to supply a standard cable such as this. With a parallel IDE drive there might be an unused port that can be utilised for the new drive. Where such a port is available, it makes sense to use it and leave any other IDE drives and ports unaltered.

In practice it is likely that there will be two IDE ports, and that there will already be at least one drive connected to each of them. In order to add another drive there must be at least one IDE port that is only connected to one existing drive. The new drive can then be used as the second drive on that port. Try to pair the new drive with an existing CD-ROM or DVD drive rather than a hard disc drive. Having a CD-ROM or DVD drive on the same IDE channel as a hard disc drive could result in the performance of the hard drive being impaired. It is likely that the IDE cables already fitted to the computer will be double types that can handle two drives. If so, the spare connector on an existing cable can be used

Fig.9.2 There is usually an analogue audio output on CD-ROM drives

with the new drive. If not, a double IDE cable must be obtained and fitted in place of the existing single type. A suitable cable is sometimes included with retail boxed drives, but it will probably have to be obtained separately.

Audio cable

With any form of CD-ROM or DVD drive there is invariably an audio output socket on the rear of the unit, usually between the configuration jumper block and the power input socket (Figure 9.2). This enables audio CDs played on the drive to be heard through the computer's sound system. This coupling is not really necessary if you will not play audio tracks on the CD-ROM drive, or if audio tracks will be monitored via the headphone socket on the CD-ROM drive. It is not essential if the new drive is in addition to an existing CD-ROM or DVD drive, and the original unit is coupled to the audio system. CDs can simply be played through the

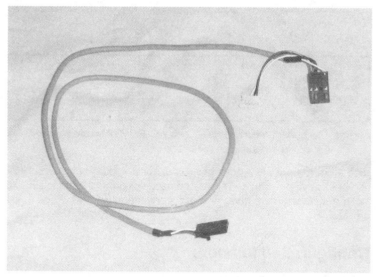

Fig.9.3 An audio lead that has two types of connector at the end which connects to the motherboard or soundcard

original drive. However, it makes sense to connect the socket just in case you need to play audio tracks on the new drive via the soundcard.

There are a couple of potential snags, one of which is simply that more than one type of connector has been used at both the CD-ROM and the soundcard ends of these cables. An audio cable is usually supplied with any form of CD-ROM or DVD drive provided you buy the retail boxed version and not a "bare" OEM unit. This usually has a relatively large and flat connector at each end, which is the only type used in current equipment. Where an old PC is being upgraded it is possible that the soundcard or motherboard will use a different type of connector. The audio cable supplied with the drive might have two connectors at one end (Figure 9.3). One or other of the connectors at this end should suit the connector on the soundcard or motherboard. It will otherwise be necessary to buy a suitable cable.

The other potential problem is that there might not be a spare audio input on the soundcard or motherboard. Soundcards are more accommodating in this respect, and any reasonably modern type should have at least two audio input ports. The integrated audio circuits on

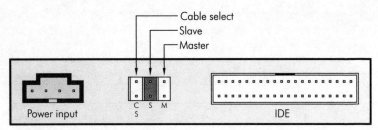

Fig.9.4 The configuration jumpers for a CD-ROM drive are buried in
        the connectors at the rear of the unit

motherboards are often fairly basic, but some motherboards do have
two or three audio inputs. There is no easy solution if the audio system
lacks a suitable input, and the audio connection will then have to be
omitted.

Configuration jumpers

The configuration jumper block of a CD-ROM or DVD drive is usually
quite basic, using the arrangement shown in Figure 9.4. The configuration
jumper block of a CD/RW drive can be seen to the right of the audio
connector in Figure 9.2. There are no complications of the type
encountered with some other types of drive, with just the three basic
settings, which are master, slave, and cable select. It is best to configure
the drive before mounting it in the case, because the jumper block is
likely to be inaccessible once the drive is in position. The convention is
for the drive to be set as the master unit when it is the only drive on an
IDE channel.

The new drive will presumably be the slave unit if it is added as the
second unit on an IDE channel that is already in use. The existing drive
should not require any changes to its configuration jumper if it is a CD-
ROM or DVD type. The situation is different for an IDE hard disc drive,
which often has different settings depending on whether it is the master
in a master/slave setup, or the master and only drive on that IDE channel.
This was covered in the previous chapter and will not be considered in
detail here. If you add a new drive and the computer has problems
booting into Windows or the hard drive seems to be slow and erratic, the
most likely cause is that the hard disc drive needs to have the settings of
its configuration jumpers altered to accommodate the new drive.

Note that serial ATA drives do not normally have any configuration
jumpers, because there is only one drive per channel. If there are any

CD-ROM and DVD drives 9

configuration jumpers or switches on a drive of this type, there should be an instruction leaflet that explains their significance and how to set them up correctly.

BIOS

Normal IDE and serial ATA drives will only work properly if they have the correct parameters set in the BIOS (see chapter 12). Depending on the particular BIOS and how it is set to operate, the new drive will either be recognised automatically or just ignored by the BIOS. If the new drive is ignored, it is a matter of going into the BIOS Setup program to see if there is specific support for the type of drive you are using. There are often options for CD-ROM/DVD, Zip, and LS120 drives, but you are unlikely to find specific settings for any drives that are out of the ordinary. Note that DVD drives, CD-RW types, etc., are all plain CD-ROM drives as far as the BIOS is concerned. It is the operating system and supporting software that takes them beyond basic CD-ROM operation.

The drive's instruction manual should give advice on the BIOS settings for any non-standard drives, but in most cases it is just a matter of setting the appropriate IDE channel as occupied, but with all the parameters set to zero. The drive should be supplied with drivers for the popular operating systems, together with full installation instructions.

When buying removable hard disc drives, CD/RW drives, DVD writers, etc., you need to make sure you know exactly what you are buying, and that it is suitable for use in your system. IDE versions of some drives are only usable if they are supported by the BIOS in your PC. If not, either an external parallel port, USB, or SCSI version of the drive will have to be used. This is unlikely to be a problem unless your PC is quite a few years old, but it is as well to check this point before buying a drive for an old PC.

If the drive requires a SCSI or other form of controller card, is it supplied as standard or is it an optional extra? A suitable controller card can be quite expensive, and in some cases it costs nearly as much as the bare drive it controls. With a CD-ROM writer or CD-RW drive, is it supplied with full supporting software? These drives can be used in Windows 95/ 98/ME much like any other drive, albeit with some restrictions. However, they can only do so with the aid of suitable software, such as Adaptec's Easy CD Creator or Nero. Again, this type of software can significantly add to the cost of a drive if it has to be bought as an extra. Windows XP has some built-in support for CD-RW drives as does Vista, but additional

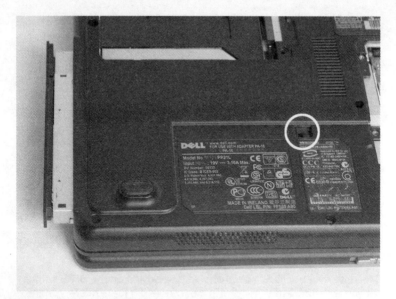

Fig.9.5 Removing a single mounting bolt frees the drive

software is still needed in order to fully exploit this type of drive. If you are using an old version of Windows, is any supplied software compatible with this version. Getting new hardware to operate with old operating systems is notoriously difficult, and in many cases is not possible to do so. Make sure that drives, or any other new hardware, is compatible with your PC and its operating system before buying it.

Laptop CD/DVD drives

An ordinary CD or DVD drive is totally out of proportion to a modern laptop PC, and in terms of height they are probably larger than most notebook PCs. Some form of CD or DVD drive is an essential part of a modern PC though, and it is difficult to install any software unless a PC has a drive of this type. Modern miniaturisation has made it possible to fit a CD or DVD drive into a laptop PC, and even the smallest notebook PCs are now supplied complete with one of these drives. G.24 in the Colour Gallery shows a standard CD-ROM drive with a laptop DVD writer on top, and the difference in size is self-evident.

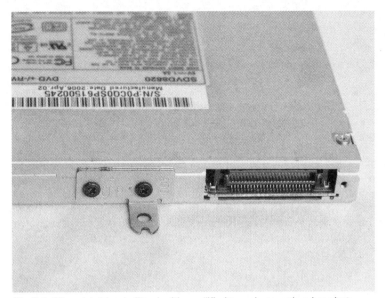

*Fig.9.6 The old drive is fitted with an "L" shaped mounting bracket.
This must be transferred to the new drive so that it can be
bolted in place*

It is highly unusual for a laptop PC to have provision for two CD/DVD
drives, so any additional drive of this type must be an external unit. There
are plenty of external CD and DVD drives available, and any of these
should be suitable provided the computer has a port of the appropriate
type.   Firewire and USB 2.0 offer optimum performance, but adequate
results should be obtained using a USB 1.1 port or drive. However, the
maximum rate at which data can be transferred will be relatively slow
using a USB 1.1 interface.

All change

With most modern laptop PCs it is possible to remove the old drive and
replace it with a more capable type, such as removing a CD/RW drive
and replacing it with a DVD writer.   This is dependent on the existing
drive being a standard slim-line type, or a non-standard type where it is
possible to obtain a suitable upgrade drive from a specialist supplier. It
is also dependent on you being able to figure out how to remove the old

drive! As always when dealing with a laptop PC, it should be disconnected from its mains adaptor and the battery should be removed before starting work.

In the example of Figure 9.5, it has only been necessary to remove one screw from the underside of the computer. The white circle indicates where the mounting bolt has been removed. It has then been possible to pull the drive forwards to disconnect it from the PC, and from here it can be moved forwards and right out of the drive bay. A slight snag in this example is that, as supplied, a new drive will slide into position properly and will work, but there is no way of fixing it in place properly. There is a small "L" shaped bracket fixed on the original drive (Figure 9.6), but this will probably not be present on the new drive. However, with this type of thing it is usually possible to remove the bracket from the old drive and fit it onto the new one. It is then just a matter of sliding the new drive into the bay, pushing it fully home so that connects to the computer correctly, and then replacing the mounting bolt.

External
storage

External drives

External versions of hard disc, CD-ROM and DVD drives were probably produced with portable computing in mind. They provide a means of adding storage to a PC while it is used at base, that does not have to be taken with you when computing on the move. However, users of desktop PCs soon found uses for them. For example, external hard disc drives are often used for archiving old data, which can be easily retrieved if necessary, but does not clog up the main hard disc drive in the meantime. They are also popular with users of digital cameras. Large amounts of picture data can be stored on a high capacity external drive, with no risk of rapidly using up the main drive's capacity. Another approach is to use an external hard disc drive to store the older data. If necessary, the disc, complete with all its data, is easily transferred to another PC.

Drive enclosures

External hard drives and CD-ROM/DVD drives were covered in the previous two chapters, and will not be discussed in detail here. Something not covered in these chapters is drive enclosures, and Figure 10.1 shows a typical unit of this type. A drive enclosure has a built-in interface that can connect an ordinary parallel ATA or SATA hard disc drive to a USB port. The enclosure normally comes complete with any additional equipment that will be needed, such as cables and a power supply unit, but they do not come complete with a disc drive.

These enclosures are primarily aimed at people who have a spare hard disc drive, perhaps after upgrading a desktop PC. The drive can be added into a low-cost enclosure to produce a neat external drive. Of course, you can buy a hard disc drive specifically for use with one of these enclosures, and it in terms of cost it might be competitive with a normal external hard disc drive. This method certainly gives a huge

Fig.10.1 This is a 3.8-inch hard disc enclosure and interface

choice of drive units. However, you have to be careful to buy an enclosure having an interface that matches that of the hard disc drive.

Power source

Some external hard disc drives require their own battery supply or mains adaptor while others can be powered from the host PC. Most seem to have their own power source rather than relying on the host PC for power. Bear in mind that there will probably be only a limited amount of power available from the USB port of a laptop computer. This means that it can power small peripherals such as mice, but anything more substantial is unlikely to work unless it has its own power source.

Firewire ports on laptop computers are usually of the 4-pin variety, which means that no power output is available from these ports. Consequently, they can only be used with peripherals that have their own power source. Using a 4-pin to 6-pin adaptor lead will not work in such cases. The lead will provide the required data coupling between the computer and the peripheral, but no power will be supplied to the peripheral device.

Flash memory

Where huge amounts of external storage are not required, Flash memory, which is sometimes in the form of a so-called "pen drive", offers a useful alternative to hard, DC-ROM, and DVD drives. A "pen drive" is a gadget that looks rather like a large pen, but removing the top reveals a USB connector (see G.25 and G26 in the Colour Gallery). It is not really a drive in the conventional sense, since the data is not stored on some form of disc or tape. There are no moving parts, and a device of this type is purely electronic. These devices are also known as "Flash drives", which is a bit more accurate but is still a little misleading. The "drive" part of these names is derived from the fact that the gadget is accessed as a drive in the operating system and when using application software.

The data is stored on Flash memory, which is the same type of memory that is used in digital cameras and various portable electronic devices. Unlike the main memory of a PC, Flash memory does not get a severe case of amnesia when the power is switched off. You may sometimes encounter references to "non-volatile" or just "NV" memory, and this name is used to describe any form of memory that retains its contents when the power is switched off. Flash memory is of the non-volatile variety, which makes is suitable for backing up data or transferring it from one PC to another.

In addition to the Flash memory itself, a pen drive includes a USB interface and some electronics. Together with the driver software built into modern versions of Windows, this makes the unit appear as a normal drive to the operating system. Note that versions of Windows prior to XP and ME will require suitable drivers to be installed in order to make a pen drive usable. The necessary software is normally supplied with the drive, but it is advisable to check this point if you are not using a current version of Windows. The Plug and Play feature of Windows ME, XP, and Vista will recognise a pen drive and automatically install the software to support it. However, with Windows ME you might need the Windows installation disc in order to complete the installation.

The pen drive will normally be added to the end of the existing series of drive letters. For example, if the PC already has drives from A to F, the newly added pen drive will be drive G. In the example of Figure 10.2, Windows Explorer has found the Flash drive and it is listed as drive H. Windows usually refers to Flash drive as a "Removable Disk", which means that it is effectively an outsize floppy disc as far as the operating system is concerned. The practical importance of this is that removing the drive will not have dire consequences for the smooth operation of the PC.

Note though, that it might be necessary to switch off the drive via software control before it is removed. In fact this will almost certainly be necessary. There is otherwise a risk of an error message being produced, and the

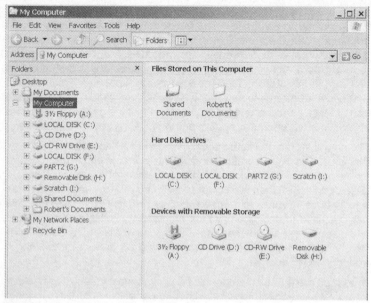

Fig.10.2 An external drive is given a drive letter by the operating system

operating system could become confused. The deactivation process usually requires little more than operating a button in the Windows taskbar. The instructions provided with the drive should explain how to switch the drive on and off.

The small size of pen drives makes them ideal for use with a portable PC. You can take two or three of these drives with you when computing on the move, and the increase in the size and bulk of the equipment will be so small that it is unlikely to be noticeable. Pen drives are widely used as a means of swapping data between a laptop PC and a desktop computer.

The capacities of early pen drives were often quite low, with something in the region of 16 to 32 megabytes being typical. This is equivalent to about one or two dozen floppy discs, and is sufficient for many purposes. Flash memory technology has moved on quite fast in recent years, resulting in much higher capacities and massive price reductions. Capacities of around 1 gigabytes to 16 gigabytes are now commonplace, making it possible to transfer large amounts of data via these drives.

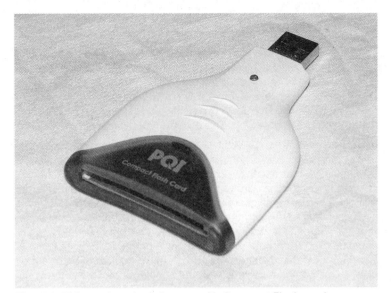

Fig.10.3 This card reader is for use with Compact Flash cards

Card reader

Pen drives are useful gadgets, but they have an obvious limitation in that it is not possible to change the "disc". In other words, you really have something more like an external hard disc drive than a floppy disc drive. You can unplug one drive and fit another, but it is not possible to leave the drive in place and change the "disc". For many purposes it would be better if the drive could be left connected, with some interchangeable Flash memory cards being used rather like very high capacity floppy discs. Provided all your PCs were equipped with a suitable drive, data could be written to a memory card on one PC and then read on any of the others. Where a large amount of data has to be backed up to Flash memory, you would simply need a few high capacity Flash cards, which would be used in the drive, one after the other until all the data had been saved.

A big advantage of this method is that it would not involve switching off a drive before removing the "disc". Unplugging a memory card would leave the drive connected to the USB port, so there would be no vanishing hardware to confuse the operating system. The "discs" would appear and disappear as they were moved from one PC to another, but Windows is not fazed by simple disc changing of this type. The memory cards could therefore be freely exchanged between PCs, just like floppy discs.

There is a device called a "card reader" that is the flash memory equivalent of a floppy disc drive. The card reader connects to a USB port, and like a pen-drive, and it is used by the operating system as a "Removable Disk". The difference is that there is no built-in memory. Some card readers are designed for use with a single type of memory card, such as the one shown in Figure 10.3. This accepts type 1 Compact Flash cards.

Other card readers can be used with half a dozen or more different types of memory card. Some printers and other peripheral gadgets have a built-in card reader, and these usually have slots for all the popular types of memory card. The card reader in a printer is primarily included so that prints can be made direct from the files on memory cards. However, it will usually act as a normal card reader when the printer is connected to a PC. Some PCs have a built-in card reader, but this feature is still something of a rarity for anything other than media PCs. Whatever "flavour" cards the reader accepts, they are the equivalent of the floppy discs. One card can be removed and another one can be fitted in its place.

Disc swapping

Swapping discs other than the floppy variety has sometimes caused problems in the past. The usual snag was that on changing the disc the operating system refused to acknowledge that a change had been made. It still showed the contents of the original disc in file browsers, and attempts to access any of these files obviously failed and produced an error message. Fortunately, this does not happen with card readers, which are treated by the operating system as a truly removable disc drive. If you remove one card and fit another, file browsers should show the files on the second card, and there should be no difficulty in accessing them.

Although the cards are used like high-capacity floppy discs, they have high capacities and are formatted more like hard disc drives. Originally they were mostly formatted using the old FAT16 system, but with large cards the more recent FAT32 system is normally used. In fact the very high capacity cards must use FAT32 formatting, since the FAT16 system can not handle capacities of more than two gigabytes.

FAT16 and FAT32 drives can be read by any version of Windows, including Windows 2000, XP, and Vista systems where the hard disc drive uses the NTFS file system. Consequently, there should be no

Fig.10.4 Compact Flash, Secure Digital, and XD memory cards

difficulty in reading a card produced using a PC running Windows ME even if the card reader is connected to a PC running Windows Vista or XP. A transfer in the opposite direction should be equally successful. In fact many gadgets that use memory cards also use the FAT16 or FAT32 file systems. Memory cards from most digital cameras, for instance, can be read on a PC that is equipped with a suitable card reader. Note though, that some devices use their own system of formatting, and that cards from older digital cameras are often unreadable via an ordinary card reader.

Several different types of memory card are available, but it is a good idea to use one of the most popular types unless there is a good reason to do otherwise. The more popular types of card are available in high capacity versions and are relatively cheap. The maximum capacities of the less common types are sometimes quite low, and they can easily cost more than twice as much as an equivalent card in a more popular format.

The two most popular types of Flash card are Type 1 Compact Flash (CF) and Secure Digital (SD) cards. Type 1 Compact Flash cards are the most widely used, and almost certainly represent the best choice for

PC data transfer and storage. Secure Digital cards are also very popular though, and they also represent a good choice. Normal SD cards have a maximum capacity of 2 gigabytes, but there is a high capacity version (SDHC) which can have capacities of up to 32 gigabytes. SDHC devices are backwards compatible with SD cards, but SDHC cards can not be used in ordinary SD card slots. Compact Flash and SD/SDHC cards having capacities of up to a few gigabytes are now readily available. Figure 10.4 shows Compact Flash, Secure Digital, and XD Flash cards.

Speed

The "Flash" name tends to give the impression that this type of memory is extremely fast. Unfortunately, the name refers to the process used when writing data to the card, and it is not meant to imply super-fast operation. The reading and writing speeds of Flash memory are actually quite slow by current standards, and they are not even very fast when compared to various types of true disc storage. Most Flash memory manufacturers use a speed rating that is essentially the same as the one used for CD-ROM drives. There is a slight difference in that the rating used for a CD-ROM drive is the maximum it can achieve, and the actual speed obtained near the middle of the disc is usually much lower. There is no Flash memory equivalent to this, and the quoted speed should be obtained when writing to any part of the disc.

A speed rating of X1 is equivalent to about 150k per second. Most memory cards are not actually marked with a speed rating, although this information is usually included in the manufacturer's data. A card that has no marked rating usually has a speed of about X4 to x12, and can read or write data at about one megabyte or so per second. Note that there is no point in using a faster card with a reader that has a USB 1.1 interface, or is connected to a USB 1.1 port. A "bog standard" memory card can transfer data at a rate that is about double that of a single device on a USB 1.1 port.

At the time or writing this, cards that have speed ratings of up to about X200 are readily available, and even faster cards can be obtained if you are prepred to pay a relatively high price for them. It seems likely that significantly faster cards will be developed before too long. These cards are mainly intended for use with electronic gadgets that handle large amounts of data, such as digital video cameras and the more upmarket digital cameras. However, they also offer the potential for moving large amounts of data from one PC to another in a reasonably short time, or for backing up data. A card having a rating of x60 for example, can read and write data at up to nine megabytes per second, and a x200 card can transfer data at around 30 megabytes per second. In theory at any rate, a gigabyte of data could written to the x200 card in 30 seconds or so, and then copied onto another PC in a similar amount of time.

Of course, transfer speeds of this order requires a reader that supports a high speed interface such as USB 2.0 or Firewire. Using either type of interface and a matching card reader should enable data to be read and written at something very close to the maximum speed rating of the card. Where high-speed operation is needed it is important to check that a USB card reader is a genuine USB 2.0 type. Some are described as "USB 2.0 compatible", which means that they are actually USB 1.1 devices that can operate at USB 1.1 speeds with a USB 2.0 interface.

Note that some manufacturers do not use speed ratings such as X20 and X40. Instead they simply state the maximum rate at which data can be read from and written to the card. In order to compare the speeds of various cards it might be necessary to do a conversion from one type of speed rating to the other. I have a SanDisk Ultra II card that has quoted read and write rates of 9 and 10 megabytes per second respectively. Dividing these figures by 0.15 gives their equivalent ratings in the Xn system.

This gives read and write speeds of X60 and X67 respectively. The read speed of a Flash card is usually a little faster than the write speed. In the Xn system it is the slower rate that is used, so my SanDisk Ultra II card is an X60 type and not an X67 card. To convert an Xn rating into its equivalent in megabytes per second, multiply its speed rating by 0.15. An X80 card, for example, can transfer data at up to 12 megabytes per second.

PCMCIA FLASH

It is perhaps worth mentioning that there is an alternative to using a USB or Firewire card reader if your laptop has a spare PCMCIA slot. It is possible to obtain PCMCIA cards that are complete with some FLASH memory, and PCMCIA card readers for use with FLASH cards. The latter are the more practical proposition. A PCMCIA card reader has the advantage of providing a reader that is largely built into the computer, which makes it a neater solution for computing on the move. The only real drawback is that this type of card reader seems to be significantly more expensive than the USB or Firewire variety.

Power
supplies

Why upgrade?

On the face of it, one computer power supply is very much like another, and there is no point in upgrading. In reality there are PC power supplies of various shapes and sizes, and there are a couple of reasons that could warrant an upgrade. The less likely reason is noise, and here I am talking in terms of noise in the sound sense, rather than electrical noise on the outputs of the supply. Modern PCs have more powerful processors than those of the past, more memory, more ports, and more of just about everything in fact. Although advances in modern electronics have reduced the power consumed by each transistor, the number of transistors in a PC's integrated circuits has mushroomed over the years. A typical PC now has several billion of them in its memory circuits alone!

Gone are the days when a PC had a 200 watt power supply and actually required only about half that power. A modern PC power supply is likely to be rated at around 300 to 450 watts, and in use it will probably have little spare capacity. Modern power supplies are quite efficient, but the higher the rating of the supply, the more power that is wasted. This wasted power manifests itself in the form of heat, and this is removed from the PC using metal cooling fins and a fan. In electronic circles the cooling fins are known as a heatsink. In order to get rid of the excess heat the cooling fans have become more powerful over the years, and this is reflected in generally higher sound levels. This noise is unwelcome in most environments, but it is particularly unhelpful if the PC is being used for multimedia applications.

Quiet power supplies are produced, and they are becoming quite popular despite their relatively high prices. It is only fair to point out that a quiet power supply will not render a PC silent. There are other sources of noise, such as the hard disc and the processor's cooling fan. However, in most cases the fan in the power supply is the main culprit. Replacing it with a quiet unit will usually give a very noticeable reduction in the noise level, especially if the original power supply unit is one of the more noisy types. If you have to raise your voice in order to be heard above the sound of the computer, replacing its power supply with a quieter type is probably a good idea.

It might seem better to simply replace the cooling fan in the power supply with a quieter unit. This is possible, but is not the approved way of doing things. Delving into the interior of a PC power supply is something that should only be undertaken by those having the necessary experience. Another problem is that the replacement fan might be much quieter, but it could also be less efficient. You will have the ultimate in quiet PCs if the power supply starts to overheat and shuts down!

Power mad

The more common reason for upgrading a power supply is that so many upgrades have been added that the original supply can no longer cope. Adding more drives, a bigger and better video card, more memory, a faster processor, or just about any internal upgrade, results in greater loading on the power supply unit. In the past it was normal for external units to have their own power source. This situation has changed with the arrival of Firewire and USB. Although the total amount of power drawn by external units is unlikely to be very high, it all adds to the loading on the power supply unit. Particularly with older PCs, where the original power supply is likely to be rated at about 250 to 300 watts, more than a modest amount of upgrading can result in the supply being "caught short".

I have heard of people upgrading a power supply because the original unit lacked sufficient power connectors to accommodate newly added drives. Possibly those concerned have assumed that the power supply does not have the wherewithal to operate more than one drive per connector. Actually, a supply is quite capable of powering two drives from one connector with the aid of a suitable adaptor. The main proviso is that the additional drive must not result in the current drain from any of the supply's various outputs being exceeded.

Obviously the supply might have been operating "at the edge" prior to the new drive being added, and a power supply having a higher rating will then be required. On the other hand, there is a good chance that the original supply will have sufficient spare capacity to accommodate the new drive. The cost of a PC power supply of reasonable quality is not

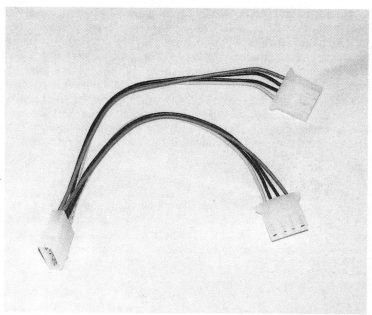

Fig.11.1 A supply splitter having 5.25-inch drive power connectors

particularly high, but I would certainly opt for a supply splitter first. It could turn out to be a waste of money, but these adaptors are quite cheap. They can often be picked up at computer fairs for pence rather than pounds. If the adaptor does not have the desired result, it is a useful gadget to have in the spares box. It may well prove useful at some later date.

There are various power supply adaptors available, so it is necessary to make sure that you obtain a suitable type. Most PC power supplies have two power connectors for 3.5-inch floppy drives. These connectors are only used for 3.5-inch floppy drives, with 3.5-inch hard drives, CD-ROMS, etc., using the larger power connector. Most PCs only have one floppy disc drive. This leaves a spare 3.5-inch power connector, which can be connected to a CD-ROM drive, etc., via the appropriate adaptor. The alternative is to use a splitter cable that enables two drives to be powered from one of the larger power connectors. Figure 11.1 shows an adaptor of this type. The power supply's connector fits into the female connector of the adaptor. The other two connectors of the adaptor supply power to the two disc drives.

With modern PCs there is a further complication, which is that the power connector used for serial ATA drives is different to the standard 5.25-inch type. Some serial ATA drives actually have both types of power connector, and can therefore be used with a power supply that only has the normal 5.25-inch power connectors. However, many are only equipped with a serial ATA power connector, and are unusable with ordinary 5.25-inch power leads. Although the two types of power connector are different, the voltages they provide are exactly the same. A simple adaptor is all that is needed in order to use an old power supply unit with a modern serial ATA drive (see G.27 in the Colour Gallery).

AT or ATX supply

The power supply for an ATX case and motherboard is different to that for an AT type. You therefore have to determine which type your PC uses before a more powerful or quieter unit can be obtained. One way is to measure the size of the power supply's case. An ATX case should be approximately 150 by 140 by 84 millimetres. If it is slightly smaller on one or more of these dimensions it is almost certainly an AT power supply.

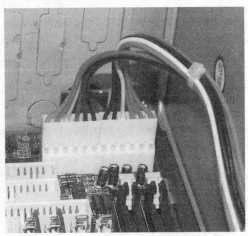

Fig.11.2 AT motherboard power connectors

You definitely have problems if the supply is not reasonably close to these dimensions, as it is a non-standard type. One or two manufacturers have gone their own way with power supplies, and many Dell PCs have non-standard supply units. In other instances a case of unusual design requires an equally unconventional power supply unit. The manufacturer of the computer might be able to sell you a power supply that suits your requirements. If not, it will probably not be possible upgrade the power supply unit.

The most reliable method of differentiating between an AT power supply and an ATX type is to look at the connectors that supply power to the motherboard. If there are two of them side by side, as in Figure 11.2, the supply is an AT type. An ATX supply unit uses one large connector, as in Figure 11.3. Replacing a power

Fig.11.3 A single power connector is used for ATX motherboards

supply is much the same whether it is an AT or ATX type, and it is an ATX type that will be used for this example. However, the computer is quite old if it uses an AT supply. Finding a replacement supply could be very difficult, and it is probably not worth spending much money on a PC of this vintage.

Out with the old

Clearly the first task is to remove the original power supply, and this should not be difficult. First you must disconnect the PC from the mains supply and unplug the power lead from the supply unit. If the monitor is powered via the PC, its power lead must also be disconnected from the supply unit. In fact

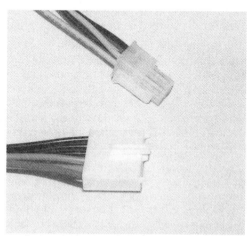

Fig.11.4 The additional connectors for a Pentium 4 motherboard

Fig.11.5 Four screws hold the power supply in place

it is a good idea to disconnect everything from the PC, since it is difficult to work on a unit that has leads connecting to a variety of peripherals.

Next the supply is disconnected from the motherboard and drives. The larger drive connectors are notoriously stiff, and they are unlikely to pull free without a bit of a struggle. Do not disconnect one by pulling on the leads. Get a firm grip on the plug and wiggle it free of the socket. If there are any cooling fans or other gadgets that are powered from one of the drive connectors via an adaptor, these should also be disconnected at this stage. Make a note of how everything fits together so that you can reassemble everything correctly when the new supply has been installed.

The motherboard connectors usually have a simple locking mechanism, so it is necessary to press the unlocking lever and then pull the plug free. If you have a close look at the connectors it is fairly obvious how the locking mechanism functions. If some of the connectors are inaccessible with the power supply in place, and the motherboard connectors may well fit into this category, they can be disconnected once the supply unit has been removed from the case.

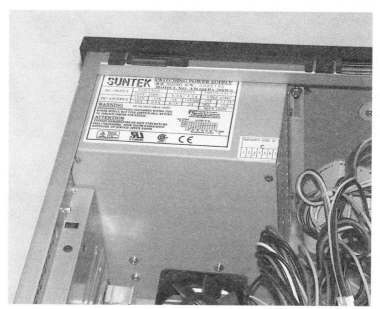

Fig.11.6 Some ATX power supplies also have a mounting bracket

Extra connectors

Most ATX supplies only have one connector to carry power to the motherboard. Some have one or two extra connectors (Figure 11.4) to carry additional power to motherboards that require it. Most motherboards do not require the additional connectors, but some Pentium 4 motherboards will not function unless one or other of them is implemented. Check for the extra connections to the motherboard before

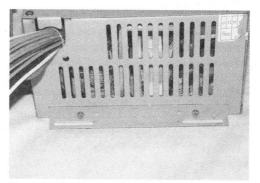

Fig.11.7 The bracket can be seen more clearly here

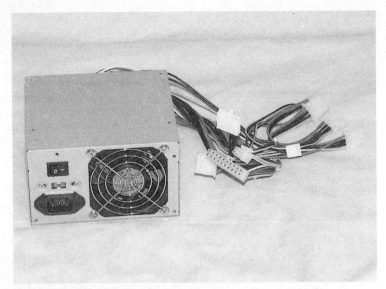

Fig.11.8 The replacement power supply is an ultra-quiet type

ordering a new power supply, and where appropriate make sure that you buy a power supply that has them. These supplies are usually described as something like "Pentium 4 ready" or "Pentium 4 equipped" supplies. The additional connectors are locking types, rather like miniature versions of the main ATX motherboard connector. Accordingly, the unlocking lever must be operated before the connector will pull free from the motherboard.

Most AT and ATX power supplies are only secured to the case by four screws. These fix the supply to the rear panel of the case, and they can be seen in Figure 11.5. Some ATX cases are bolted to the top or side of the case via a right-angle bracket. This bracket and fixing screw can be seen in Figure 11.6, and Figure 11.7 shows a clearer view of the bracket. Check for the additional bracket and fixing screw, and remove the screw if they are present. Then remove the four main fixing screws, being careful to support the supply unit so that it can not drop into the PC when the last fixing has been removed. Carefully manoeuvre the supply out of the case, and disconnect any leads if necessary.

It is then just a matter of reversing the process to install the new supply. In this example the new supply unit (Figure 11.8) looks much like the

Fig.11.9 The replacement power supply installed in the PC

original, and has the same power rating of 300 watts. It is an ultra quiet power supply though, and should help to make the PC much quieter in use. It is unlikely that the new supply will be fitted with a mounting bracket, and it was certainly absent from the new supply unit in this case.

However, the new supply should have mounting holes that permit a mounting bracket to be fitted. Therefore, if necessary, remove the bracket from the old supply and fit it to the new one. If the power connectors on the motherboard will be obscured when the supply is in place, connect the supply to the motherboard before fitting it in place. It is best to fit all the mounting bolts loosely at first, and then tighten them once they are all in place. This avoids fitting one in place and finding that the others can not be fitted because the mounting holes are out of alignment.

The larger drive connectors can only be fitted to the drives the right way around, and it usually requires quite firm pressure to fully push them into place. In theory it is not possible to connect the power to a 3.5-inch floppy drive incorrectly, but in practice many drives have a slightly too

Fig.11.10 The mounting bracket has been transferred to the new supply

minimalist version of the connector. It might be possible to fit the connector with the terminals one row out of alignment or even with it upside down. The broader, slightly concave surface is the one that goes down against the floppy drive, and the smaller convex surface faces upwards. Make sure that the five pins on the drive's connector are in proper alignment with the power connector. A mistake here could destroy the drive.

Figure 11.9 shows an external view of the new power supply bolted in place, and Figure 11.10 shows an internal view. The size of an ATX supply is well standardised, and although it is a tight fit inside the case, the new one fits in just like the original. The right-angle bracket has also fitted in perfectly with the new supply. The exterior view shows that the new supply has a space for a voltage selector switch, but no switch is actually fitted. It is unusual for a modern PC power supply to have one of these switches, and most supplies will automatically adjust to suit mains voltages from about 90 to 250 volts. However, it is a good idea to check for a voltage selector switch, and where present it must obviously be set to the appropriate voltage before the supply is connected to the mains.

Unlike the original power supply, the new one does not have a mains outlet for a monitor. Presumably this change has come about due to changes in the safety regulations, and modern PC supplies have an on/ off switch in place of the mains outlet for a monitor. Either a new power lead for the monitor will be required, or the plug on the existing lead will have to be changed to a normal mains plug. Use a two or three amp fuse in the plug.

Before reconnecting everything to the PC and testing the new supply it is as well to check that no power connections have been omitted and that none of the other cables have come adrift during the swap. Make sure that the power supply is switched off (the "O" symbol of the on/off switch is pressed down) before reconnecting the mains lead. With everything connected up and ready to go, switch on the power supply and then switch on the PC itself. Everything should power up as normal, and the PC should be switched off at once if there are any obvious signs of a malfunction.

The most likely problem is that there will be no response at all when the computer is switched on. This is usually caused by the power connector to the motherboard not being fully pushed down into place. This connector should lock, so it has not been connected properly if it can be pulled free without operating the locking lever. If the connection to the motherboard is correct, check any secondary motherboard connectors and the drive leads. The floppy drive's connector being out of alignment is the most likely cause of problems.

Monitoring

It is perhaps worth mentioning that many motherboards are now equipped with sensors that monitor various temperatures and voltages. With a PC that has this facility it is worthwhile using it to check the voltages from a power supply that seems to be giving problems. It could be that the supply is faulty or is being overloaded, and that a replacement or upgrade is needed. On the other hand, power supplies tend to be blamed for problems that have their origins elsewhere.

Figure 11.11 shows the HW Doctor program in action. Some of the monitored voltages might be produced by regulators on the motherboard rather than the power supply itself, so you need to read the documentation

11 Power supplies

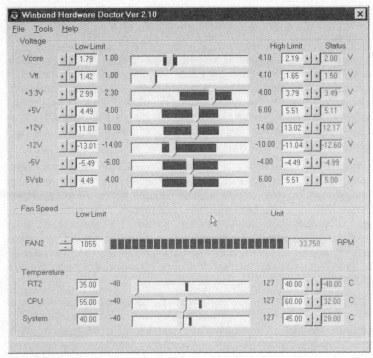

Fig.11.11 Many PCs are supplied with monitoring software

for the program to determine what is actually being monitored. An apparent fault in the power supply could actually be a problem with the motherboard. If a voltage drops well below its normal level when (say) a CD-ROM drive is used, and a malfunction then occurs, it is likely that the supply has an inadequate rating.

The BIOS

Centre of things

The basics of the BIOS were explained in chapter 1, and it should be apparent from this that the BIOS is very much at the centre of things. Consequently, when upgrading other parts of a PC you may well find it necessary to get involved with the BIOS. It is by no means a foregone conclusion that an upgrade will involve the BIOS, and the largely automatic nature of a modern BIOS means that it will often adjust automatically to suit changes. However, when you are involved with PC upgrading it is inevitable that before too long you will need to upgrade the BIOS or use its Setup program to make adjustments. The BIOS will therefore be considered in some detail in this chapter.

Essentials

The BIOS is used by the computer when it is communicating with drives, memory, etc., and it is largely "transparent" to the user. When you make adjustments to the BIOS you use the BIOS Setup program. With early PCs a simple utility program was needed in order to control the parameters of the BIOS, but with current PCs the program is effectively part of the BIOS itself. A modern BIOS Setup program enables dozens of parameters to be controlled, many of which are highly technical. This tends to make the BIOS intimidating for those who are new to PC building, and even those who have some experience of PC construction.

However, when building a new PC or upgrading to a new motherboard it is not necessary to go through the BIOS, setting dozens of parameters in order to get the PC to perform satisfactorily. The BIOS should be customised to suit the particular motherboard it is fitted to, and it should set sensible defaults. In order to get the PC running well it is usually necessary to do nothing more than set a few basic parameters such as the time, date, and some drive details. Some "fine tuning" of a few other parameters might bring benefits, but is not essential.

Fig.12.1 The BIOS is a program stored in a ROM chip

We will therefore start by considering the BIOS essentials before moving on to consider some of the other features that can be controlled via the BIOS. A detailed description of all the BIOS features would require a large book in itself, so here we will concentrate on those that are of most importance.

BIOS basics

Before looking at the BIOS Setup program, it would perhaps be as well to consider the function of the BIOS again. Its basic function is to help the operating system handle the input and output devices, such as the drives, and ports, and also the memory circuits. The BIOS is also involved with some other items of hardware, such as the video circuits. Also, some of a PC's ports are internal, such as the expansion slots, and the BIOS is often involved with these and not just external ports. Most of a PC's hardware is in some way tied into the BIOS.

The BIOS is a program and data store that is contained in a ROM on the motherboard. These days the chip is usually quite small and sports a holographic label to prove that it is the genuine article (Figure 12.1). The

Fig.12.2 An older style ROM BIOS chip

old style ROM is a standard ROM chip, as in Figure 12.2. Either way its function is the same.

Because the BIOS program is in a ROM on the motherboard it can be run immediately at start-up without the need for any form of booting process. It is the BIOS that runs the test routines at switch-on, or the POST (power on self test) as it is known. With these tests completed successfully the BIOS then looks for an operating system to load from disc. The operating system appears to load itself from disc, which is a bit like pulling oneself up by ones bootlaces. It is said to be from this that the term "boot" is derived. Of course, in reality the operating system is not loading itself initially, and it is reliant on the BIOS getting things started.

Another role of the BIOS is to provide software routines that help the operating system to utilize the hardware effectively. It can also store information about the hardware for use by the operating system, and possibly other software. It is this second role that makes it necessary to have the Setup program. The BIOS can actually detect much of the system hardware and store the relevant technical information in memory.

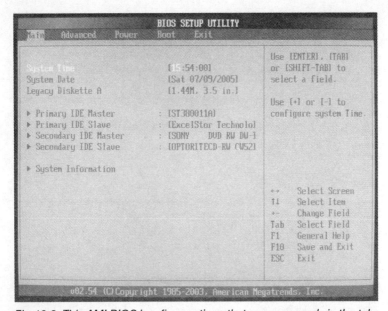

Fig.12.3 *This AMI BIOS has five sections that are accessed via the tabs*

However, some parameters have to be set manually, such as the time and date, and the user may wish to override some of the default settings. Note though, a modern BIOS has some settings that can only be set automatically. With memory for example, you can usually set various timing parameters, but the amount of memory can not be set manually. If the BIOS does not detect some of the memory, then that memory is effectively non-existent. In practice it is virtually certain that any memory or other hardware that the BIOS can not detect is faulty, and unusable. It is very unusual for a modern BIOS to make a mistake with this type of thing.

The Setup program enables the user to control the settings that the BIOS stores away in its memory. A battery powers this memory when the PC is switched off, so its contents are available each time the PC is turned on. Alternatively, some form of non-volatile memory such as a Flash type might be used. Unlike the normal memory circuits used in a PC, this type retains its contents when the power is switched off. Once the correct parameters have been set it should not be necessary to deal with the BIOS Setup program again unless some major upgrade is undertaken.

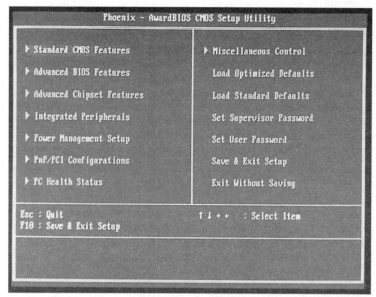

Fig.12.4 The main menu of a Phoenix-Award BIOS

Entry

In the past there have been several common means of getting into the BIOS Setup program, but the most common method in use at present is to press the Delete key at the appropriate point during the initial testing phase just after switch-on. The BIOS will display a message, usually in the bottom left-hand corner of the screen, telling you to press the "Del" key to enter the Setup program. The instruction manual for your PC or its motherboard should provide details if the motherboard you are using has a different method of entering the Setup program.

The manual for the motherboard should also have a section dealing with the BIOS. It is worth looking through this section to determine which features can be controlled via the BIOS. Unfortunately, most motherboard instruction manuals assume the user is familiar with all the BIOS features, and there will be few detailed explanations. In fact there will probably just be a list of the available options and no real explanations at all. However, a quick read through this section of the manual will give you a good idea of what the BIOS is all about. A surprisingly large number of

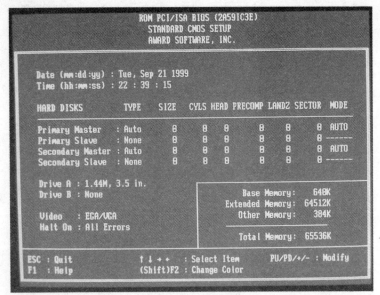

Fig.12.5 An example of a Standard CMOS Setup screen. Not every BIOS now permits manual entry of drive parameters

PC users who are quite expert in other aspects of PC operation have no real idea what the BIOS and the BIOS Setup program actually do. If you fall into this category the section of the manual that deals with the BIOS should definitely be given at least a quick read through.

There are several BIOS manufacturers and their BIOS Setup programs each work in a slightly different fashion. With motherboards available to the do-it-yourself builder it is probably the ones from Award, Phoenix, and AMI that are most likely to be encountered. At one time the AMI BIOS had a Setup program that would detect any reasonably standard mouse connected to the PC. With the aid of a mouse it offered a simple form of WIMP environment, although keyboard control was still available. This system seems to have been dropped, and a modern AMI BIOS uses a more conventional approach with tabs at the top of the screen providing access to the various sections of the program (Figure 12.3). The required tab is selected via the keyboard and not using a mouse. The Award BIOS is probably the most common and as far as I am aware it only uses keyboard control. Figure 12.4 shows the main menu for a modern Phoenix-Award BIOS.

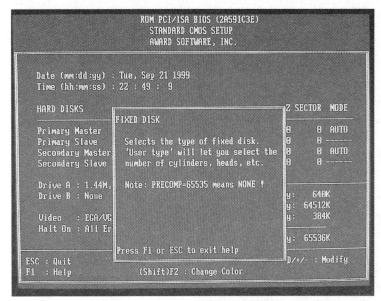

```
                  ROM PCI/ISA BIOS (2A59IC3E)
                     STANDARD CMOS SETUP
                     AWARD SOFTWARE, INC.

   Date (mm:dd:yy) : Tue, Sep 21 1999
   Time (hh:mm:ss) : 22 : 49 : 9

   HARD DISKS                                           Z SECTOR  MODE
                        FIXED DISK
   Primary Master                                       8     8  AUTO
   Primary Slave        Selects the type of fixed disk. 8     8  -----
   Secondary Master     'User type' will let you select the 8  8  AUTO
   Secondary Slave      number of cylinders, heads, etc. 8    8  -----

   Drive A : 1.44M,     Note: PRECOMP=65535 means NONE !
   Drive B : None                                        y:    640K
                                                         y:  64512K
   Video   : EGA/VG                                      y:    384K
   Halt On : All Er
                                                         y:  65536K
                        Press F1 or ESC to exit help
   ESC : Quit                                            D/+/- : Modify
   F1  : Help                   (Shift)F2 : Change Color
```

Fig.12.6 Pressing F1 will usually bring up a brief Help screen

Apart from variations in the BIOS due to different manufacturers, the BIOS will vary slightly from one motherboard to another. This is simply due to the fact that features available on one motherboard may be absent or different on another motherboard. Also, the world of PCs in general is developing at an amazing rate, and this is reflected in frequent BIOS updates. The description of the BIOS provided here has to be a representative one, and the BIOS in your PC will inevitably be slightly different. The important features should be present in any BIOS, and it is only the more minor and obscure features that are likely to be different. The motherboard's instruction manual should at the least give some basic information on setting up and using any unusual features.

Standard CMOS

There are so many parameters that can be controlled via the BIOS Setup program that they are normally divided into half a dozen or so groups. The most important of these is the "Standard CMOS Setup" (Figure 12.5), which is basically the same as the BIOS Setup in the original AT style PCs. The first parameters in the list are the time and date. These can

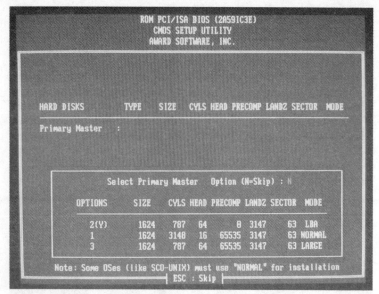

Fig.12.7 An IDE automatic detection screen in operation

usually be set via an operating system utility these days, but you may as well set them from the Setup program while you are in that section of the program. There are on-screen instructions that tell you how to alter and select options. One slight oddity to watch out for is that you often have to use the Page Up key to decrement values, and the Page Down key to increment them.

With virtually any modern BIOS a help screen can be brought up by pressing F1, and this will usually be context sensitive (Figure 12.6). In other words, if the cursor is in the section that deals with the hard drives, the help screen produced by pressing F1 will tell you about the hard disc parameters. It would be unreasonable to expect long explanations from a simple off-line help system, and a couple of brief and to the point sentences are all that will normally be provided.

Drive settings

The next section is used to set the operating parameters for the devices on the IDE ports, including any serial ATA ports. For the sake of this example we will assume that the hard disc is the master device on the primary IDE channel (IDE1), and that the CD-ROM is the master device on the secondary IDE channel (IDE2). Note that CD-RW and DVD drives are straightforward CD-ROM drives as far as the BIOS is concerned. The additional features of these drives are provided by applications software such as Nero and Power DVD. Windows XP and Vista have some built-in support for CD-RW drives, but this is the operating system providing the extra features and not the BIOS.

If the manuals for the drives provide the correct figures to enter into the CMOS memory, and they certainly should do so in the case of hard disc drives, you can enter these figures against the appropriate device. In this case the hard disc drive is the "Primary Master". A modern AMI BIOS should have a setting specifically for a CD-ROM drive, and this can be used for the "Secondary Master" device. Simply setting everything at zero usually works where no CD-ROM setting is available. There are no primary or secondary slave drives, so simply enter "None" for these.

If you do not know the appropriate figures for your drives it does not really matter, because there is always an "Auto" option. If this is selected, the BIOS examines the hardware during the start-up routine and enters the correct figures automatically. This usually works very well, but with some drives it can take a while, which extends the boot-up time.

There is an alternative method of automatic detection that avoids this delay. If you go back to the initial menu you will find a section called "IDE HDD Auto Detection" (Figure 12.7), and this offers a similar auto-detection facility. When this option is selected the Setup program examines the hardware on each IDE channel, and offers suggested settings for each of the four possible IDE devices. If you accept the suggested settings for the hard disc drive (or drives) they will be entered into the CMOS RAM. There may actually be several alternatives offered per IDE device, but the default suggestion is almost invariably the correct one.

After using this auto-detection facility it is a good idea to return to the "Standard CMOS Setup" page to check that the settings have been transferred correctly. Also, make sure that "None" is entered for the drive type where appropriate. Note that the BIOS will not automatically detect any changes to the drive onfiguration when the second method of auto-detection is used. It avoids the auto-detection delay at start-up, but changes to the drives will almost certainly make it necessary to go into the BIOS and make any changes required to the settings.

The last parameter for each IDE drive is usually something like Auto, Normal, LBA (large block addressing), and Large. Normal is for drives

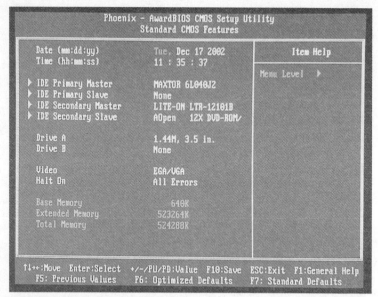

Fig.12.8 This Standard CMOS screen only permits automatic detection of the IDE devices

under 528MB, while LBA and Large are alternative modes for drives having a capacity of more than 528MB. Modern drives have capacities of well in excess of 528MB, and mostly require the LBA mode. The manual for the hard drive should give some guidance here, or you can simply select Auto and let the BIOS sort things out for itself.

Some users get confused because they think a hard drive that will be partitioned should have separate entries in the BIOS for each partition. This is not the case, and as far as the BIOS is concerned each physical hard disc is a single drive, and has just one entry in the CMOS RAM table. The partitioning of hard discs is handled by the operating system, and so is the assignment of drive letters. The BIOS is only concerned with the physical characteristics of the drives, and not how data will be arranged and stored on the discs.

Non-standard IDE

If you are using IDE devices other than hard discs and an ordinary CD-ROM drive it is advisable to consult the instruction manual for these drives

to find the best way of
handling their BIOS
settings. As pointed
out previously, CD-
RW and DVD drives
are normally entered
into the BIOS as
normal CD-ROM
drives. A modern
operating system
such as Windows XP
should then
recognise and install
the drive, but only as
a simple CD-ROM
type. Some
additional software,

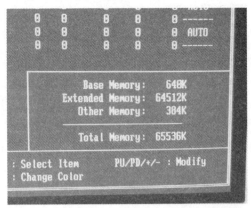

*Fig.12.9 The BIOS reports the memory it finds.
The user can not alter these settings*

which is usually but not always supplied with the drive, will be needed in
order to exploit the additional capabilities of these drives. When
upgrading it is a good idea to obtain a drive that comes complete with
some bundled software since the extra cost is minimal, and buying the
software separately can be quite expensive.

Other drives such as LS120 and Zip drives often have some specific
support in the BIOS. It may even be possible to boot from these devices,
although not necessarily with all operating systems. The instruction
manuals for the drives should give detailed instructions on how to
integrate them with any common BIOS.

Auto-only

There is a trend towards automatic detection with no manual override.
With the Phoenix-Award BIOS shown in Figure 12.8 the Page Up and
Page Down keys permit parameters such as the time and date to be
changed, but they have no effect on the IDE drive types. The BIOS
automatically detects the drives, displays its findings in the Standard
CMOS page, and sets the correct parameters. As most users opt for
automatic detection anyway, the lack of manual control is not likely to be
of any importance. On the other hand, if you should happen to use an
IDE device that the BIOS can not identify, it will probably be unusable
until a BIOS update becomes available.

Floppy drives

The next section in the "Standard CMOS Setup" is used to select the floppy disc drive type or types. All the normal types of floppy drive are supported, from the old 5.25-inch 360k drives to the rare 2.88M 3.5-inch type. You simply select the appropriate type for drives A and B. Select "None" for drive B if the computer has only one floppy drive. It used to be necessary for at least one floppy drive to be fitted, since most operating systems needed a drive of this type during the early stages of installation. This is not the case with modern operating systems, and many PCs now have no floppy drives at all. If this is the case, "None" must be entered for drives A and B.

In days gone by you had to enter the amount of memory fitted, but with a modern BIOS the amount of memory is automatically detected and entered into the CMOS RAM. The "Standard CMOS Setup" screen will report the amount of memory fitted, and will display something like Figure 12.9. It is unlikely that there will be any way of manually adjusting this setting.

As pointed out previously, there is no way of altering the memory settings if they are wrong. If the BIOS reports the wrong amount of RAM there is a fault in the memory circuits, and the correct amount will be reported if the fault is rectified. Sometimes what appears to be an error is just the way the amount of memory is reported by the BIOS. For those who are new to computing the way in which the amount of memory is reported can seem rather strange. It should look very familiar to those who can remember the early days of IBM compatible PCs. The original PCs had relatively simple processors that could only address one megabyte of RAM, but only the lower 640k of the address range were actually used for RAM. The upper 384k of the address range was used for the BIOS ROM, video ROM, and that sort of thing.

Modern PCs can address hundreds of megabytes of RAM, but the lowest one megabyte is still arranged in much the same way that it was in the original PCs. The BIOS therefore reports that there is 640k of normal (base) memory, so many kilobytes of RAM above the original one megabyte of RAM (extended memory), and 384k of other memory. This "other" memory is the RAM in the address space used by the BIOS, etc.

The final section of the standard Setup enables the type of video card to be specified, and the degree of error trapping to be selected. The BIOS will probably detect the video card and set the appropriate type, which for a modern PC will presumably be a EGA/VGA type. It might be possible

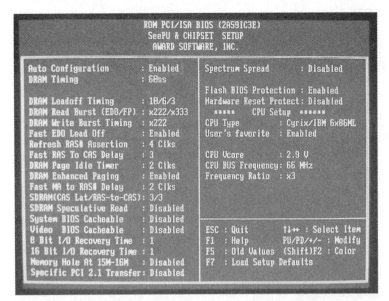

Fig.12.10 This screen provides control over the chipset features

to select the old CGA and mono adaptors, but these are obsolete and not used in modern PCs. The error trapping controls the way in which the computer responds to errors that are found during the BIOS self-testing routine at switch-on. The default of halt on all errors is probably the best choice, particularly when you are testing a new PC. Once the PC has been fully tested and is running properly you may prefer to alter this setting, but I would not bother.

Chipset

Setting up the standard CMOS parameters is probably all you will need to do in order to get the computer running properly, but it is a good idea to look at the options available in the other sections of the Setup program. There will be a section called something like Chipset Setup or Advanced Chipset Setup (Figure 12.10), which controls things such as the port and memory timing. There are so many parameters controlled by a modern BIOS that a multi-level menu system is sometimes used. In the example of Figure 12.11 the DRAM timing option produces the submenu of Figure 12.12. You can "play" with these settings in an attempt to

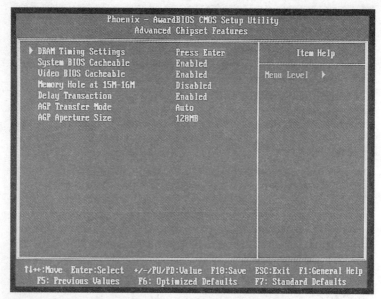

Fig.12.11 The Chipset Features menu might contain some submenus

obtain improved performance, but higher speed may well produce lower reliability. Results should be quite good if you simply leave this section with the auto configuration enabled.

If you make a complete "dogs breakfast" of these settings it is possible that the PC could become unusable. This is not as drastic as it sounds because you can always go back into the BIOS and select the default settings from the initial screen. There will probably be an option to return to the "old" settings, which usually means the settings saved prior to the last time the BIOS Setup program was used.

I suppose it is conceivable that changes made in the BIOS could render the computer unable to start up at all. I think that this is highly unlikely, but remember that the contents of the CMOS memory can always be wiped clean using the appropriate jumper on the motherboard. No matter how badly you scramble the BIOS settings it should always be possible to get back to the default settings and then "fine tune" things from there. If it is not possible to do so, the most likely cause is a hardware fault rather than something amiss with the BIOS settings.

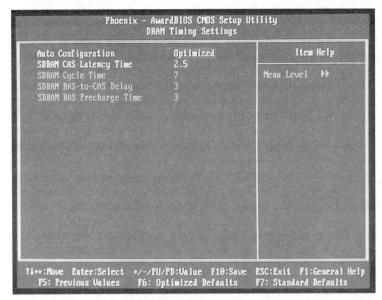

Fig.12.12 This is the DRAM Timings submenu

It is worth remembering that no changes are made to the settings unless you opt to save the changes when exiting the Setup program. If you know you have made a complete mess of things, simply exit the Setup program without saving the changes. The PC will then reboot, the Setup program can be entered again, and you can start from scratch with the changes.

Timing

If the PC is fitted with some form of SDRAM, which it almost certainly will be, one of the timing settings will be the SDRAM CAS Latency. The default setting will probably be suitable provided the Standard Default settings are used. If the Optimised Default settings are used, or a low figure is set manually, make sure that the DIMMs used are up to the task. Trying to use memory modules beyond their ratings is not usually successful and can produce major problems when running applications programs.

The AGP Aperture Size controls the amount of system memory that is set aside for use with a graphics adaptor for such things as texture storage. Of course, this parameter will not be included if the motherboard does not have an AGP slot, and modern motherboards mainly have the PCI Xpress type instead. There might still be an equivalent of this setting though. Anyway, where appropriate, the default value should be a sensible one for the amount of system memory installed in the PC and the amount of video memory fitted to the video card. There are various formulas for calculating the optimum setting, and you can try these if maximum video performance is important. In most cases any change in performance will be quite small.

The amount of memory allocated by default might seem to be large relative to the total amount of system memory. However, bear in mind that it is actually the maximum size that is being set. The actual amount of memory used depends on the video activity, and system memory is only used when it is essential to do so.

Cache

There are various BIOS address ranges listed or there may be just a list of BIOS names. There is the option of enabling or disabling shadowing of each one. By default the video BIOS will be shadowed, and possibly the video RAM as well, but the system BIOS and any others listed will probably not be cached. Shadowing of a BIOS is where it is copied into the computer's RAM and then run from there. The top 384k of the base memory is given over to the main BIOS, plus any other device that needs its own BIOS. In a modern PC this part of the memory map is occupied by RAM, but this RAM is normally disabled.

When shadowing is enabled, the relevant block of RAM is activated, and the contents of the BIOS at that address range are copied into it. The point of this is that the RAM is faster than the ROM used for the BIOS, and using shadowing should speed up operation of the video card. Usually the only peripheral that has its own BIOS is the video card, but shadowing of other parts of the top 384k of memory can be enabled if necessary. If you have a peripheral device that will benefit from this treatment its manual should say so, and specify the address range that must be shadowed.

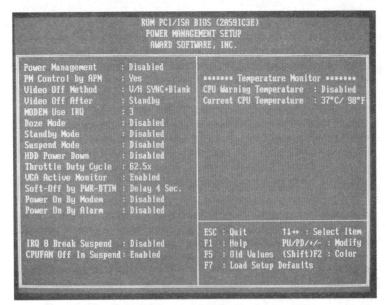

Fig.12.13 A typical Power Management Setup screen

Power Management

Most operating systems and all modern motherboards seem to support some form of power management facility. In other words, the computer goes into some form of standby mode if there is no mouse or keyboard activity for a certain period. Most motherboards can also be switched to and from a standby mode via a peripheral such as a modem, and this also comes under the general heading of power management. A modern BIOS usually has a section dealing solely with power management (Figure 12.13).

The Power Management Setup will probably be set to Disabled, and with some operating systems this is probably the best way to leave it. A lot of power management features can be controlled via the operating system these days, and you can sometimes get into a situation where the BIOS and the operating system are both trying to rule the power management roost. Where possible I totally disable this feature and only enable it if there is good reason to do so.

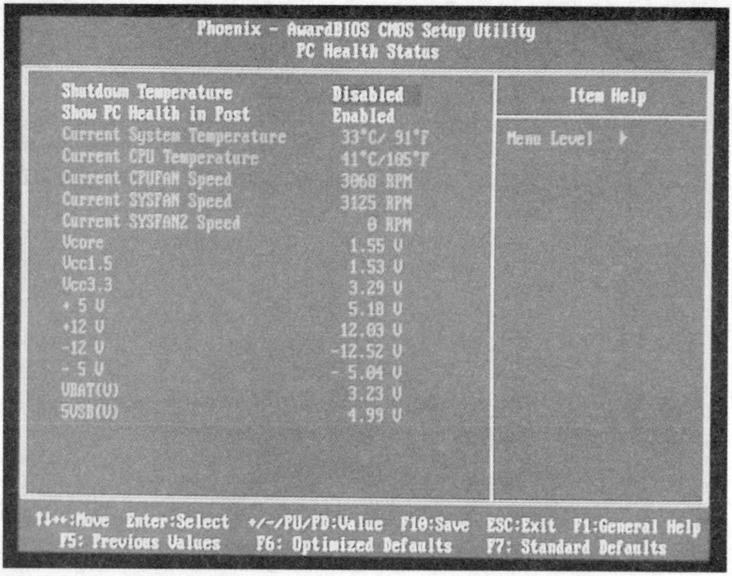

Fig.12.14 Voltages and temperatures can be monitored via the PC
          Health Status screen

These days it is not uncommon for the motherboard to support more
than one standby mode. The idea seems to be that the computer
progressively shuts down the longer it is left unused. It will typically go
from normal operation into the "doze" mode, followed by the "standby"
and "suspend" modes. Operating the mouse or keyboard should always
result in the computer returning directly to the "normal" mode, but it may
take a few seconds to become fully operational if the motor of the hard
disc has been switched off. Due to the high rotation speed of a hard
disc it takes several seconds for it to reach its normal operating speed.

The BIOS Setup program will probably permit adjustment of the delay
times before each standby mode is entered, plus other details such as
whether the processor fan is switched off when the "suspend" mode is
entered. Of course, all this type of thing is only relevant if the power
management feature is enabled. You may wish to "fine tune" the power
management feature at a later time, but when initially setting up a PC it is
probably best not to get deeply embroiled in this type of thing.

If the motherboard supports some form of external power management,
and you wish to use this feature, it will have to be enabled in this section

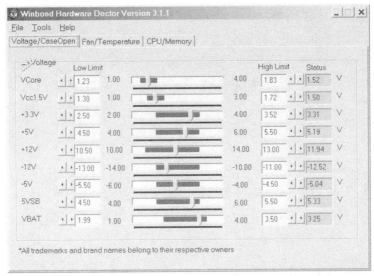

Fig.12.15 Many motherboards are supplied with a monitoring program that runs under Windows

of the BIOS. Any feature of this type is always disabled by default. Any feature of this type will, of course, only operate if it is properly supported by the peripheral device or devices, and any extra cabling that it needed is properly installed.

Monitoring

Most motherboards now support at least a basic over-temperature detection circuit for the processor, and there are often various CPU threshold temperatures that can be selected. Figure 12.14 shows a typical BIOS screen that provides temperature and voltage monitoring. This screen usually shows the system temperature (the temperature inside the PC's case) in addition to the processor's temperature and various operating voltages. If the CPU goes above the selected temperature a warning can be produced, and the PC usually shuts down as well. It is probably best to activate this feature and simply leave the threshold temperature at its default setting.

The normal operating temperature varies considerably from one type of processor to another. In general, the processor should operate below

241

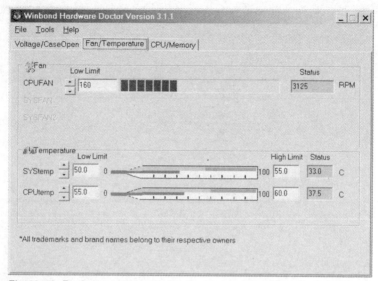

Fig.12.16 Further screens allow more parameters to be monitored

about 50 degrees Celsius. However, some AMD chips seem to operate quite happily at around 60 degrees while many Intel chips settle down at around 40 degrees or even less. Unless you know what you are doing it is not a good idea to alter the default alarm temperatures.

Note that many motherboards are supplied complete with so-called health monitoring software that enables parameters such as the CPU temperature, fan speeds, operating voltages, etc., to be monitored while running Windows. It is well worthwhile installing any bundled software of this type. Figure 12.15 shows the main window of the Winbond Hardware Doctor program while it is monitoring a Pentium 4-based PC. A range of voltages are measured by this window, including the core voltage of the processor and the main 5-volt supply.

Whether monitoring via the BIOS or a Windows program, do not be surprised if the measured voltages are slightly different to the nominal voltages. There is a tolerance of plus and minus 5 percent or more on most voltages, and the measuring circuits will produce small errors that effectively widen the tolerance ratings. Another window of the Hardware Doctor program enables the processor's temperature, the system

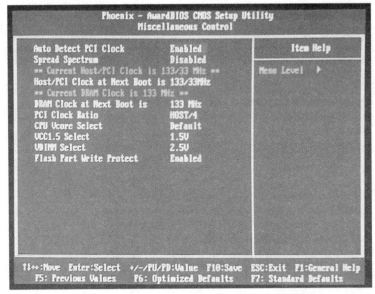

Fig.12.17 The CPU Settings menu of the Phoenix-Award BIOS

temperature, and the speed of the processor's fan to be monitored (Figure 12.16). Most of these monitoring programs can sound an alarm if (say) an excessive temperature is detected.

CPU settings

If the motherboard is one that uses software control to set the correct parameters for the PC there could be a separate page for this (Figure 12.17), but it is sometimes included in the chipset settings or in a miscellaneous section. The BIOS will automatically detect the processor type and should set the correct core voltage, bus frequency, and processor multiplier values. It is advisable to check that the BIOS has correctly identified the processor and set the correct values. It should be possible to set the correct figures manually if the BIOS makes a mistake, although it is very unlikely that it would do so. Otherwise, it should only be necessary to exercise manual control if over-clocking is to be tried. Over-clocking is taking the CPU and other components beyond their normal speed ratings in order to boost the computer's speed, and is only for those who possess the necessary expertise.

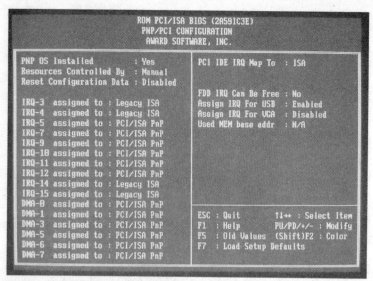

Fig.12.18 The PNP/PCI Configuration menu

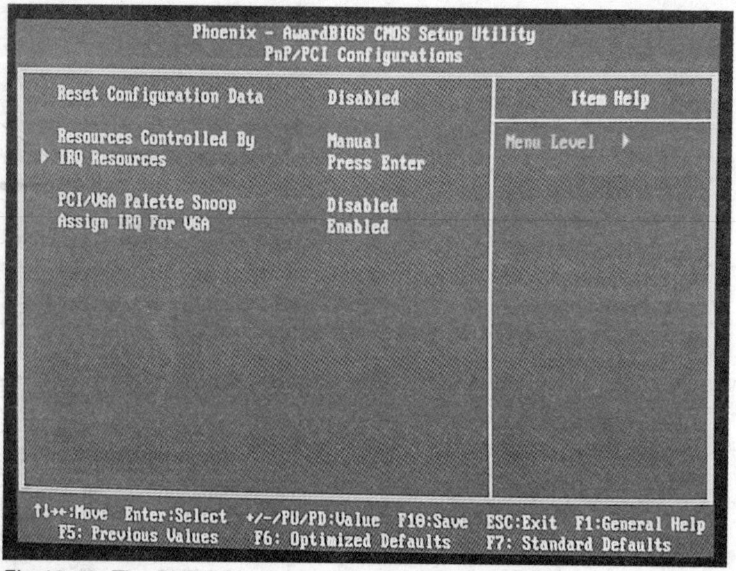

Fig.12.19 The PNP/PCI menu might rely on submenus

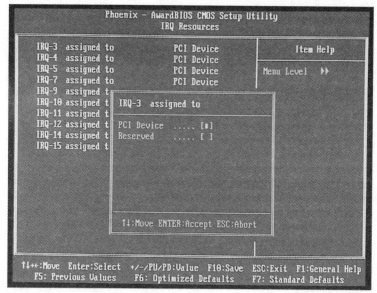

Fig.12.20 The IRQ Resources submenu

Note that any changes you make to the CPU settings may be ignored unless you activate an override setting. Also, with any modern Intel or AMD processor the motherboard will automatically set the correct multiplier value by reading information from the processor itself. It is not normally possible to set the multiplier manually even if the override setting is activated. The BIOS may seem to accept the new multiplier value, but when you exit the BIOS and reboot the computer it will operate with the multiplier value set by the chip.

PNP/PCI

Unless you know what you are doing it is not a good idea to mess around with the PNP/PCI settings (Figure 12.18). The initial screen might be lacking in options (Figure 12.19), but things like the IRQ assignments will be tucked away in submenus like the one of Figure 12.20. The defaults should work perfectly well anyway. There will be the option of selecting "Yes" if a PNP (Plug-N-Play) operating system is installed or "No" if a non-PNP type is installed. Windows 95 and 98 are PNP operating systems, and the obvious setting is "Yes" if you still use either of these. In practice

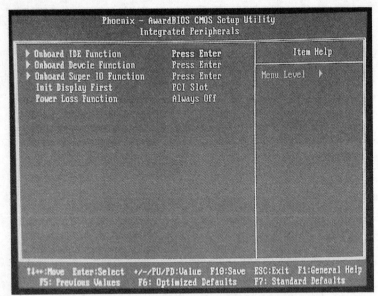

Fig.12.21 *The Integrated Peripherals menu will probably use submenus*

I have sometimes encountered problems if "Yes" is selected when using Windows 95. Assuming that a modern operating system such as Windows XP or Vista is used, there should be no problem if "Yes" is selected.

It should only be necessary to alter the IRQ (interrupt request) settings if there are problems with hardware conflicts. While this problem was not exactly unknown in the past, the widespread use of PCI expansion cards and USB external peripherals has greatly eased the problem. It is definitely not a good idea to alter these settings unless you know exactly what you are doing. With this type of thing it is much easier to make matters worse than it is to cure a problem.

Integrated Peripherals

The Integrated Peripherals section (Figure 12.21) provides some control over the on-board interfaces. In particular, it allows each port to be switched on or off, and in the case of the serial and parallel ports it also enables the port addresses and interrupt (IRQ) numbers to be altered.

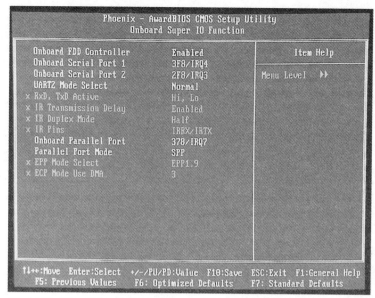

Fig.12.22 This is the Onboard Super IO Function submenu

This can be useful when trying to avoid conflicts with hardware fitted in the expansion slots, but is unlikely to be necessary with a modern PC. The number of integrated peripherals on current motherboards is such that the options in this section of the BIOS will largely be handled by sub-menus.

With the example BIOS the serial and parallel ports are covered by the Super IO submenu (Figure 12.22). Recent PCs tend not to have any serial ports, and some now lack a parallel port as well. There is a possibility of encountering a slight anomaly, with a PC that lacks serial and parallel ports, but still has BIOS entries for them! This could be an error in the BIOS, but it is more likely to be the result of the port hardware being present on the motherboard, but not implemented by the PC's manufacturer. In other words, the electronics for these ports is present on the motherboard, but no serial or parallel port connectors are included on the case. Making connections to them is therefore impossible, except where the necessary connectors and leads are available as optional extras.

Where the serial and parallel ports have an entry in the BIOS there will be various parallel port modes available, but with a modern BIOS it is

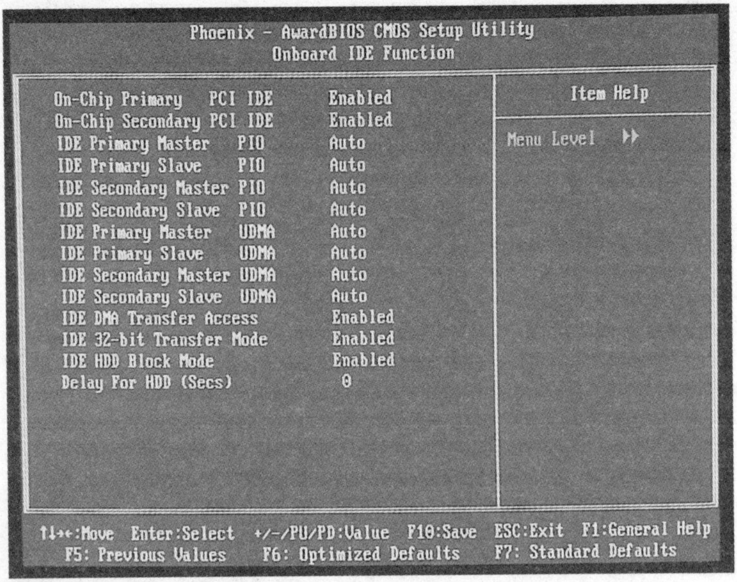

```
                 Phoenix - AwardBIOS CMOS Setup Utility
                         Onboard IDE Function

    On-Chip Primary   PCI IDE      Enabled           Item Help
    On-Chip Secondary PCI IDE      Enabled
    IDE Primary Master   PIO       Auto          Menu Level    ▶▶
    IDE Primary Slave    PIO       Auto
    IDE Secondary Master PIO       Auto
    IDE Secondary Slave  PIO       Auto
    IDE Primary Master   UDMA      Auto
    IDE Primary Slave    UDMA      Auto
    IDE Secondary Master UDMA      Auto
    IDE Secondary Slave  UDMA      Auto
    IDE DMA Transfer Access        Enabled
    IDE 32-bit Transfer Mode       Enabled
    IDE HDD Block Mode             Enabled
    Delay For HDD (Secs)           0



   ↑↓→←:Move  Enter:Select  +/-/PU/PD:Value  F10:Save  ESC:Exit  F1:General Help
      F5: Previous Values    F6: Optimized Defaults    F7: Standard Defaults
```

Fig.12.23 The Onboard IDE Function submenu. Automatic detection should set suitable operating modes

unlikely that there will be a Standard (output only) mode. The choices will probably be SPP, EPP, and ECP, which are all bi-directional modes. For most purposes either SPP or EPP will suffice. Only set ECP operation if you use the port with a device that definitely needs this mode. There might be further options, such as a mode that can provide both EPP and ECP operation, and a choice of ECP versions. It is unlikely to matter which version is selected, but the relevant one should obviously be selected if the instruction manual states that a peripheral requires a certain ECP version.

If the motherboard supports infrared communications it may be possible to switch serial port two (COM2) between normal operation and infrared operation. When set to infrared operation it is possible for the PC to communicate with suitably equipped notebook computers and digital cameras that support infrared communications. However, the correct hardware add-on is needed on COM2 before this cordless communication will be possible.

This dual role for serial port two seems to be less common these days and most motherboards now have entirely separate hardware to

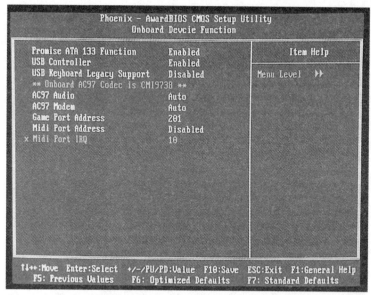

Fig.12.24 The Onboard Device Function menu. The Promise ATA 133 Function controls the built-in RAID controller

implement the IrDA facility. It is likely that the BIOS Setup program will give some control over the settings for this port, but simply accept the default settings. Only change the settings if this port is used with a piece of equipment that requires changes to be made. If any changes should be required, the instruction manual for the device concerned should explain exactly what needs to be altered.

Support for IrDA seems to be dwindling, presumably due to the increased use of alternatives such as Bluetooth. This method of interfacing never achieved much of a user-base. With a modern PC it is quite likely that there will be no support for it on the motherboard, and therefore no section for it in the BIOS Setup program. The BIOS Setup program might give the option of deactivating the parallel and serial/IrDA ports. It makes sense to do so if they are not actually implemented on the PC, or if they are simply not used.

The Onboard IDE Function submenu (Figure 12.23) enables the IDE controllers to be switched on and off and permits the modes to be set manually. Auto operation will be selected by default, and manual control should only be contemplated if the automatic mode selection fails for some reason. This is very unlikely to happen.

Onboard Device

The Onboard Device submenu (Figure 12.24) covers an assortment of onboard hardware. Many motherboards now have a built-in RAID interface with two additional IDE ports. This was once an expensive option, but it is a feature that is now found in quite low-cost motherboards. This means that your chosen motherboard may well come complete with a RAID interface that you do not actually need. It is unlikely that leaving the RAID hardware switched on will cause any major problems, but the boot process will be lengthened while the BIOS looks for absent drives on the RAID ports. It is therefore a good idea to switch off the RAID hardware if it is not needed.

If there is a built-in audio system there will probably be the option to disable it in this section of the BIOS. This should not be necessary unless a PCI soundcard will be used. In theory it should be possible to have both sound systems installed, but in practice there could be difficulties. Since having both audio systems installed is unlikely to bestow any advantages, it is advisable to disable the built-in sound circuits. Similarly, it is probably best to disable the integral USB ports if a USB expansion card is used instead for some reason. It is possible to add more USB ports to a PC by adding a USB card, but in practice this can be problematic. Using a powered USB hub to expand an existing USB port is likely to be a cheaper and less troublesome way of handling things.

It is only necessary to alter the game and MIDI port addresses and the MIDI port IRQ setting in the event that hardware conflicts occur. This is unlikely to be a problem with a modern PC. Note that the MIDI port is often disabled by default. This is a common cause of problems, with users finding that they can not output data to the MIDI port. Indeed, with the port disabled it will not be listed by Windows as an output option. If you are going to use the MIDI port or might use it in the future, it is a good idea to enable it from the outset.

The MIDI port used to be part of the PC's Game port, but this was the first of the so called "legacy" ports to be phased out. The serial and parallel ports are the other two "legacy" types. Consequently, a MIDI port is is unlikely to have an entry in the BIOS Setup program of a modern PC, because the PC is unlikely to actually have a port of this type.

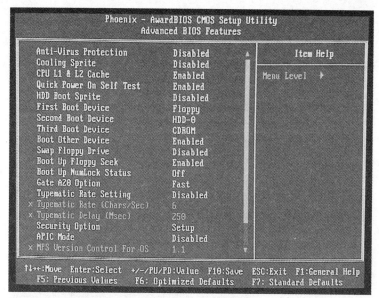

Fig.12.25 The Advanced BIOS Features menu

BIOS Features Setup

The BIOS Features Setup (Figure 12.25) controls some useful features, but once again the default settings should suffice. Note that the larger menus, which will probably include this one, can not show all the settings simultaneously. A sort of scrollbar appears down the right-hand edge of the section that contains the settings, and this indicates which section of the page is being displayed. It is not possible to scroll the page using the scrollbar and the mouse. The up and down cursor keys are used to do this. Figure 12.26 shows the scrolled version of the BIOS Features Setup screen. Once into the menu system, the right-hand panel of the screen indicates the current menu level.

Returning to the BIOS features, the internal and external caches must be enabled if the computer is to operate at full speed. There are various boot sequence options, and eventually you might like to select C Only. In the meantime the boot sequence must include drive A if Windows 95, 98, or ME is to be installed on the PC. This is the drive that the computer must boot from until drive C is made bootable. It is advisable to have drive A as the first boot drive when undertaking a major upgrade that

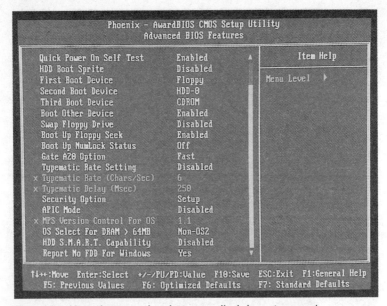

Fig.12.26 Here the menu has been scrolled down to reveal
further options

involves reinstalling the operating system from scratch, such as replacing
the main hard disc drive. There is otherwise a slight risk that the boot
process will stall when the BIOS tries to boot from a blank hard disc
drive.

Most other operating systems, including Linux and Windows XP, can be
and normally are installed from a bootable CD-ROM. Any modern BIOS
should have the option to use the CD-ROM drive as a boot drive, and
this option must be selected if you intend to use this method of installation.

The drives might be referred to as A, B, C, etc., in the BIOS Setup program,
but these days different terminology is often used. In the example BIOS
the hard drives are referred to as HDD-0, HDD-1, etc. Assuming drive C
is the hard disc that will be used as a boot drive, it is HDD-0 (not HDD-1).
To avoid possible confusion, this drive should be used as the master
drive on the primary IDE interface.

Other drives are referred to by suitable names, such as CD-ROM, Floppy,
and ZIP-100. If there are two of these drives of the same type, the BIOS
will probably try to boot from the drive with the highest priority and ignore

the other one. The primary IDE interface is searched first, followed by the secondary IDE interface. As one would expect, the master drive takes precedence over the slave device on the same interface.

If this option is present, make sure that the IDE HDD Block Mode is enabled, because the hard disc performance will be relatively poor if it is not. In a modern BIOS this function might be in the Onboard IDE Function submenu. After boot-up the NumLock key is normally on, but there is an option that enables it to be switched off after boot-up. Unfortunately, this useful option has apparently been omitted from some recent BIOS Setup programs.

Floppyless

There are usually several options relating to the floppy disc drive or drives. One of these enables drives A and B to be swapped over. I am not sure why it would ever be necessary to have drive A operate as drive B and vice versa, but this facility is there if you should need it. Although at one time a floppy disc drive was an essential part of a PC, this is no longer the case. Other forms of removable disc are available, and with modern operating systems it is now possible to install the system from a bootable CD-ROM. This removes the need to boot initially from a floppy disc.

This makes it possible to have a PC that lacks a floppy disc drive, and most modern PCs fall into this category. The problem with leaving out the floppy disc drive is that the BIOS will produce an error message each time that the computer is booted. There should be an option called something like Floppy Seek or Boot Up Floppy Seek, and by disabling this option the BIOS will not check for a floppy drive, and the error message will be suppressed. In some cases there might be a setting called something like Report No FDD for Windows, and could be necessary to set this to No as well.

The Rest

Other sections of the BIOS Setup program allow you to select a user password that must be entered before the PC will boot-up, load standard or optimised default settings, save the new settings and exit, or exit without saving any changes to the settings. Being able to load the standard set of default settings is clearly useful if you experiment a little too much and end up with totally unsuitable settings. It is worth repeating that no settings are actually altered unless you select the Save and Exit option. If you accidentally change some settings and do not know how to restore the correct ones, simply exiting without saving the new settings will leave everything untouched. You can then enter the Setup program again and have another try.

Flash upgrade

If you look through the specifications for motherboards you will often encounter something like "Flash upgradeable BIOS" or just "Flash BIOS". In days gone by the only way of upgrading the BIOS was to buy a new chip, or pair of chips as it was in those days. Some of the ROMs used to store the BIOS were actually re-programmable, but only by removing them from the PC and putting them into a programmer unit. This was not a practical proposition for most users. New BIOS chips were very difficult to obtain and you were usually stuck with the BIOS supplied with the motherboard.

The rate at which modern computing changes makes it beneficial to upgrade the BIOS from time to time in order to keep PCs up to date, and not just to accommodate a major upgrade such as a change of processor. The BIOS sometimes has to be updated to cure compatibility problems with certain items of hardware. There could even be one or two minor bugs in the original BIOS.

With a modern BIOS there is no need to replace the BIOS ROM chip or to remove it from the motherboard for reprogramming. The ROM for a modern BIOS can be electronically erased and reprogrammed while it is still on the motherboard. This is why it is possible to download a new BIOS and a "blower" program and upgrade the BIOS. Of course, an upgrade of this type is dependent on the motherboard having the BIOS in Flash memory. However, there is little likelihood of a new motherboard lacking support for the Flash method of upgrading the BIOS. It is many years since I last used a motherboard that lacks this facility.

Write protection

If you get an error message such as "Flash type unrecognised" during the upgrade, this does not mean that the BIOS is a non-reprogrammable type. It usually just means that the Flash memory is write-protected, making it impossible for the upgrade program to alter its contents. Write protection is used as a means of preventing viruses and other malicious programs from corrupting the BIOS and rendering the PC unusable. It

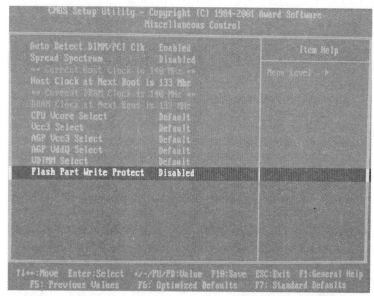

Fig.12.27 The BIOS can not be upgraded unless write protection is disabled

would be prudent to check for write-protection before trying to upgrade the BIOS.

The manual for your PC or its motherboard should give instructions for disabling this facility. In some cases the write protection is provided via a switch or jumper on the motherboard. These days it is more usual for this facility to be controlled via a setting in the BIOS itself (Figure 12.27), but you may have to do some searching to find the appropriate menu. There should be no difficulty in upgrading the BIOS once the write-protection has been switched off. Having completed the upgrade it is a good idea to enable this facility again, so that the BIOS is protected from attack.

Risk factor

It is only fair to point out that a BIOS upgrade is a bit risky. For a start, you need to be absolutely certain that the data file you are using is the correct one for your motherboard. Using the wrong BIOS data file could easily render the computer unusable, and if it will not boot-up correctly it is impossible to restore the original BIOS.

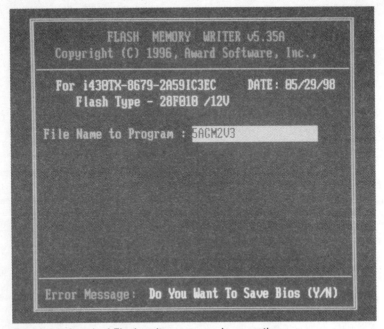

Fig.12.28 A typical Flash writer program in operation

Another slight worry is that a power failure during the upgrade could leave the PC with a BI (half a BIOS)! With an incomplete or corrupted BIOS it is unlikely that the PC could be rebooted to restore the original or complete the upgrade. It only takes a few seconds to carry out the upgrade, so you would be very unlucky indeed if a power failure interrupted the process, but there is a slight risk. A serious error when upgrading the BIOS could necessitate the fitting of a complete new motherboard.

The upgrade program usually has to be run from MS-DOS, and is very simple to operate (Figure 12.28). After you have supplied the name of the data file for the new BIOS (including any extension to the filename) the program should give the option of saving the existing BIOS onto disc. It is as well to do this so that you can revert to the original BIOS if the new version proves to be troublesome. After you have confirmed that you wish to continue with the upgrade the new data will be written to the BIOS ROM chip. Do not touch the computer during the flash upgrade, just stand back and let the upgrade program get on with it. The computer is then ready for rebooting and checking to see if the new BIOS has the desired effect.

Boot disc

The boot disc used when upgrading has to be a very basic type that does not run some form of memory management software such as EMM386. Making a suitable boot disc from a system running Windows XP or Vista is very straightforward. Place a blank disc in the floppy drive, launch Windows Explorer, and then locate drive A in Windows Explorer. Right-click on the entry for drive A and select the Format option from the pop-up menu. This produces the window for the Format program. Tick the Create an MS-DOS Startup Disc checkbox and then operate the Start button. A warning message will probably appear, pointing out that any data on the disc will be lost. Operate the Yes button to continue and create the boot disc. Exactly the same method is used to make a boot disc when running Windows Vista,

When the formatting has been completed, copy the BIOS data file and upgrade program to the floppy disc. Leave the disc in the floppy drive and restart the computer. With luck the floppy drive will be used as the boot drive and you will be ready to proceed with the upgrade once the boot process has been completed. It is possible that the computer will simply boot into Windows. This occurs because the floppy drive is not set as the first boot disc in the BIOS. The BIOS therefore looks for the hard drive first, finds it, and then boots into Windows as normal. Restart the PC, go into the BIOS and set the floppy as the first boot disc, then save the changes and exit the BIOS Setup program. The computer should then boot into MS/DOS using the floppy disc in drive A.

Unfortunately, the Windows ME Format program does not provide a boot disc option. It is possible to make a Startup disc via the Control Panel and the Add/Remove Programs facility. However, this option results in various utilities being placed on the disc, and some of these could interfere with the upgrade process. Make sure that the Minimal Boot option is selected from the boot options menu during the initial boot process, and the memory management programs, etc., will not be run. It should then be safe to go ahead with the BIOS upgrade.

Switches

Most BIOS upgrade programs allow certain switches to be added after the command name. For example, it is possible to specify the file containing the data for the new version of the BIOS. Another common option is one that clears the CMOS memory of all the BIOS settings. It is generally considered advisable to use this switch, since some of the original settings might be inappropriate to the new BIOS. Using this switch means that the BIOS will have no setting when the PC is restarted, and you must enter the Setup program so that the Load Setup Defaults option can be selected. If necessary, the defaults can then be "fine tuned" to suit your requirements. The date and time will have to be reset, but this can be done from the Windows Control Panel.

If the BIOS has been updated correctly a new BIOS version number and date should be displayed on the initial screen at start-up. It is also likely that Windows will detect that there has been a change and respond with various messages to the effect that new hardware has been detected. Actually, it is just detecting the same old hardware and reinstalling the drivers for it. The change in BIOS presumably fools Windows into "thinking" that a different motherboard has been installed. Once this reinstallation has been completed the computer should perform much the same as it did before.

Some motherboards are supplied with a Windows program that permits the BIOS to be easily updated. In fact most motherboards now seem to be supplied with a program of this type. Since many PCs now lack a floppy disc drive, the earlier method of booting from a floppy disc is often inapplicable, making an alternative essential. Anyway, a facility that enables the BIOS upgrade to be performed from within the operating system should make the process much simpler and easier, but as always with a BIOS upgrade, make sure that the manufacturer's instructions are followed "to the letter".

13

Modems

Hard and soft

A modem used to be a strictly a device for communicating via an ordinary telephone connection. These days broadband is gaining in popularity, and low-cost ADSL services are proving to be very popular. In fact cable and telephone broadband services are now more popular than the dial-up variety. Many users still have ordinary telephone modems though, and these will be covered first. Telephone modems are available in two basic types, which are external USB, and internal PCI card modems.

Internal modems are offered in two types, which are the software and hardware varieties. These do not look much different (Figure 9.1 and 9.2 respectively), but software modems have relatively simple hardware.

Fig.13.1 A software modem uses relatively simple hardware, leaving the software to do most of the work

*Fig.13.2 A hardware modem places little loading on the processor.
All external modems are hardware types incidentally*

They are really just soundcards, and software is used to provide the encoding and decoding. The drivers for a software modem are therefore rather more than normal Windows drivers. There are often two or three sets of drivers, so make sure that all the necessary drivers are installed. A hardware modem uses the hardware to provide the encoding, decoding, and error correction.

Both types of modem are capable of excellent results, but the hardware type tends to be held in higher regard. I suppose that hardware modems are much less demanding on the PC, leaving plenty of processing power for applications programs. Software modems will only work at all with a suitably powerful PC, but the minimum specification is usually very low by current standards, so this should not be a problem.

Horse to water

Physically installing a modem is usually quite straightforward, and you can use a USB type if you would prefer not to open up the PC and install a PCI type. Installing the drivers supplied with the modem should not provide any problems either. Getting the modem to do something useful once it is installed is perhaps more troublesome. In general this is not as difficult as it used to be, but things can still go wrong, and occasionally do. Problems with software provided by an ISP are best sorted out by the customer support department of the ISP. They should be aware of any common problems with their installation software, and the easiest ways of sorting things out.

No dialling tone

An error message along the lines of "no dialling tone detected" is not an uncommon problem. Obviously this can occur because there is genuinely no dialling tone present, but this is not necessarily the cause of the problem. It is easy to check this point by picking up the telephone and listening for the usual dialling tone. There is probably a minor problem

with the lead from the modem to the telephone wall socket if the dialling tone is present and correct.

Try disconnecting and reconnecting the lead at both the modem and the telephone socket. If an extension lead is in use, disconnect and reconnect this as well. Make sure that all the plugs are properly locked into the sockets. The connectors used for

Fig.13.3 The two styles of telephone plug

telephones and modems are quick and easy to use, but they are not the toughest of components. Leads tend to get kicked around and tripped over, and the connectors are damaged occasionally. Look carefully at all the connectors and replace any leads that have a seriously damaged plug or socket.

The connection to the telephone socket is via a standard BT plug, but the connection to the modem is by way of a smaller American style telephone plug. Both types of plug are shown in Figure 13.3. The American style plugs and sockets seem to be something less than rigidly standardised, or perhaps some of them are made to rather low standards. Some plugs do not lock into the sockets properly, while others are difficult to fit into place at all. Unfortunately, a few seem to fit into place perfectly but do not make reliable connections.

When installing a new modem or PC it is normal to use the existing lead to connect the modem to the telephone socket. However, this can give problems and it is safer to make the connection to the modem via the lead supplied with the modem or PC. This should be a good and reliable match for the socket fitted to the modem. On the other hand, if the lead supplied with the modem does not work, try another lead. Mistakes can be made, and it is possible that a lead for a mainland European country or the USA has been supplied instead of a UK lead.

A faulty modem can sometimes result in the telephones on the system failing to work properly. Typically, as soon as the modem is plugged into the wall socket the telephones on the same circuit ring until the modem is disconnected again. This can also be caused by a faulty cable or one of the wrong type. Cables for use in America and Europe will not give the correct set of connections between the modem and socket and will often produce this fault. Once again, it is a matter of using the cable provided with the modem wherever possible and making sure that any extension cables are of the correct type. Try another cable if the one supplied with the modem seems to be of the wrong type.

ADSL

Having a broadband Internet connection installed by one of the ISP's engineers is a very easy way to get everything installed. In theory anyway, you simply sit back while it is installed and then start surfing the Internet at high speed. The big drawback is that it tends to be quite costly, and most small business and home users now opt for the do-it-yourself approach, or "self installed broadband as it is known. An engineer still has to test the line from the telephone exchange to your premises to ensure that the line quality is adequate, and some changes have to be made to your connection to the exchange. However, the cost of these services is relatively low, and are sometimes waived by the ISP.

Provided you live close enough to a broadband equipped exchange and the line quality proved to be adequate, you are then ready to install the equipment at your end of the system. First a microfilter (Figure 13.4) must be added at each telephone socket in the house. These are now very cheap and the cost should be quite low even if there are several sockets to contend with. Note that a microfilter is needed at every socket including any where an ADSL modem will not be used.

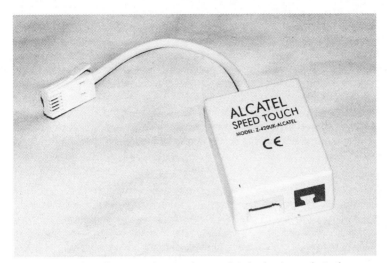

Fig.13.4 A microfilter must be used at each telephone socket when a broadband Internet connection is installed

The purpose of a microfilter is to mix the high frequency broadband signal with the audio signal from the telephones connected to the system. It also ensures that the two types of equipment do not interfere with each other. One socket on the filter takes an ordinary BT telephone plug, and the telephone is plugged into this socket. The other socket is smaller and this is the one that connects to the modem, which should be supplied with a suitable lead. A huge advantage of ADSL is that it can carry the Internet connection while the telephone is in use.

ADSL modems are mainly in the form of external USB devices, like the example shown in G.28 of the Colour Gallery, but PCI types are also available. There are also external types that have a standard 10/100 Ethernet port, and some have the option of using a USB or Ethernet connection (see G29 in the Colour Gallery). The internal PCI and external USB types are both installed and set up in more or less standard fashion. Of course, if your ISP provides a modem and a Setup disc as part of the deal, you should follow their installation instructions and use their installation software. This might largely automate the installation process.

Modern versions of Windows have wizards to help with the creation of a new Internet connection. Windows XP is used in this example,and it is the New Connection Wizard that is needed. This is accessed by going to the Start menu and then selecting All Programs, Accessories,

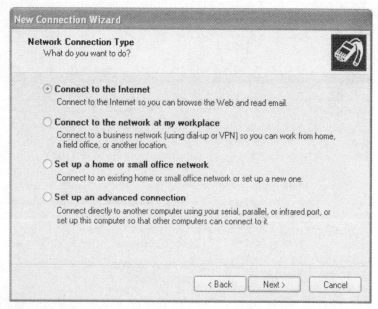

Fig.13.5 Choose the default option (Connect to the Internet)

Communications, and Network Connections. Here the existing network and (or) Internet connections are listed. Left-click the Create new connection link near the top left-hand corner of the window, which will launch the New Connection Wizard. Then operate the Next button to move on to the first set of options (Figure 13.5). Here the default option, Connect to the Internet, is required. At the next window the bottom option can be used if you have a suitable Setup disc, but in most cases the Manual option has to be selected.

Operating the Next button then moves things on to the window of Figure 13.6. On the face of it, either the middle or bottom option should be selected, as these are both for DSL connections. However, most do-it-yourself ADSL connections are actually treated as normal dial-up types. Unless your ISP recommends otherwise, it is therefore the top option that is selected. The next window will look like the one of Figure 13.7 if there is more than one modem installed in the PC. It is a good idea to leave the ordinary modem in place when upgrading to ADSL. It can be used to provide emergency Internet access via a "pay as you go" Internet service, and it will still be needed if faxes have to be sent or received.

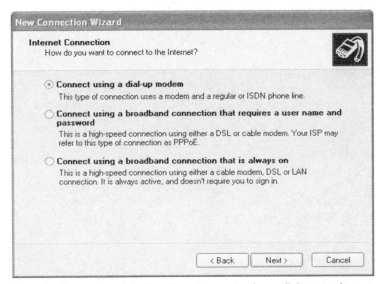

Fig.13.6 Accept the default option, Connect using a dial-up modem

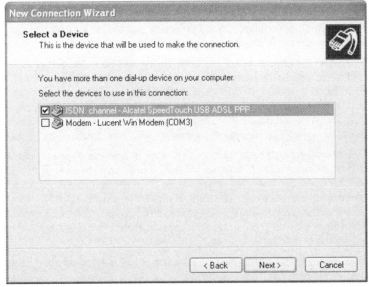

Fig.13.7 Select the appropriate modem, which is the ADSL type

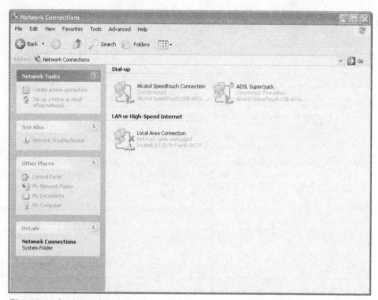

Fig.13.8 An icon for the new connection will appear in the Network Connections window

Anyway, the new connection will obviously use the new ADSL modem, and the appropriate checkbox must be ticked.

A name for the new connection is added in the textbox of the next window, and this is usually the name of the service provider, but any name can be used here. The next window asks for the ISPs telephone number to be added in the textbox, but with an ADSL connection there is no telephone number. It is probably best to add some random numbers here since the Wizard might be reluctant to move on unless a number is added.

Operating the Next button moves on to a window where your user name and password must be entered. These should have been supplied to you by your ISP, and it is not possible to produce a dial-up Internet connection without them. The three checkboxes provide useful options, and if necessary the default settings should be amended. Unless firewall software will be used to protect the system from hackers it is advisable to use the built-in firewall protection of Windows XP.

That more or less completes the creation of the new connection. The next window has a checkbox that gives the option of creating a desktop shortcut to the new connection. Operate the Finish button to create the

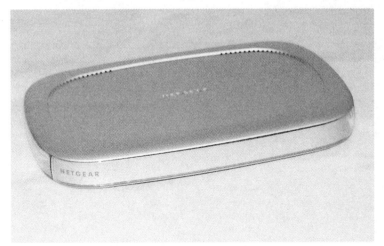

Fig.13.9 A combined router and ADSL broadband modem

new Internet connection. Enter your user name and password at the next window, and try out the new connection. If you did not opt to have a shortcut placed on the desktop, the new connection can be activated by double-clicking on its icon in the Network Connections window (Figure 13.8). The Windows Copy and Paste facilities can be used to copy this shortcut to the desktop.

Modem/router

Probably the most popular means of sharing a broadband connection between a few computers is to use a combined modem and router, such as the one shown in Figure 13.9. A router has several Ethernet sockets, and these connect to the various PCs in the system. In the example shown in G.30 of the Colour Gallery there are four Ethernet sockets on the rear panel. There is also a telephone socket which is connected to a telephone wall socket via a microfilter. A combined modem and router is used in a standard network, but with the important difference that any PC connected to the router is automatically provided with Internet access. It is possible to obtain much the same effect using a separate router and broadband modem, but combining the two units gives a neater solution.

Things can be taken a stage further with a combined broadband modem, router, and wi-fi access point (see G.31 in the Colour Gallery). A unit of this type is used in essentially the same fashion as a combined modem and router, but it can also be used with wi-fi enabled PCs. The wi-fi approach is especially useful with portable PCs, but a lack of connecting wires is also a convenient way of doing things with desktop PCs. There is insufficient space available here to cover the subject of wi-fi and broadband, but it is covered in detail in the book Wireless Networking with Broadband Explained (BP592) from the same publisher and author as this publication.

Troubleshooting

Prevention

Provided you proceed carefully, checking and double-checking everything as you go, and observing the basic anti-static handling precautions, you will be very unlucky indeed if the upgraded computer fails to start up correctly. This is true even when undertaking a massive upgrade such as replacing the motherboard, processor, and memory, and when building a PC from scratch. However meticulous you are though, there is still an outside chance that things will not go perfectly. Should you take an "it will be all right on the night" approach to things it is likely that the outcome will be far from all right when the new PC is switched on.

This is definitely something where the old adage that "prevention is better than cure" applies. Most computer components are reasonably idiot-proof, and if an error should be made it is unlikely that any damage will occur. This possibility can not be totally ruled out though, and there is a small but real risk of mistakes proving to be quite costly. Check everything as you go along, and then carefully recheck the finished PC before switching it on.

If possible, get someone to check everything for you. Having fooled yourself into making a mistake it is easy to make the same mistake when you check the finished unit. It can be difficult to find someone willing and able to help with this type of thing, but it is worth making the effort to find someone. The mistake is often glaringly obvious to a fresh pair of eyes.

With any fault-finding it is important not to jump to conclusions. When you have, for instance, just replaced a video card, it is natural to suspect that the new card is faulty or has not been installed correctly. The replaced component is certainly the prime suspect, but it is easy to accidentally dislodge connectors in one part of a computer while working on a different part. It makes sense to check that there is nothing amiss with the newly installed component, but do not overlook the fact that the problem could easily lay elsewhere.

Try again

With a major upgrade you will probably have dismantled and rebuilt so much of the computer that checking for errors in the work you have just done will mean checking most of the computer. With a more minor upgrade it is possible to initially concentrate your efforts on a restricted part of the computer. For example, if you have installed a new PCI card in an expansion slot, the obvious starting point is to check that the card is properly installed. Give the card a close visual inspection to ensure that it is fitted in its slot correctly, and press it into place again to make sure that it is fully pushed down into place. Essentially the same thing can be done with practically any upgrade, making sure that any newly fitted connectors are genuinely connecting, and are not half-way into place with none of the metal contacts actually making physical or electrical contact.

If that fails to cure the problem, try reversing the upgrade and taking the computer back to its previous state. This might not be very practical in the case of a major upgrade, but it is advisable to do so in cases where it is a realistic proposition. The upgrade is almost certainly the cause of the problem if the computer works perfectly when restored to its previous state. It is then a matter of trying again, carefully reinstalling the upgrade, making sure that everything is exactly as it should be. If you did not bother to read any manufacturer's installation instructions the first time, it would be advisable to do so before reinstalling the upgrade. It is surprising just how often an upgrade that failed the first time works perfectly when it is reinstalled.

Matters are more difficult if the restored computer fails to work properly. The most likely cause of the problem is that a connector has been dislodged while working on the computer, or something of that ilk. It is possible that you have damaged some part of the computer while working on it, but this is unlikely if you have proceeded carefully, taking any necessary anti-static handling precautions, etc. It is also possible, if unlikely, that the computer has developed a fault, and that it is just coincidence that it happened at the time you installed an upgrade. Anyway, it becomes a matter of using general fault-finding techniques to locate the cause of the problem.

Blank expression

A faulty PC may start to go through the initial start-up routine and then fail at some stage, usually after the initial BIOS checks as the computer goes into the boot-up phase. Alternatively it may simply refuse to do anything, or sit there on the desk producing "beeping" noises with a blank screen. We will start by considering likely causes if the computer does very little, or even nothing whatsoever.

If switching on the PC results in nothing happening at all, with no sign of cooling fans operating or front panel lights switching on, the obvious first step is to check that power is getting to the computer. Is the power lead plugged in properly at both the computer and the mains outlet, and is the mains supply switched on at the outlet? It is a silly mistake to forget to plug the computer into the mains supply or to switch on the supply, but it is easily done in your haste to try out the new PC. Also check that the fuse in the mains plug is present and correct.

Overload

A PC power supply is a fairly sophisticated piece of electronics that contains numerous protection circuits. The fact that it fails to operate even though it is receiving power does not necessarily mean that it is faulty. It could simply be that a protection circuit is detecting a problem somewhere and is shutting down the supply circuit. An overload on one of the supply lines could cause this, and an overload is a definite possibility when an upgrade has just been installed.

There is a greater risk of an overload with certain types of upgrade. Short-circuits can occur when an expansion card is not fitted into its slot correctly, and this will usually result in the power supply unit immediately cutting out at switch-on. Where the upgrade involved fitting an expansion card, try removing and refitting the card, even if you have already done so. Make sure that the card is fully pushed down into its expansion slot. Another possible cause is that the upgrade has resulted in an increase in power consumption that is resulting in the power supply being overloaded. Any internal upgrade that involves adding something to a PC is almost certain to produce a significant increase in the loading on the power supply.

Less obviously, an upgrade that involves replacing an existing component with an improved one can also result in a substantial increase in power consumption. For example, where a run-of-the-mill video card is replaced by the latest super-fast type, the new card will have powerful on-board processing that the original card lacked. These on-board processing circuits will require additional power, and quite possibly large amounts of it. It should also be borne in mind that an external upgrade can result in an increase in the load placed on the power supply. Many Firewire and USB devices draw power from the computer, and although the maximum that can be drawn is not very great (10 watts for USB 2.0 devices), it could be a case of "the last straw that broke the camel's back".

If the computer works fine without an upgrade fitted, but it fails to power-up when it is installed, there is a strong possibility that the problem is insufficient power for the new hardware. This is not the only possibility, and the new hardware could be faulty. Ideally it should be tried in another PC to see if it fares any better in a different setup. A lack of power is the likely cause of the problem if the new hardware works perfectly in another PC. Another approach is to temporarily disconnect some non-essential hardware in the upgraded PC. For example, disconnecting any CD-ROM or DVD drives from the motherboard and the power supply should significantly reduce the drain on the power supply. If this results in the computer springing into life, then it seems certain that the problem is due to the power supply having an inadequate rating. A supply with a higher power rating will then have to be installed in place of the current unit.

Leads

Another possible cause is that the leads carrying the output of the supply are not connected properly. With the old AT power supplies it is possible to get the two supply connectors swapped at the motherboard, but this is not possible with modern PC supply units due to their single main power connector. In theory, with a single connector it is impossible to get things wrong, but in practice this type of power connector can be difficult to get properly into place. In fact this applies to most types of power connector, and I suppose it is a byproduct of making the connectors fit very firmly together so that good connections are produced.

It is worth removing and refitting the power connector to the motherboard to make quite sure that it is fully pressed down and into place. These connectors lock into place, a connector is not fitted properly if you can free it without releasing the locking mechanism. In normal use an ATX power supply is switched on and off via a simple pushbutton switch on the front of the case, and not by way of a conventional on/off switch in the mains supply. Check that the on/off switch is connected to the motherboard correctly. Fitting the leads that connect vaious items on the case to the motherboard tends to be rather fiddly, and mistakes are easily made when installing these leads, and once in place they are easily dislodged.

If the PC uses a motherboard that requires one or two supplementary power leads, make sure that these are both connected to the motherboard correctly. The larger of the two additional connectors is normally left unused with modern Pentium 4 motherboards, but it is advisable to check this point and not make assumptions. An ordinary 20-pin power connector can only be used with a 24-pin connector on the motherboard if the instruction manual states that this is acceptable, or the appropriate adaptor is used.

AMD approved

Occasionally there is a problem with a PC that seems to power-up correctly, but does not go into the POST routine. In fact the PC will usually start correctly on some occasions, but not on others, with the fault occurring randomly. This seems to occur more with PCs based on AMD processors than those having Intel chips. It possibly stems from a problem with the power supply, which is probably failing to establish the main supplies with suitable rapidity, or perhaps there is some initial noise on the supply lines that is causing problems.

Anyway, whatever the cause, you either have to learn to live with the problem or try fitting a new supply. When building a PC or upgrading to one based on an AMD processor it is advisable to obtain a power supply that is AMD approved. This should avoid these start-up problems. Also, if the supply should fail to work properly with a motherboard fitted with an AMD processor, you then have good grounds for complaint.

If the mains supply seems to be getting through to the power supply unit all right, and the on/off switch, motherboard and power supply are all connected together correctly, it is time to look further afield for the problem. It is unlikely that a faulty drive is causing an overload, but it is as well to check this by disconnecting the drive power and data cables.

It is worth making the point that you should not disconnect and reconnect any leads with the computer switched on. Doing so with power or data leads could result in costly damage, with you creating more faults than you fix! If any changes to the cabling are required, switch off the computer, make the changes, and then switch on again. Ideally the drive data cables should also be disconnected when making this test. With no power supplied to the drives they could provide abnormal loading on the data cables and could conceivably cause damage to the motherboard, although the chances of this occurring are admittedly quite remote.

Cutting out

As pointed out previously, it is possible that the problem is simply that the power supply is overloaded. This is very unlikely to happen provided the supply has a rating of at least 450 watts, but it is a real possibility with a low-cost supply rated at around 300 to 350 watts. Actually, a supply that has a genuine rating of 350 watts is usually adequate, but some supply units seem to be rated rather optimistically. Of course, if you are massively upgrading a PC, fitting it with the latest superfast processor and video card, adding more drives, and so on, do not expect a supply rated at 350 to 400 watts to be adequate. A supply having a rating of at least 450 to 500 will probably be needed. With this type of thing, fitting the most powerful supply you can find is probably the best approach.

An overloaded power supply may not simply result in the PC refusing to start. In my experience it is more likely that the PC will start up all right but it will tend to sporadically reset or switch off for no apparent reason. The power drain varies from one instant to another depending on what the PC is actually doing. Presumably one of the supply rails drops to an inadequate level during peaks of power consumption, causing the PC's monitoring circuits to reset or switch off the computer. Anyway, if a PC behaves in this fashion after an upgrade has been installed, and no other cause can be found, it is quite likely that the problem is due to a power supply unit that has a slightly inadequate rating.

On the cards

If tests indicate that the power supply unit is probably not the cause of the problem, it is time to look for other possible causes. Switch off the computer, remove all the expansion cards, and then switch on again. In my experience the expansion cards are often the cause of problems, and removing them will often result in an otherwise "dead" PC bursting into life. If the cause of the problem is a faulty card, reinserting the cards one by one will soon reveal which card is at fault. When the computer ceases to start up again, the last card restored is the faulty one. Of course, the computer must be switched off before each card is installed. Adding or removing a card with the computer switched on does not guarantee that something will be damaged, but it nearly does.

Do not be surprised if having restored all the cards in the computer it still starts up properly. This will not be due to the faulty card having been miraculously cured, but is simply due to the fact that it was not originally installed correctly. As pointed out previously, if a card is not slotted into

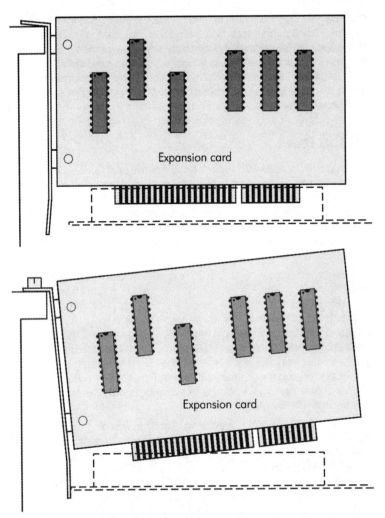

Fig.14.1 A mounting bracket can cause problems if it does not have the correct right-angled bend

the motherboard correctly it can cause short circuits that will prevent the power supply from operating. The expansion card system used in PCs is a decided asset, which makes it easy to produce custom PCs that exactly suit given requirements. It also makes it easy to change the configuration of a PC to suit changing circumstances.

The drawback of this system is that there are numerous contacts on the expansion card connectors, and the card and motherboard connectors must be accurately aligned if everything is to work properly. Some PCs fit together better than others, but it can sometimes be difficult to get the cards into place, and nothing seems to fit correctly. When this happens the usual cause is the motherboard being slightly out of position on the base panel of the case.

On the level

Do not simple wrestle with the expansion cards until they are eventually forced into place. Apart from the very real risk of damaging the cards and the motherboard, boards forced into place in this fashion are unlikely to stay in place very long. If expansion cards are proving troublesome it is usually possible to sort things out by slightly loosening the screws that hold the motherboard in place. Fit the expansion cards and then tighten the motherboard's mounting bolts again.

You may occasionally find that an expansion card plugs into place perfectly well, but when its retaining bolt is tightened it tends to lift up out of its expansion slot. In most cases it is only the front end of the card that shifts out of position. The usual cause of this is the metal mounting bracket on the card not having a proper 90-degree bend at the top where it bolts to the rear of the case. This results in the card tending to lift out of the expansion slot at one end when the fixing bolt it tightened. This is shown in somewhat exaggerated form in Figure 14.1. The cure is to carefully bend the bracket to the correct angle with the aid of a small vice or some sturdy pliers.

Note that it only needs the card to lift slightly at one end or the other to totally "gum up" the computer. There are only minute gaps between the metal contacts on the connector of an expansion card (Figure 14.2). If the connector fits into the expansion slot at a slight angle this produces short-circuits along the rows of terminals. This in turn produces short-circuits on the supply lines, causing the power supply to shut down. With luck this should prevent any damage from occurring, but it is much better if you can spot a badly fitting card before you switch on the PC.

Another occasional cause of problems is a mounting bracket that is too high or too low on the expansion card. If it is mounted too low down on the card it will prevent the card from going down into the slot correctly. When this occurs it is usually possible to loosen the screws that fix the bracket to the card, pull the bracket into the correct position, and then retighten the screws.

Another problem with the expansion card system is that it only needs one bad connection to prevent the entire computer from working properly. This is something that tends to be more of a problem after a computer has been in use for some time and the connectors start to corrode slightly. Nevertheless, even with new equipment it is possible that the metal terminals on one or other of the connectors could be slightly dirty or

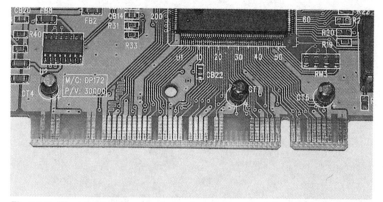

Fig.14.2 The gap between adjacent contacts on an expansion card is very small, making accurate alignment of the card and slot absolutely essential

corroded, and that bad connections could cause problems. This is a very real possibility if you build a "bargain" PC using components that have been in storage for some time prior to you purchasing them. There are special cleaning fluids, etc., for use with connectors, but simply inserting and removing an expansion card a few times should do the trick.

The problem could be due to a faulty memory module short-circuiting the supply, and removing the module or modules from the motherboard might bring results. It could also be that the processor is faulty and is overloading the supply, but this is not very likely. It is not a good idea to power up the motherboard without a processor installed, so unless you have another processor that can be tried on the motherboard it is difficult to test for this.

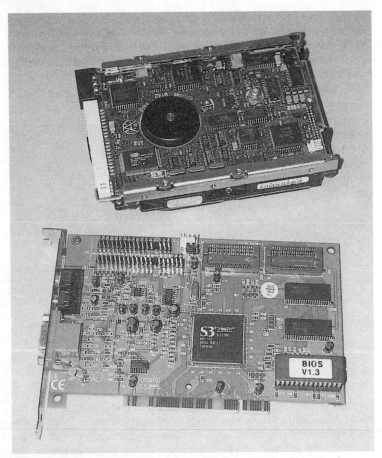

Fig.14.3 *Keep old hard disc drives, video cards, etc. They can be invaluable when things go wrong*

Substitution

If none of this gets the power supply operating it is likely that either the motherboard or the power supply itself is faulty. Do not be tempted to open up the power supply unit and prod around inside to see if you can see what is wrong. A modern PC power supply is a complex piece of equipment that uses a lot of specialised components and quite advanced techniques. Many electronics engineers are not qualified to sort out this type of equipment and it is certainly well beyond the scope of an electronics handyman. Also, it is potentially lethal to dabble with any equipment that connects direct to the mains supply, and it is certainly not something that should be undertaken by anyone who is not properly qualified.

So how can you determine whether it is the supply or the motherboard that is at fault? Sorting out problematic PCs is much easier if you have some old parts that can be used as an aid to fault finding. This is one reason for me not recommending do-it-yourself PC building to people who have little or no previous experience with PCs. Most long-standing PC users have a collection of old components that have been replaced by more up-to-date components. These days they often have one or two complete but ageing PCs.

I would certainly recommend that you hold on to any PCs or PC components that are working and not totally obsolete, as these can often be useful when sorting out a troublesome PC. Items such as old PCI audio cards, AGP or PCI video cards, and low-capacity IDE hard disc drives (Figure 14.3) can be invaluable when trying to sort out a faulty PC. In these days of SATA hard discs I suppose that old IDE drives are less useful than was once the case. A useful ploy is to obtain an IDE to SATA converter (Figure 14.4), which is a simple gadget that enables IDE drives to be used with the SATA interfaces of motherboards. Converters of this type are available quite cheaply, and enable an IDE drive to be used when checking IDE or SATA interfaces. Old but working floppy or CD-ROM drives are also valuable for fault finding and are well worth keeping for this purpose.

In this case an old motherboard could be temporarily installed in the case to see if the power supply can be persuaded to burst into action. Alternatively, the new motherboard could be installed in an old case to see if it functions correctly. In either example there could be problems if the new case and motherboard are of the ATX variety, and the old equipment has AT connectors. For some years now it has been standard practice for AT motherboards to be ATX compatible, so unless the "spare" motherboard is really old it should be compatible with a new case. The old power supply might have a low power rating by current standards, but it should be sufficient to power a basic PC having a minimal set of drives and expansion cards.

If the new motherboard works in an old case, then clearly the new motherboard is not faulty. Presumably it is the new power supply that has the problem. If the old motherboard works properly in the new case, then the new power supply is functioning correctly and it is almost

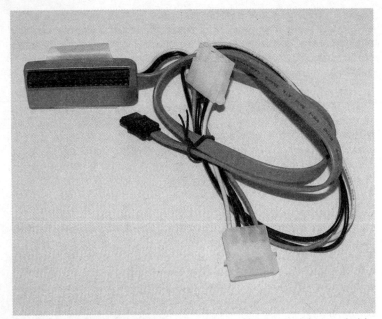

*Fig.14.4 An IDE to SATA converter can increase the usefulness of old
         IDE hard disc drives*

certainly the new motherboard that is faulty. This method of substituting
a component that is known to work for one that is thought to be faulty is
the basis for much PC faultfinding. Without specialised and expensive
pieces of test equipment to check individual components it is the only
practical method of determining which parts of a faulty PC work properly,
and which do not.

Incidentally, if you return a component that is suspected of being faulty,
it is unlikely to be tested on a special test bed or using some advanced
piece of test equipment. It is much more likely that it will be installed in
a working PC to see what happens. In other words, professional testers
make great use of the substitution method, which is the quickest, easiest,
and most reliable method of testing practically any computer component.

Partial failure

It is unusual for a faulty PC to simply "play dead" at switch-on, and the
more usual problem is the computer starting up but reporting an error

and failing to boot-up. Sometimes it fails to boot because the error brings things to a halt before the boot-up phase is reached. In other cases the error message will include a phrase like "boot failure", which means that the BIOS has tried to boot the PC but has failed to find a valid operating system. We will consider pre-boot failures first.

If the computer seems to be starting up normally, but there is no video signal, the obvious initial check is to see whether or not the video card is installed correctly. In the past it was the video card that was most likely to give problems if there was a problem with physical alignment of the cards. These days the video card will presumably be an AGP type or one of the PCI Express variety, complete with a locking mechanism to prevent any lifting at the front of the card. It is still worth checking that the card is properly in place, and that the locking lever has properly hooked into the card's cut-out and locked into place.

Also check that the signal lead for the monitor is connected properly to the video card and at the monitor if it is detachable at this end as well. If none of the monitor's indicator lights switch on it is likely that the problem is a complete lack of power to the monitor rather than an absence of video output from the computer. There is normally an indicator light switched on even if a modern monitor is receiving no video signal. Either another light switches on or the light changes colour when a video signal is received.

If the monitor is completely "dead", it is not receiving power and the power lead and plug must be checked. In the unlikely event that the monitor is powered via the power supply unit, try powering it directly from the mains supply. This will require a different power lead, but monitors can normally use a standard mains lead of the type used with many modern electrical and electronic gadgets.

If necessary, borrow the computer's power lead and try using the monitor on its own. Obviously you will not get any response from the screen, but an indicator light should switch on if power is getting through to the monitor. If this results in it working, either the original power lead is faulty or the power supply unit is faulty and is not providing any power on the mains output socket.

If the monitor itself appears to be faulty, do not be tempted to open the case and start delving around inside. There are very high voltages present inside a conventional (CRT) monitor, and these voltages can remain for some time after the unit is switched off. The interior of a monitor is potentially lethal and only trained engineers should attempt repairs to this type of equipment.

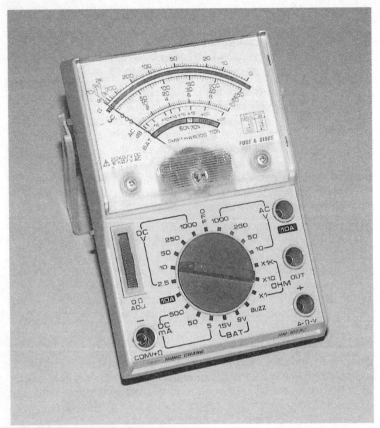

Fig.14.5 A cheap analogue multimeter is useful for checking leads

Lead checking

When faultfinding on PCs you will soon need to check leads for broken wires. There are inexpensive test meters available that have a continuity tester setting that is ideal for this sort of thing. In addition to any visual indication, the unit normally produces a "beep" if a short-circuit is detected across the test prods. A miniature digital instrument is well suited to this type of testing, but is somewhat over-specified. A basic analogue multimeter (Figure 14.5) will do the job well, but these days it is unlikely to cost much less than one of the more basic digital units.

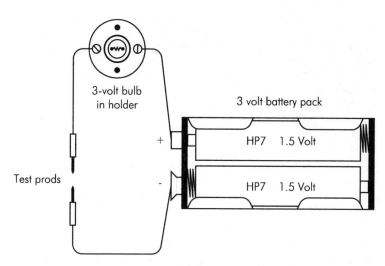

Fig.14.6 A simple continuity checker for testing leads

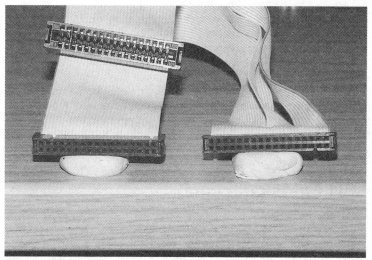

*Fig.14.7 Fixing both connectors to the work table makes it much
easier to test leads*

Something much more basic than a test meter is adequate for testing leads, and even an old torch bulb and battery style continuity checker (Figure 14.6) will do the job perfectly well. The test prods and leads can be the genuine article, but they need consist of nothing more than two pieces of single-strand insulated wire with a few millimetres of the insulation stripped away to produce the prods. This is admittedly a bit crude, but when testing computer leads it is often necessary to get the prods into tiny holes in the connectors. With the improvised prods there is no difficulty in doing so because they are so narrow, but with proper prods they are often too thick to fit into the connectors.

Testing cables is often rather awkward because you need four hands! You require one hand per test prod and another hand per connector. The easy way to tackle the problem is to fix both connectors to the workbench using clamps, or something like Bostik Blu-Tack or Plasticine will often do the job quite well (Figure 14.7).

With heavier cables such as printer types it is better to clamp the connectors in place, because Blu-Tack and the like may not have sufficient sticking power to keep everything in place. With the connectors fixed to the bench and the metal terminals facing towards you it is easy to check for continuity because you then have both hands free to hold the test prods. Provided the workbench is well lit you can also see exactly what you are doing, which should help to avoid errors.

Incidentally, if you use a test meter for cable testing, on the face of it the meter is also suitable for checking the supply levels on the motherboard and other simple voltage checks. I would definitely advise against prodding around on the motherboard or an expansion card using a test meter. With the intricacy of modern boards it is quite tricky to do this, and there is a high risk of the test prods causing accidental short circuits. These could in turn ruin expensive items of hardware. The meter can be used to check for the correct voltages on a disc drive power cable and for simple continuity tests on cables that have been totally removed from the PC, but it is advisable to go no further with it than that.

Error messages

Returning to the subject of problems during the initial testing by the BIOS, it is possible for things to simply grind to a halt, but a more likely cause of the problem is that the BIOS has detected a problem and brought things to a halt. The screen may display a message along the lines "Press F1 to continue", but there is probably no point in trying to continue with the boot process if there is a major fault present in the system.

The error message may be rather cryptic, giving nothing more than a number for the error. The computer may also do a certain number of "beeps" from the internal loudspeaker over and over again, which is another way of indicating the nature of the fault. Unfortunately, motherboard instruction manuals do not usually give any information about the exact meaning of the error messages, but this information might be available at the web site of the BIOS manufacturer. It is worthwhile looking in the manual to see if it gives any guidance. Some instruction manuals are much more comprehensive than others.

These days the error message usually gives some indication of what is causing the problem, with an error message along the lines "keyboard error or no keyboard present". With the BIOS telling you the cause of the problem you can obviously go straight to the component that has failed to work properly. It is then a matter of checking that the keyboard is connected correctly, the memory modules are seated correctly in their holders, or whatever.

Once again, the substitution method can be used to nail down the exact nature of the fault. It the BIOS reports something like a memory or keyboard problem and everything seems to be plugged in correctly, there is a tendency to jump to the conclusion that the keyboard or a memory module is faulty. This could well be the case, but it is also possible that the problem is due to a fault in the motherboard.

If the keyboard is not functioning, try swapping over the keyboard with that of another PC. If the new PC fails to work with the replacement keyboard, but the other PC works perfectly well with the keyboard from the newly constructed PC, it is clearly the motherboard that is faulty. On the other hand, if the new PC works with the replacement keyboard and the other PC fails to work with the keyboard from the new PC, it is clearly the keyboard that is faulty.

Anomalies

Things in the computing world are not always as clear-cut as they should be, and if you are very unlucky you may be faced with an anomaly. For example, in our keyboard substitution example you might find that on swapping the keyboards both computers work fine, but on swapping them back again the new PC fails to work again. I can not say that I have ever experienced this problem with keyboards, but I have certainly encountered one or two memory modules and expansion cards that are rather selective about the computers they will work in. I have also heard of others having similar problems with mice and CD-ROM drives.

It is difficult to explain this sort of thing, and there is probably more than one cause. In days gone by there were certainly problems with expansion slots and cards that were not engineered with adequate accuracy. Some combinations of motherboard and expansion card would just about fit together well enough to work while others would not. Obviously there should never have been any problems of this type, but a lot of PC components were in the "cheap and cheerful" category, and were simply not up to the task.

This sort of thing seems to be extremely rare these days, and the more likely cause of problems is some slight electrical incompatibility, or two components in the system refusing to peacefully coexist for some obscure reason. Some makes of hard disc drive do not get on well together for example, particularly when trying to use an old drive alongside a new one. Some CD-ROM drives and hard drives seem to suffer from a lack of compatibility, although it is not advisable to use this combination on the same IDE interface for performance reasons.

If you are unlucky enough to find yourself saddled with one of these incompatibility problems you may be entitled to return the item that is causing the trouble. The difficulty is in determining which component is the cause of the problem, and it is understandable if suppliers are reluctant to take back items that work fine when they try them in their test PCs. If you persist with your complaint most suppliers will reluctantly do so, but you may prefer to be pragmatic about this sort of thing and rearrange the PCs slightly so that they all work, and the incompatibilities are avoided.

It is probably not worthwhile spending large amounts of time trying to get incompatible components to function together. Bitter experience suggests that in most instances they will never do so. Fortunately, this type of thing is relatively rare these days, so you would be very unlucky to encounter a serious problem of this type. Problems with device drivers rather than with genuinely incompatible hardware are another matter. If you have a PC that almost works but there are a few obscure problems it is odds on that the trouble is due to a faulty device driver. As pointed out previously, a visit to the relevant manufacturer's web site will usually produce a fully working device driver that cures the problem. Failing that, the manufacturer's product support team might have a solution or a way of working around the problem.

Memory

In some cases the BIOS will detect and report a memory problem, but if there is a total failure of the memory circuits or a problem with the processor the BIOS start-up routine may grind to a halt or never get started properly in the first place. Often the PC will slowly beep away without entering the POST, rather than doing the usual one or two beeps and then starting the POST routine. There are other problems that can cause this, but in my experience it usually indicates a memory problem.

When a memory fault is suspected, carefully check again the section of the motherboard's manual that deals with memory matters. Make sure that you are using an acceptable memory arrangement, and that the motherboard is not fitted with an unacceptable mixture of memory types. Unlike SIMMs, DIMMs can usually be used in multiples of one. Also, it does not usually matter which DIMM holders are used and which are left empty.

However, check the motherboard's instruction manual to make sure that there are no restrictions on the way that the memory modules are used. It might be necessary to fit the modules in the correct bank of sockets for the memory to work correctly. There are usually a few restrictions when using DDR2 memory modules, such as having to use memory modules of the same size in each bank. In practice it is advisable to always use identical memory modules, and I do not just mean modules of the same capacity. Experience suggests that the best reliability is obtained by using memory modules from the same manufacturer, and having identical ratings for CAS latency, etc.

DIMM capacities

When the memory is in the form of DIMMs, the motherboard will probably not accept DIMMs of all capacities. Are you using memory modules that are supported by the motherboard? Where the motherboard has provision for both standard DIMMs and the DDR variety it will probably not be possible to use all the memory sockets. In most cases a mixture of normal DIMMs and the DDR type is not allowed at all, and you can therefore only use one or the other.

Modern motherboards are generally more accommodating than those of a few years ago, but when choosing the memory for a modern PC it is still essential to read the "small print" in the relevant section of the motherboard's manual. Also be very careful to avoid expensive mistakes and obtain the right type of memory first time.

A problem with the memory is most likely to be caused by one of the memory modules not fitting into its holder correctly. The quality of holders for memory modules is often quite poor even on some of the more up-

*Fig.14.8 A close-up showing the locking arm of a holder within
         the notch of a DIMM*

market motherboards. This tends to make it quite difficult to fit the
modules into the holders, and in some cases they can be difficult to
remove as well. When in place correctly the modules should lock into
position, so try giving the modules a gentle tug to see if they pull free
from the holders. If a module pulls away from its holder, even at just one
end, it is not fitted in the holder correctly, and is unlikely to work reliably.

Although polarised, it was often possible to fit SIMMs the wrong way
round. DIMMs are less problematic than SIMMs, and I have not
experienced a similar problem with them. Nevertheless, perform a visual
check to ascertain that the DIMMs are fitted the right way round, fully
pushed down into their sockets, and fully locked in place. If a DIMM is
fully pushed down into its holder the locking arms on the holder should
fit into the cutouts at the ends of the module. One end of a properly
locked DIMM is shown in the close-up shot of Figure 14.8.

With two polarising keys, one of which is well off-centre, there is no excuse
for trying to fit a DIMM the wrong way around, and in theory anyway, it
should not even start to fit into the holder. Whenever problems with the

memory are suspected it is a good idea to remove the memory modules and refit them. This often seems to cure the problem.

Processor

The chance of a problem occurring with the microprocessor are very low, because the processor will only fit onto the motherboard the right way round, and very high quality ZIF sockets are used on even the cheapest of motherboards. If the processor fails to function properly the most likely cause is the motherboard being configured incorrectly. If the motherboard has some form of automatic processor detection facility, check that the right processor is specified on the initial start-up screen. If the wrong processor is identified it will be necessary to go into the appropriate section of the BIOS Setup program and set the processor parameters manually.

Note that if you are using a processor that has a clock frequency that is actually lower than its "equivalent" speed rating, it may well be the true clock frequency that the BIOS will use on the initial start-up screen. This depends on whether or not the BIOS specifically supports the processor you are using, and in most cases it will. Usually the name of the processor and its actual clock frequency will be displayed by the POST routine. Obviously there is a problem if the reported speed does not match up with the nominal or actual clock frequency of the processor.

If the motherboard is configured via jumpers or DIP switches, check the motherboard's instruction manual carefully again to ensure that you are using precisely the required settings. Sometimes there is a problem with the reported speed of the processor being about 25 percent slower than the correct figure. This usually means that the motherboard's bus frequency is too low, and that it is running at 100MHz instead of 133MHz for example.

Setting the correct bus frequency via the BIOS or a jumper on the motherboard, as appropriate, will take the processor's clock frequency to the correct figure and take the PC up to full speed. An error in the opposite direction is rarer, since the BIOS will usually default to the lower setting. Similarly, where the bus frequency is set via a jumper, the default setting will usually be the lower operating frequency. Erroneously setting the bus frequency to the higher frequency would probably result in the PC grinding to a halt soon after switch-on, so it is worth checking the relevant jumper if the PC exhibits this problem.

It might also be worthwhile clearing the CMOS memory in case this has become scrambled and is causing start-up problems. This is achieved by removing the relevant jumper from the motherboard, waiting about half a minute or so, and then replacing it. Most manufacturers recommend that the power supply should be disconnected from the motherboard while the CMOS memory is cleared. Presumably there is otherwise a slight risk of a residual charge in the power supply keeping the memory operational.

Discs

Discs and the BIOS were covered in chapter 12, and this topic will not be covered in detail again here. With the automatic detection systems of the average BIOS, the discs may all function perfectly well without the user altering any settings. Even so, it is advisable to carefully check the relevant BIOS settings if any drive problems are experienced. It is definitely a good idea to go into the BIOS Setup program to check the main settings when a new PC is first switched on, or when a PC has been given a motherboard upgrade.

As pointed out previously, there can be rare problems with incompatibility between certain IDE devices. This mainly occurs when using an old hard disc drive and a new one, and it can also occur when using some hard drive and CD-ROM combinations. This seems to be an innate problem with the drives, but it can often be resolved by shifting one of the drives from one IDE interface to another. In most cases this means having the problem devices on separate IDE interfaces, but apparently in some cases it can be necessary to move them from separate interfaces to the same IDE channel.

Note that if you are using a UDMA33 or later disc drive, special drivers will be needed in order to get maximum performance from these. These days any new hard disc drive will be UDMA100 or later, and some CD-ROMs, etc., have UDMA33 or faster interfaces. The motherboard and (or) drive should be supplied with any necessary Windows drivers and full installation instructions. However, these drivers will not always be required, since many of them are included as part of a modern version of Windows. Remember that UDMA66 and later hard disc drives require a cable specifically for this type of drive and not an ordinary IDE cable. In the interest of performance, try to avoid having fast and slow devices on the same IDE interface. This is not a problem with most modern PCs, which have the slower drives on the IDE interface and the faster drives

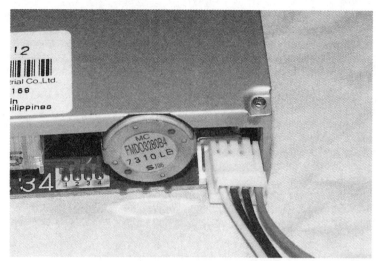

Fig.14.9 *The power connector is erroneously fitted one set of terminals to the right*

on serial ATA types. In fact serial ATA interfaces avoid many of the problems of the past.

Floppy problems

The most common mistake with floppy disc drives is to get one of the connectors on the data cable fitted the wrong way round. If you try to boot from the floppy drive it is inevitably unsuccessful, but it can also result in the data on the disc being corrupted. Having cleared the fault you try to boot from the disc, but this again proves to be unsuccessful. This gives the impression that the floppy disc drive is faulty or still installed incorrectly, but it is actually the corrupted disc that is causing the problem. It is advisable to have one or two spare boot discs handy so that you can try an alternative disc if the computer refuses to boot from the floppy disc for no apparent reason.

If there is a problem with a floppy connector fitted the wrong way round, or with the wrong ends of the cable connected to the drive and the motherboard, this should be immediately obvious. During the initial BIOS checks and the boot-up sequence the drive light of the floppy disc drive will usually switch on and off a few times, but with the cable connected wrongly the light usually stays on continuously. If the drive light comes on at switch-on and stays on, switch off and check the data cable. Of course, these days it is quite common for the floppy drive to be omitted. Make sure that the BIOS is set up correctly if the floppy drive is omitted, as it might otherwise produce an error when it fails to find the nonexistent drive.

The 5.25-inch power connectors are reasonably foolproof, but they are often a very tight fit. If a drive that uses one of these power connectors fails to do anything at all, make sure that the connector is fully pushed into the drive. The smaller power connectors used on 3.5-inch floppy discs are a different matter. Some drives have properly polarised connectors that only permit the power lead to be fitted correctly. Unfortunately, most 3.5-inch drives seem to have very "cheap and cheerful" power connectors that do permit errors to occur. Mistakes here can result in damage to the drive and (or) the power supply unit, so it is definitely a good idea to get it right first time.

The most common mistake is for the power connector to be shifted one terminal out of alignment. In Figure 14.9 the connector is fitted one terminal too far to the right, and it is not difficult to see that there is something wrong. Apart from the fact that the connector is too far to the right, it is also at a slight angle to the drive's connector. It is easy to spot the mistake with the drive outside the case, but it can be more difficult to see this problem in a real-world situation with the drive installed in the case. Often you will be able to feel that the connector has not fitted into place properly, because it will not fully push into place. The mistake should be obvious if you take the time to look carefully at the connector.

Late problems

Problems do not always come to light when a PC is going through its initial testing or booting into Windows. Everything might seem to be all right until the operating system has been installed, after which some of the hardware may fail to work properly. Having installed Windows on a new PC it is always a good idea to go into the Windows Device Manager to check for any problems.

To do this with Windows Vista, operate the Start button and then select Control Panel, the Classic View link near the top left-hand corner of the screen, and then operate the Device Manager icon. Operate the Continue button if a warning message appears. You can then look down the list of devices in search of the dreaded yellow exclamation marks that indicate a problem (Figure 14.10). With Windows XP it is a matter of first selecting

Control Panel from the Start menu and then double-clicking the System icon. Then operate the Hardware tab and finally operate the Device Manager button.

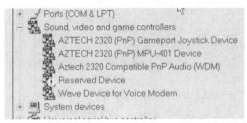

Initially there will usually be a few problems reported by the Device Manager,

Fig.14.10 The exclamation mark indicates a problem with one of the soundcard's device drivers

and this is simply because some of the drivers for the motherboard's built-in hardware have not been installed. These days motherboards are invariably supplied with a disc and (or) CD-ROM with various driver programs that have to be installed before everything will operate to perfection. The motherboard's instruction manual should give full details of the drivers provided, and how to install them. With the particular configuration you are using you may not need all the drivers supplied, so read the manual carefully to determine which software must be installed.

The ports can often be switched on and off via the BIOS Setup program, so if there is a problem with a port it is as well to go into the BIOS and check that any absent port is actually turned on. If a port is active, but is not detected by the operating system or an error is reported, it is likely that the port hardware is faulty. Unfortunately, since the standard ports are integrated with the motherboard these days, this means that the motherboard is faulty and must be replaced.

One possible exception is if you are having problems with the USB ports under an old operating system such as Windows 95. Most versions of Windows 95 do not have proper USB support, and it is advisable to upgrade to Windows XP or Vista if you intend to use the USB ports. Note that it can be impossible to run an old operating system on a modern PC due to a lack of suitable drivers. Users of an old version of Windows can be left with no option other than an upgrade to a modern version of Windows. Unfortunately, it is likely that some of your old software will not run properly using a modern version of Windows.

Some soundcards have a game port that can also act as a MIDI port, although this is becoming something of a rare feature. Integrated audio systems sometimes have the same facility. These days it seems to be the convention to have the MIDI port switched off by default, so it is

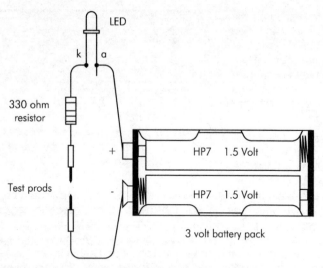

Fig.14.11 A low-current continuity tester using a LED

usually necessary to enable this port before it can be used. Where appropriate, the manual for the soundcard or motherboard should explain how the port is switched on and off. In the case of an integrated audio system, the MIDI port is usually controlled via the BIOS Setup program. Note that this form of MIDI port is not a standard type and that it can not be used with standard MIDI data cables. Special PC MIDI cables are required, and these include a small amount of interface electronics.

I have very occasionally had Device Manager show a problem with a piece of hardware that actually performs flawlessly. This was not exactly a rarity with Windows 95, but it seems to be much less common with later versions of Windows. I am far from certain about the cause of this problem, but there is presumably a minor flaw in the device drivers that "fools" Windows into thinking that there is a problem. In this situation it is best to take a pragmatic approach and not waste time trying to cure a nonexistent problem.

The opposite problem can also occur, with Device Manager reporting that everything is all right when there is clearly a problem. This is rare, but it can happen from time to time. One possibility is that the device drivers for the hardware are faulty or that the wrong ones have been installed. Try going into Device Manager, uninstalling the drivers, and

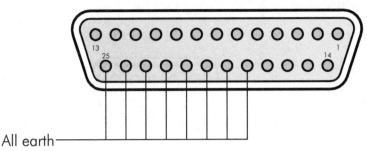

All earth

Fig.14.12 The earthed pins on a parallel port connector

then reinstalling them again. If that fails to cure the problem, visit the hardware manufacturer's web site and look for updated device drivers. It is likely that there is a hardware fault if loading the correct drivers fails to cure the problem. Windows will detect some hardware faults, but by no means all of them. The "all clear" in Device Manager is not a reliable indicator that the hardware is functioning perfectly. It just means that the hardware is present and connected to the rest of the PC correctly, and does not guarantee that it is fully operational.

Right leads

When you have been building PCs for some time you inevitably end up with a lot of leads and other odds and ends. When building a PC based on an AT motherboard it is tempting to simply grab the first serial or parallel port lead and blanking plate that comes to hand. This is not really a good idea though, since leads that look much the same may actually be wired up very differently. The serial, parallel, USB, and Firewire port leads supplied with motherboards are not all the same, and you could certainly end up with a non-operating port by using the lead from one motherboard with a different motherboard.

When dealing with apparently faulty serial and parallel ports that connect to the motherboard via a lead, it can be helpful to use a continuity check to determine whether or not the port is connected properly to the motherboard. However, a torch bulb continuity tester of the type described earlier is not suitable for this type of testing. The test current used is too high, and could damage the port hardware. Only use a proper test meter that is designed for this sort of testing.

Alternatively, use a modernised version of the continuity tester that uses a LED rather than a torch bulb. Figure 14.11 shows a suitable

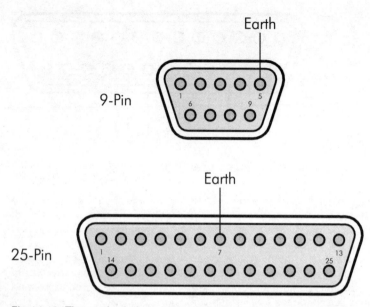

Fig.14.13 The earthed pins of 9 and 25-pin serial port connectors

arrangement. All the parts should be available from a shop or mail order company selling electronic components and equipment. Note that the LED will only work if it is connected the right way round. The cathode ("k") terminal is normally indicated by that lead being shorter than the anode ("a") lead and the cathode side of the body is usually (but not always) flattened slightly. Do not omit the resistor. Without this component a high current will flow, resulting in almost instant destruction of the LED.

Down to earth

The quick and easy way of checking that the leads are connected properly is to check for continuity between the chassis of the computer and whichever terminal or terminals of the port connector should be earthed. For a parallel port it is pins 18 to 25 that should be earthed (Figure 14.12). For 25 and nine pin serial ports it is respectively pins seven and five that should be earthed (Figure 14.13). If the right pins are not earthed and some of the other pins are, either the cable is connected incorrectly at the motherboard or you are using an unsuitable cable and bracket assembly.

The port connectors on motherboards are often simplified versions of IDE connectors. Unless some form of polarizing key is incorporated into the design, it is possible to connect the leads either way round. With a motherboard of this type you must refer to the manual to find pin one on each

Fig.14.14 The power LED connector is out of position

of the connectors, and then make sure that the red lead of the cable connects to this pin. It is also possible to fit many of these connectors one row of pins out of alignment. Fortunately, these cut-down connectors are now relatively rare, but due care needs to be taken if you should encounter a motherboard that uses them.

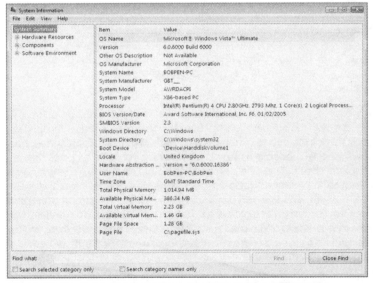

Fig.14.15 Some basic information about the finished PC can be obtained from the built-in facilities of Windows

Fig.14.16 The opening screen of Sisoft Sanda 2003. Double-clicking an icon runs the appropriate utility program

Of course, these days the vast majority of motherboards are of the ATX variety, with the main ports fitted direct on the motherboard. On the face of it, this largely avoids problems with leads to off-board port connectors. However, ATX boards usually have a number of optional ports that are implemented by way of a lead and back-plate assembly. This method is used to implement additional USB ports, front-panel mounted audio connectors, and this sort of thing. Note that the leads and back-plate assemblies are often optional extras and not supplied as standard with the motherboard. With this type of thing always be careful to obtain the correct items for the make of motherboard and to fit them correctly.

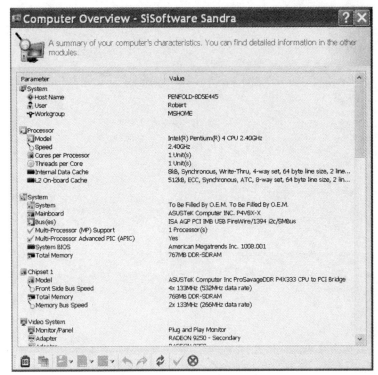

Fig.14.17 This screen provides some general information about the PC

Minor problems

Most problems with a newly constructed PC are actually quite minor.
Probably the most common of these is one of the front panel lights failing
to operate. As pointed out in chapter five, these lights are light emitting
diodes (LEDs) and not miniature light bulbs. Consequently they will
only operate properly if they are fed with a supply of the correct polarity.
If a light fails to operate, try reversing the connector to see if that cures
the problem.

If the integral loudspeaker or any of the LEDs and switches that connect
to the motherboard fail to work, carefully check the connections to the
connector block on the motherboard. Getting these items plugged into
the motherboard tends to be a bit fiddly, and it is often difficult to see
what you are doing. Unless you have small fingers it will probably be

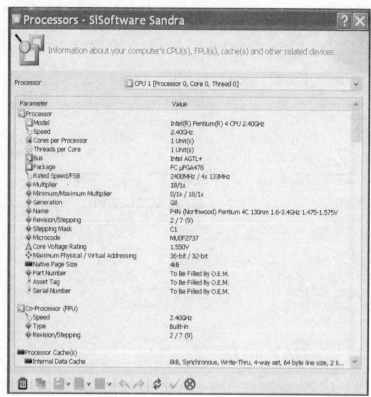

Fig.14.18 This window provides some detailed information about the processor

easier using a pair of long-nose pliers or tweezers to manoeuvre the connectors into position. Incidentally, these tools are also useful for setting jumpers on the motherboard.

It can be helpful to shine a torch on the connector block so that you can see exactly what connects to where. Better still, get a helper to hold the torch so that you are free to concentrate on the connections. It is easy to get a plug shifted along the block by one set of pins so that one pin is unconnected, or it connects to the wrong pins. In the example of Figure 14.14 the power LED connector is shifted one row of pins to the left. A close visual inspection should soon reveal any problem of this type.

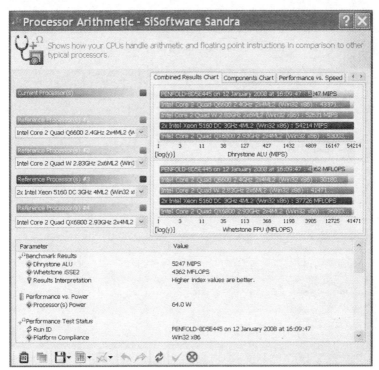

Fig.14.19 This test of the maths coprocessor shows that it is operating at an appropriate speed

Be meticulous

Obscure problems can occur with a new PC, but they are relatively rare with modern PCs. In the vast majority of cases the computer will boot-up properly and work well if you are careful to get everything connected properly. When a newly assembled PC fails to work properly it is hardly ever due to a faulty component, and is usually due to something very fundamental like a connector that has come adrift or is fitted the wrong way around.

When something goes wrong we would all rather blame someone else, but if you check through a troublesome PC and fix any mistakes it will almost certainly work flawlessly when you try it out again. Always resist the temptation to rush at things. Trying to put a PC together in the shortest possible time more or less guarantees that mistakes will be made.

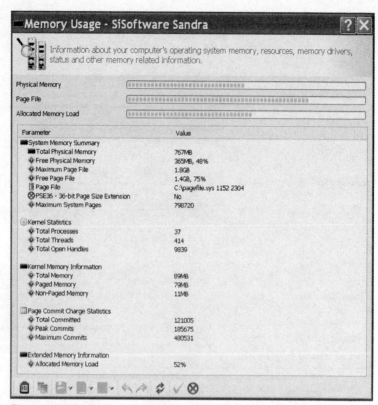

Fig.14.20 Information about the memory and its use is provided here. In diagnostics and testing programs the RAM is usually referred to as "physical memory"

Concentrate on getting everything right and give each part of construction as much time as it requires. The newly completed PC should then work first time.

Check-up

Having completed the PC and installed the operating system, many users like to check that the computer is running reliably and that the amount of memory, processor speed, etc., is all correct. Windows can provide some basic information about the processor and the amount of memory installed. With Windows XP or Vista, go to the Start menu and then

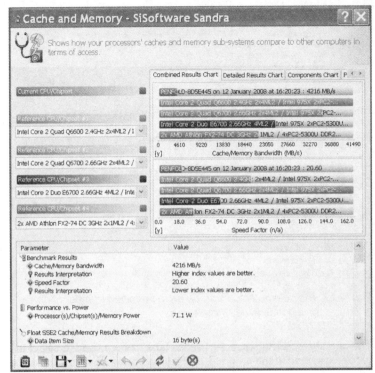

Fig.14.21 *The memory seems slow in comparison to the reference figures, but this is simply due to the test PC being fitted with relatively slow memory*

select Accessories, System Tools, and System Information. The System Information will take a few seconds to probe the system and then a Window like the one in Figure 14.15 will appear. This indicates the type of processor, its clock speed, and the amount of memory fitted (Total Physical Memory).

There are numerous diagnostic and testing programs that can provide further information and test the reliability of various parts of the PC. The basic version of Sisoftware's Sandra is a very useful program that can be downloaded free of charge. A more advanced version is available as a commercial product. This is the web address to visit:

www.sisoftware.co.uk/sandra

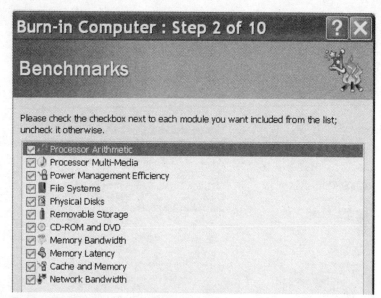

Fig.14.22 The selected tests can be run a specified number of times, or run indefinitely if preferred

The opening screen (Figure 14.16) has tabs that are used to select the required section of the program, and icons that are used to access the various test and information screens. The two screens of Figures 14.17 and 14.18 respectively show some general information about the PC and some detailed information about the processor. Figure 14.19 shows the result of testing the maths coprocessor of a 2.4GHz Pentium 4 PC. Typical test results for a range of processors are provided in addition to the results from the PC being checked. This makes it easy to assess the results, and in this case the test figures seem to be in line with the typical results for a 2.4GHz Pentium 4 PC.

Memory testing

Detailed memory information is available (Figure 14.20) and the speed of the memory can also be tested (Figure 14.21). In this example the memory seems to be rather slow compared to the reference memory figures, but the memory in the test PC is slower than the memory types supplied for comparison purposes. The memory of the test PC is actually performing quite well for its type.

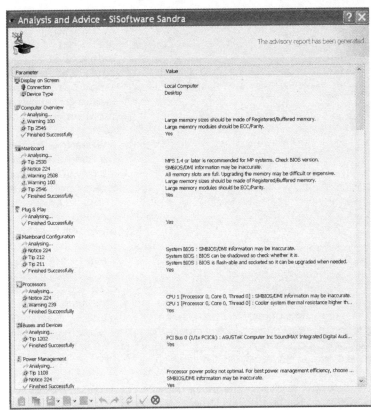

*Fig.14.23 The analysis section of the program has produced a long list
of test results, with advice included where appropriate*

Various tests and information are available from the other modules, and
one of these provides benchmark speed tests (Figure 14.22). Another
produces a test report that points out possible problems and includes
suggestions for improving the computer's perrformance (Figure 14.23).
In order to make the most of this type of thing it is necessary to have a
certain amount of technical knowledge, and in some cases some in-
depth technical know-how is needed. However, some useful pointers
can sometimes be gleaned from one of these test and analysis reports.
Be warned though, that this type of thing is a bit like reading a medical
book. You can find that your PC has practically every known computer
ill, plus a few that were previously unheard of! Many of the possible

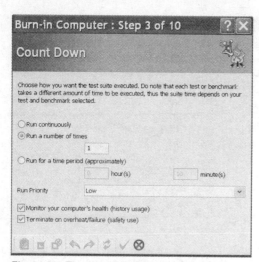

Fig.14.24   The benchmark tests can be run a certain number of times or indefinitely

problems pointed out by this type of report are not really problems at all. In some cases it is simply that for some reason the analysis program has not been able to properly analyse that part of the computer. With removable disc drives for example, there are often problems reported by analysis programs simply because there are no discs in the drives being tested. It helps read the documentation for that part of the program, and make sure that you are using the correct test conditions. Another cause of reported problems is that the hardware in your PC does not do things "by the book", but it is quite likely that most other PC hardware uses the same shortcut, and that it is of no real consequence. In a few cases it is possible that something is genuinely not quite right, and that some simple corrective measures can be taken. However, do not be tempted to tinker with the BIOS, hardware, or the operating system unless your are sure that you know exactly what you are doing. It is probably easier to make things worse than it is to make a worthwhile improvement.

Like most programs of this type, with Sisoft Sandra you can select a set of tests that are then carried out a large number of times so that the computer's reliability can be checked. The selected benchmark tests (see Figure 14.22) can be run a specified number of times or indefinitely (Figure 14.24). It is certainly a good idea to give a new PC the "once over" with some test and diagnostics software. Some of these programs can also be used as an aid to diagnosing faults.

Index

Index